S0-CKS-210

Manufactured Exports of East Asian Industrializing Economies

NF

Manufactured Exports
of
East Asian Industrializing Economies

Possible Regional Cooperation

Shu-Chin Yang, editor

M.E. Sharpe
Armonk, New York
London, England

382.45
M294

Copyright © 1994 by M.E. Sharpe, Inc.

All rights reserved. No part of this book may be reproduced in any
form without written permission from the publisher, M.E. Sharpe, Inc.,
80 Business Park Drive, Armonk, New York 10504.

Library of Congress Cataloging-in-Publication Data

Manufactured exports of East Asian industrializing economies
and possible regional cooperation / edited by Shu-Chin Yang.
Includes bibliographical references and index.
ISBN 1-56324-245-1 (cloth)   ISBN 1-56324-462-4 (pbk.)
1. Exports—East Asia—Congresses.
2. East Asia— Manufactures—Congresses.
I. Yang, Shu-Chin.
HF3820.5.M36
1994
382′.457′0954—dc20
93-27326
CIP

Printed in the United States of America

The paper used in this publication meets the minimum requirements
of American National Standard for Information Sciences—
Permanence of Paper for Printed Library Materials, ANSI Z39.48—1984.

JK

∞

BM (c)	10	9	8	7	6	5	4	3	2	1
BM (p)	10	9	8	7	6	5	4	3	2	1

CONTENTS

University Libraries
Carnegie Mellon University
Pittsburgh, PA 15213-3890

LIST OF TABLES

PREFACE AND ACKNOWLEDGMENTS

The past generation's phenomenal economic growth of the so-called East Asian four tigers, or newly industrialized economies (NIEs)—Singapore, Hong Kong, Taiwan, and South Korea—has often been cited as a success story. The core of their impressive growth has been industrialization, with the rapid expansion of manufactured exports playing a crucial role. Their experiences in focusing on an export-led industrialization strategy and devising policy measures to carry it out; adjusting their macroeconomic policies to a changing international economic environment; and upgrading their industrial structures, can provide valuable lessons to latecomers to industrialization, particularly in the rest of East Asia, including a newly market-oriented People's Republic of China.

However, the international trade climate today is quite different from what it was when the four East Asian NIEs were taking off. Huge international payments imbalances, increasingly saturated markets, and growing threats of protectionism have created serious problems of global economic restructuring. These new developments make it extremely difficult for latecomers to expand their exports, and the challenge is formidable even for the NIEs. East Asia's economies have to make more concerted efforts to deal with these multifaceted and interrelated problems.

Against this background, the Institute of International Economics (IIE) of Nankai University in Tianjin, China, the International Trade Research Institute (ITRI) in Beijing, and the Center for Asian Pacific Studies (CAPS) of Lingnan College in Hong Kong jointly organized a Seminar on Manufactured Export Expansion of Industrializing Economies in East Asia (SMEEA), which took place June 7–9, 1989. The purposes of the seminar were threefold: (1) to exchange experiences of postwar promotion of manufactured exports by various East Asian economies; (2) to discuss current problems facing the manufactured exports of these economies and their policies for dealing with them; and (3) to explore the possibilities for regional cooperation. These topics were considered important and timely. The inclusion of China for the first time in such a seminar was particularly important.

To add practical elements to the seminar's academic nature, several high-level government officials and business executives were invited to participate on a personal basis. The seminar brought together twenty-nine participants and/or contributors from nine countries/areas of the region; the United States; Canada; and the World Bank. The chapters of the present volume present thirteen papers that were contributed to the seminar: nine cover individual countries and four cover the region as a whole. Some of the country papers were briefer than the others; this was due to the seminar's design rather than authors' choice. The seminar discussions were lively, pointed, and had wide participation. My concluding remarks were expanded into a full overview, *Open Industrialization in East Asia and the Quest for Regional Cooperation*, which includes new material and incorporates the essential points in all the participants' papers and discussions (see chapter 1). Except where comments are attributed to individual authors, the overview represents my own analysis and views.

Being pressed by time for publication and owing to difficulties in reaching the authors, I took the liberty in updating several chapters to include as many recent developments as possible. The updating was so extensive for chapter 8 on Singapore and chapter 10 on Malaysia that it became more appropriate to make them joint authorship. I am of course responsible for any errors remaining in the parts of my contribution.

I would like to thank the Ford Foundation for sponsoring the seminar; Zhang Peiji, director of ITRI, and Frances Lai, director of CAPS, for their cooperation in organizing it; and Dr. Lai and her energetic staff for administering the event. I also thank the contributors of papers and participants in the seminar, whose efforts make this volume possible. Dr. Yung Whee Rhee's paper (chapter 3) was also presented at a World Bank Economic Development Institute (EDI) Seminar and subsequently published in *Increasing the International Competitiveness of Exports from Caribbean Countries* (edited by Yin-Kann Wen and Jayshree Sengupta, 1991, Washington, D.C.). I am grateful to EDI for permission to include the paper in this volume. Finally, I thank Dr. Harold Pilvin for his helpful comments on my overview chapter; any remaining errors are mine.

Dr. Bela Balassa, a colleague and renowned international economist at the World Bank, passed away after the seminar. For his many contributions to international economics as well as to this volume, we offer our sincere gratitude.

Manufactured Exports of East Asian Industrializing Economies

CHAPTER 1

Open Industrialization in East Asia and the Quest for Regional Cooperation: An Overview

SHU-CHIN YANG

This overview places in a broad development perspective various aspects of the expansion of manufactured exports by nine East Asian industrializing economies: Hong Kong, Singapore, South Korea, Taiwan, Indonesia, Malaysia, the Philippines, Thailand, and China. It also considers the issue of regional trade cooperation.

This chapter is based on my concluding remarks to the Seminar on Manufactured Export Expansion of Industrializing Economies in East Asia (Yang 1990). I have added new material and analysis and included further points from other papers presented at the seminar. While this overview stands by itself and represents my personal views, it is also intended to link the individual chapters.

The first section analyzes the progress of industrialization that has been led by manufactured exports in the nine East Asian developing economies. Their trade and development performance during the past thirty years or so indicates clearly that the preferred path is "open industrialization" (a term coined by the author in preference to "outward-looking strategy," which is somewhat ambiguous).

The second section discusses the theoretical implications of progress in the structure of industrialization in relation to dynamic changes in these categories of manufactured products: labor-intensive, resource-based, capital-intensive, and technology-intensive. It describes Pearson's export ladder analysis and Balassa and Noland's factor endowments thesis and emphasizes the importance of developing the various factors of production and increasing their supplies to effect dynamic changes in comparative advantage.

Section three discusses the government's role, strategy, and incentives in promoting open industrialization. It points out the differences between China's planned economy and the private-enterprise market economies in all the other East Asian countries. The cycle of import substitution and export promotion, first

3

in light industries and later in heavy industries, is treated as an inevitable sequence, leading to a smooth, quick transition to open industrialization.

Section four puts expansion of the East Asian industrializing economies' manufactured exports into a global perspective. It highlights growing protectionism and trade regionalism as well as their adverse impacts, and explores the feasibility of regional cooperation.

The conclusion summarizes the chapter's main points.

Progress of Open Industrialization in the East Asian Developing Economies

Economic history teaches the important lesson that industrialization has been the core of economic development. This is demonstrated once again by the phenomenal growth of the newly industrializing economies (NIEs) of East Asia since the mid-1960s and some other countries in the region more recently. Many aspects of industrialization have a common focus: establishing new industries by initiating or imitating technological innovation developed elsewhere to manufacture new or improved products (for a summary of the importance of technology in economic growth, see World Bank 1991: 12–14). The demand for such manufactured goods is much more varied and income-elastic than the demand for agricultural products. The expansion of manufacturing industry adds new occupations and raises employment and productivity above levels found in the traditional sectors. Agricultural development and increased productivity facilitate the transfer of labor to industry, causing both rural and nonrural incomes to increase more rapidly and reinforcing growth. A number of development economists have explored this mechanism of industrialization (see, for an earlier exposition, Singer 1952).

Various approaches have been used to start and sustain industrialization. In the early postwar period, development economists and developing country policymakers pursued "closed industrialization," that is, establishment of new industries under protection to make products that could substitute for imports. More recently, the great majority of economists and policymakers have favored "open industrialization," relying on exports to lead industrialization and growth, or opening the industrialization process to the world market, and emphasizing the expansion of manufactured exports to support the development of the manufacturing industry, eventually liberalizing imports (see Yang 1964 for an early treatment of this topic).

The remarkable development experience of the four tigers or East Asian NIEs—Singapore, Hong Kong, Taiwan, and South Korea—has demonstrated the success of open industrialization. From 1965 to 1980, their average annual real GDP growth rate ranged from 8.6 percent for Hong Kong to 10 percent for Singapore. This far exceeded the world GDP growth rate of 4 percent. Although the growth rates of these four NIEs slowed slightly in the 1980s, even the lowest—Singapore's 6.6 percent annual rate for 1980–91—was more than dou-

Table 1.1

Population and GDP/GNP of East Asian Economies, 1965–91

Country/Area	Population mid-1991 (millions)	GDP Growth Rate (annual %)		GDP 1991 (U.S.$ billions)	GNP per capita Growth rate 1980–91
		1965–80	1980–91		
NIEs (total & %)	72.4 (1.4)			566.4 (2.6)	
Singapore	2.8	10.0	6.6	40.0	5.3
Hong Kong	5.8	8.6	6.9	67.5	5.6
Taiwan	20.5	9.8	7.7	175.9	6.5
South Korea	43.3	9.9	9.6	283.0	8.7
ASEAN-4 (total & %)	319.6 (6.0)			301.7 (1.4)	
Malaysia	18.2	7.4	5.7	47.0	2.9
Thailand	57.2	7.3	7.9	93.3	5.9
Philippines	62.9	5.7	1.1	44.9	−1.2
Indonesia	181.3	7.0	5.6	116.5	3.9
CHINA (total & %)	1,149.5 (21.5)	6.8	9.4	369.6 (1.7)	7.8
TOTAL (% of world)	1,541.5 (28.8)			1,237.7 (5.7)	
Japan	123.9 (2.3)	6.4	4.2	3,362.3 (15.5)	3.6
United States	252.7 (4.7)	2.7	2.6	5,610.8 (25.9)	1.7
WORLD (total & %)	5,351.0 (100.0)	4.0	3.0	21,639.1 (100.0)	1.2

Sources: World Bank, *World Development Report* (Washington, D.C., 1993); and Council for Economic Planning and Development, *Taiwan Statistical Data Bank* (Taipei), 1992.

ble that of the world, and the highest—South Korea's 9.6 percent—more than tripled the world's rate. Similarly, the four NIEs' real per capita GNP increased at fairly rapid average annual rates of 5.3 percent to 8.7 percent from 1980 to 1991. In 1991, Hong Kong and Singapore with a per capita GNP exceeding US$10,000, and Taiwan, US$8,800 (exceeded US$10,000 in 1992), have already gained the status of high-income economies, while South Korea is now an upper-middle-income economy, according to the World Bank definition (Table 1.1).

Such rapid growth is closely related to the even more rapid growth of the manufacturing sector in these economies, which increased at rates of 13.2 percent to 18.7 percent per year from 1965 to 1980 and 6.7 percent to 12.4 percent from 1980 to 1991. Consequently, manufacturing output as a share of GDP in

Table 1.2

Growth of the Manufacturing Sector of East Asian Economies, 1965–91

Country/Area	Growth Rate of the Manufacturing Sector (annual %)		Manufacturing Sector As Percent of GDP		Growth Rate of Merchandise Exports[a] (annual %)	
	1965–80	1980–91	1965	1991	1965–80	1980–91
NIEs						
Singapore	13.2	7.0	15	29	4.7	8.9
Hong Kong	—	—	24	17[c]	9.1	4.4
Taiwan	16.3	7.4[c]	22	34	18.9	11.0
South Korea	18.7	12.4	18	28	27.2	12.2
ASEAN-4						
Malaysia	—	9.6	9	—	4.6	10.9
Thailand	11.2	9.4	14	27	8.6	14.4
Philippines	6.8	0.4	20	26	4.6	3.3
Indonesia	12.0	12.3	8	21	9.6	4.5
CHINA[b]	8.9	11.0	28	38	4.8	11.5
Japan	7.8	5.6	34	29[c]	11.6	3.9
United States	2.6	—	28	—	6.4	4.0
WORLD	—	—	30	—	6.6	4.1

Sources: World Bank, *World Development Report* (Washington, D.C., 1992, 1993); Council for Economic Planning and Development, *Taiwan Statistical Data Bank* (Taipei, 1991).

[a]Based on constant price data and calculated by the World Bank.
[b]World Bank estimates.
[c]Other than the specified period.
—Not available.

these economies increased from 15 percent to 24 percent in 1965 and 17 percent to 34 percent in 1991 (except in Hong Kong, where it declined because the service sector increased more rapidly).

The significant shift in the production structure reflects clearly the process of industrialization. During this process, total merchandise trade also increased. But when we look at manufactured exports alone, a different picture among them emerges. For Taiwan and South Korea, manufactured products increased much more rapidly than other exports and their share of total exports jumped from about 40 to 60 percent in 1965 to 93 percent in 1991 (Table 1.2). These facts suggest that the rapid growth and industrialization of Taiwan and South Korea have been associated with the more rapid expansion of their manufactured exports.

The economies of Hong Kong and Singapore differ considerably from those of Taiwan and South Korea. The former are urban economies and entrepôts with virtually no agricultural sector. Their industrialization has not involved a transformation from agriculture to industry or any other major economic structural change. They began as duty-free, open economies, with trade and services as essential activities alongside manufacturing. As area and population are small in both places, their domestic markets have been small. The growth of their manufacturing sectors has been led by growth in manufactured exports. In Hong Kong, manufactured exports for a long period (1965–1991) accounted for about 95 percent of total merchandise exports. Unlike Taiwan and South Korea, Hong Kong has no other significant production and exports. Therefore, the manufactures proportion of their total merchandise exports has remained high and stable since 1965.

As duty-free entrepôts, Hong Kong and Singapore (after independence) have had to be outward-looking, following the path of open industrialization from the beginning. There has been no question of closed industrialization or protected import substitution. Making full use of their comparative advantage, their industrialization process has evolved with an upward movement in production sophistication alongside the development of production factor supplies, and orientation to the world market with little government intervention.

Singapore's government has adopted incentive policies to attract direct foreign investment but has not practiced trade intervention. The country refines imported crude petroleum and exports refined petroleum products. (In 1990, fuel imports accounted for 16 percent of its total imports, and fuel, mineral, and metal exports accounted for 19 percent of total exports.) This has apparently distorted the picture of growth in the manufactures proportion of total Singaporean merchandise exports and accounts for their 74 percent share in 1991, which was relatively low compared with the other three NIEs (see Table 1.3).

The rapid expansion of manufacturing production and exports has also prompted shifts from resource-based, labor-intensive to capital- and technology-intensive production and exports, thereby changing the economic structure and "upgrading" the content of industrialization. All four East Asian NIEs began their industrialization with high population densities and relatively low levels of education. Their abundant, unskilled labor forces received wages that were low relative to their productivity, giving the NIEs a comparative advantage in labor-intensive manufacturing. Initially, textiles, clothing, and materials-based processing (a large part of "other manufacturing" products) were the main exports of the Asian NIEs (Table 1.3). As their economies grew, more of their surplus labor was absorbed by rapidly expanding industrial, commercial, and other related activities, and real wage levels rose accordingly.

Meanwhile, savings and capital accumulated due to rapid increases in personal income and enterprise profits. At the same time, foreign capital (aid, commercial loans, and foreign direct investment) flowed into these dynamic economies. All this helped to lower their real interest rates and enhanced the development of capital-intensive industries. Improved training and education have recently upgraded the skills of the work force as well as engineering and

Table 1.3

Manufactured Exports As Percentage of Total Exports, 1965, 1991

Country/Area	Total manufactured		Machinery & transport equipment		Textiles and clothing		Other manufactured		Total merchandise exports
	1965	1991	1965	1991	1965	1991	1965	1991	1991 (US$ billions)(%)
NIEs									236.4 (7.1)
Singapore	34	74	10	48	6	5	18	21	58.9
Hong Kong	94	96	7	24	52	40	35	32	29.7
Taiwan	41	93	4	38	15	16	22	39	76.1
South Korea	59	93	3	38	27	21	29	34	71.7
ASEAN-4									97.2 (2.9)
Malaysia	6	61	2	38	0	6	4	17	34.3
Thailand	3	71	0	22	0	17	3	28	28.3
Philippines	6	67	0	14	1	9	5	48	8.7
Indonesia	4	41	3	2	0	14	1	25	25.9
CHINA	65	76	9	19	29	28	27	29	72.9 (2.2)
Total of above									406.5 (12.2)
Japan	91	97	31	66	17	2	43	29	314.4 (9.4)
United States	65	80	37	48	3	2	25	30	397.7 (11.9)
WORLD	58	75	25	37	7	6	26	32	3,336.5 (100.0)

Sources: World Bank, *World Development Report* (Washington, D.C., 1992, 1993); Council for Economic Planning and Development, *Taiwan Statistical Data Bank* (Taipei, 1992).

Table 1.4

Export Structure of the NIEs, 1970 and 1987 (percent)

Country/Area	Natural-resource-intensive		Unskilled-labor-intensive		Physical- and human-capital-intensive	
	1970	1987	1970	1987	1970	1987
Singapore	72.6	27.6	8.2	17.5	19.2	54.9
Hong Kong	4.2	2.9	76.2	51.7	19.6	45.4
Taiwan	26.3	11.6	54.3	42.8	19.4	45.5
South Korea	34.9	10.5	52.8	39.0	12.3	50.4

Source: Tan Kong Yam, "Pattern of Asia Pacific Economic Growth and Implications for China," *Intertrade* (January 1990), Beijing.

management capabilities, also contributing to the development of technology-intensive manufacturing production and exports. Thus, the exports of machinery and transport equipment as well as other non-labor-intensive manufactures have increased rapidly. For example, the machinery and transport equipment shares of total exports for the four NIEs, grew from 3 to 10 percent in 1965 to 24 to 48 percent in 1990 (Table 1.3). Following Klause's (1987) classification, Tan Kong Yam (1991) showed that among these four countries' exports, shares of both natural-resource-intensive and unskilled-labor-intensive goods declined drastically from 1970 to 1987, while physical- and human-capital-intensive exports rose from between 12.3 and 19.6 percent in 1970 to between 45.4 and 54.9 percent in 1987 (Table 1.4).

During the initial stage of open industrialization, the NIEs fully exploited their comparative advantage by exporting miscellaneous light manufactures as well as traditional labor-intensive products such as textiles, clothing, footwear, and toys, and goods created by processing local or imported raw materials such as leather, plywood, and metal. The technologies for these products were widely known and standardized, and price was the main factor in international competition. The NIEs exported mainly to the developed countries, with the United States the largest market. Gradually, as the NIE advanced, manufactured production and exports were upgraded to more capital- and technology-intensive outputs, such as steel, ships, electrical and other machinery, various assembled electronic products, and telecommunications and office automation equipment. Their manufacturing sectors are now so diversified and flexible that they have the capability and momentum to respond quickly to product innovations and demand preference changes in the international markets.

It is highly likely that the four largest member countries of the Association of South-East Asian Nations (the ASEAN–4), namely, Malaysia, Thailand, the Philippines, and Indonesia, will follow successfully the Asian NIEs' path of open industrialization. According to World Bank criteria, Indonesia is still a low-income country, while the other three are lower-middle-income countries. Although their GDP growth rates from 1965 to 1980 were slightly lower than those of the four NIEs, they were appreciably above the world average, ranging from 5.7 percent for the Philippines to 7.4 percent for Malaysia (Table 1.1). From 1980 to 1991 Thailand increased its growth momentum, Malaysia and Indonesia were slower, and the Philippines was almost stagnant, due largely to its political instability. Overall, from 1965 to 1991 all ASEAN–4 economies (except the Philippines (in the 1980s) saw their manufacturing sectors grow appreciably faster than their GDP. Their manufactures share of GDP increased from 8–20 percent in 1965 to 21–27 percent in 1991, catching up with that of the four NIEs in the late 1960s (Table 1.2).

Even more striking was the sharp increase in manufactured exports' share of total exports, from 3–6 percent in 1965 to 41 percent for Indonesia and 61–71 percent for the other three countries in 1991 (Table 1.3). Among manufactured exports, the share of textiles and clothing products increased from almost zero in 1965 to 17 percent for Thailand and 61–71 percent for the other three countries in 1991 (Table 1.3). While the machinery and transport equipment share of total exports in 1991 was still negligible for Indonesia, 14 percent for the Philippines, and 22 percent for Thailand, it rose to 38 percent for Malaysia because multinational corporations (MNCs) moved into the country's export zones. Thus, in a broad sense, the ASEAN–4 are still at the stage of exploiting their comparative advantage in low labor costs and natural resources. They have just begun to get into capital-intensive industrial development and have barely initiated technology-intensive industrial development. Clearly, their open industrialization is not yet in full play.

The Export Ladder and Factor Endowments

The advances in stage of manufactured exports in the open-industrializing East Asian economies and the dynamic changes in their comparative advantage are generalized by Charles Pearson in "The Asian Export Ladder" (chapter 2) and by Bela Balassa and Marcus Noland in "Prospects of Trade and Regional Cooperation of the Industrializing Economies of East Asia" (chapter 13).

Pearson compares various countries' progress in export product sophistication with the process of climbing a ladder. "The countries of the Asia-Pacific region exhibit a dynamic process of changing comparative advantage," he writes. "The essential feature, apart from rapid overall growth of manufactured exports, appears to be the changing structure of manufactured exports. A useful analogy may be countries at different rungs and moving up a product-sophistication 'ladder,' with labor-intensive, capital-intensive, and technology-intensive products at the lower, middle, and upper rungs, respectively."

While the ASEAN–4 have recently started the climb from the lower rungs by expanding their output of labor-intensive manufactured goods in addition to natural-resource-based manufactured products, the Asian NIEs have moved from the lower to the middle rungs. Japan has moved from the middle rung to the upper rung and now competes with the West in emerging high-technology products.

Following Kellman and Schroder (1983 cited in chapter 2), Pearson uses an export similarity index to investigate the changing structure of manufactured exports in Asia-Pacific countries/areas in the past twenty-five years or so. For each country/area he determines first the export value (in constant prices) of each of the 106 three-digit Standard International Trade Classification (SITC) sub-manufactures categories as a percentage of total manufactured exports. He then compares these percentages with the corresponding percentages of a second country. The differences, expressed in percentages, are summed and averaged to obtain the similarity index. The higher the resulting index, the more similar the two countries' manufactured export structures are; the lower the index, the likelier it is that the two countries are at different rungs of the ladder.

For example, in calculations from the 1986 data, he used the United States as the "base" country and determined the country with the manufacturing export similarity index that was highest in relation to the United States. It proved to be Japan. Using Japan as the base country, he determined the next highest manufacturing export similarity index and continued sequentially. The resulting arrangement of countries according to the ranking of their similarity indexes in the matrix confirms the expectation that their export profiles fit along a ladder: the United States and Japan at the top, followed by the Asian NIEs, then China and the ASEAN–4. The manufactured exports similarity indexes for each country for 1965 and 1986 also show the extent to which the eleven countries/areas (the nine listed on page 3 plus the United States and Japan) have experienced shifts in the commodity composition of their manufactured exports over time. In a way, Pearson's measurement of the export ladder has defined the order of and distances between levels in the "flying geese pattern" (Chen and Li, chapter 5, p. 126).

One may infer from these findings a basis for predicting the next step that a particular economy's export structure will take. However, caution is warranted. Pearson's findings show that manufactured export structures have changed least in the United States, Japan, and Hong Kong. In the United States and Japan, this may be due to the maturity of their economies. In Hong Kong, perhaps the unique urban nature (as explained above on page 7) rather than the maturity of its economy provides the explanation. Singapore, the other urban port economy, was finally excluded from this analysis because its unique structure (in petroleum products and services exports) does not fit Pearson's pattern.

China followed a path of closed industrialization until recently, when it turned, at least partially, to open industrialization. Pearson found that China's manufacturing export structure has settled at a point between the NIEs and the ASEAN–4.

Pearson's findings suggest that a dynamic process of changing comparative advantage has enabled the East Asian industrializing economies to move up the manufactured export ladder. As a country moves to a higher rung, its manufactured exports begin competing with those of countries that are more advanced in manufacturing, leaving room for the less developed countries to expand their exports. The country moving up also imports more from those that are lower as well as those that are higher on the ladder. The competition and complementarity conditions among economies change constantly. This point is also emphasized by Xiong Xingmei and associates in their discussion of China (chapter 4). Thus, the traditional fear of trade competition in a static sense may be alleviated if all countries pursue open rather than closed industrialization.

Pearson's analysis focuses essentially on the product level. However, the forces that cause dynamic changes in comparative advantage stem from the development of the factors of production. The traditional fear has been that free trade would confine the less developed countries to being exporters of primary products and importers of manufactures in order to maintain their comparative advantage. This view was particularly prevalent in the early postwar years, when many colonies became independent and Lenin's theory of imperialism (the highest stage of capitalism in exploiting underdeveloped colonies and countries) was in vogue among many less developed countries (LDCs). It led many LDCs to adopt protectionism and an import substitution strategy, in short, closed industrialization.

However, this argument overlooks the possibility that the existing supply of factors of production can be changed and improved through development as well as through international trade. Cheap domestic labor and natural resources do not effectively determine the comparative advantage in labor-intensive or resource-intensive exports. For example, making use of labor in a nonsubsistence sector involves investment to move rural laborers to locations of new industries and give them the necessary skills training. Only after such a "refining" process does cheaper labor become available immediately to industries.

Similarly, mineral resources may exist in a poor country but be inaccessible to industry because of poorly developed transportation systems. Land may be fertile but usable only after reclamation. It is only after such resource development investment that these primary resources become effective factors of production (Yang 1964: 121). The effective supply of factors of production determines the comparative advantage at any time, and that supply is greatly affected by the process of development itself: Labor is upgraded through training and education, new technologies are gradually absorbed, land is improved, capital is accumulated, and so on.

Chapter 13 focuses on potential factor endowments as a basis for trade projections. "In this model, trade flows are a function of factor endowments (labor, capital, human capital, arable land, pasture land, forest land, oil reserves, coal reserves, and mineral reserves) and transport costs," write Balassa and Noland.

Their trade projections were generated by forecasts of factor endowments for the year 2000. They made projections for forty-six industries that were aggregated into twelve categories: fuels, three nonfuel primary categories, and eight manufacturing industries.

The results suggest that for the four NIEs and the ASEAN–4, the share of manufactured exports will continue to increase, reflecting further industrialization. In Indonesia and Malaysia the share of petroleum exports will decrease. Among manufactured exports, the shares of textiles, apparel, and leather exports will fall. The accumulation of capital in the NIEs will lead to increased export shares for paper and paper products, chemicals (particularly plastics), and iron and steel, all capital-intensive products. An increase in export shares of engineering products and miscellaneous manufactures is projected only for Hong Kong, although, in the view of this overview's author, the recent emigration of trained management and production personnel from the territory might impede the growth of such human-capital-intensive exports. Also, in Singapore, Taiwan, and South Korea the relatively high education levels and policies promoting research and development may lead to more sizable increases in exports of human-capital-intensive products than the Balassa and Noland forecasts anticipate.

For the ASEAN–4, Balassa and Noland project that exports of textiles, apparel, and leather products will not play a large role in further industrialization, but resource-based agriculture exports will be increasingly important for Malaysia, as will wood products for the Philippines and Indonesia. Engineering and miscellaneous exports will be quite important for all of them, particularly Malaysia, presumably because of export zones.

Some general problems with this approach emerged during the seminar discussions. First, it is difficult to measure the growth and development of factors of production, particularly changes in technology. Second, factors of production must be turned into effective supplies before they can affect production and exports, and it is difficult to project the pace of this process. Third, the coefficients do not take into account changes in national trade policies and world trade regimes. Policy changes affect the speed and direction of factor development as well as the degree of openness in exploiting potential comparative advantage.

Nevertheless, Balassa and Noland's more detailed classification of factors of production takes a step beyond the usual analysis. Their model may be more fruitful and convincing if it is first applied empirically to historical data. If it yields a good fit, it would throw further light on Pearson's export ladder. The two approaches complement each other: one from the product level and the other from the factor level.

What are the policy implications of these two models? If the underlying development forces are there in any case, why not let the forces work by themselves so that in due course a country climbs automatically up the theoretical ladder? The underlying assumption would have to be that the private sector is dynamic enough to be left alone to improve the economy and exports automatically, without government intervention, with Hong Kong serving as an example. Another question also arises: Would the climb up the export ladder be smooth regardless of the international trade environment? Such questions require discussion of the role of government and possible regional cooperation to facilitate manufactured export expansion.

The Government's Role, Strategy, and Incentives

In East Asia, Hong Kong and Singapore are at one extreme: Each is close to being a laissez faire market economy, with few public enterprises and a very dynamic and successful private sector. China, a socialist country, is at the other extreme, with public enterprises dominant, particularly in infrastructure and the industrial sector; in foreign trade, state trading dominates. Other countries/areas fall in between but are much closer to Hong Kong and Singapore than to China. In these other countries/areas the government usually provides infrastructure funding because private enterprises seldom have enough capital for such large and long-term investment. In some of them (for example, Thailand), the government also initially invests in some large key industries with monopoly characteristics, but by and large, private enterprises dominate in direct production sectors. State trading in manufactured exports is negligible. Besides providing infrastructure investment, the government has the important role of deciding a country's development strategies and policies for providing incentives to the private sector.

This section discusses such strategies, policies to provide incentives for the promotion of manufactured exports and industrial development in the region's market economies. Then it reviews these issues in China's socialist planned economy under reform conditions.

Strategy and Incentives: The First Round

In a historically open economy of Hong Kong, industrialization has progressed with practically no help from any government incentive policy for promoting exports. In the 1960s and early 1970s, when Hong Kong experienced rapid industrialization and a high rate of income growth, the government's role was relatively unimportant; the development process represented a series of successful self-adjustments to changes in the internal and external environment. Limited by its small internal market, Hong Kong had to adopt export-oriented industrialization from the very outset (Chen and Li, chapter 5).

Singapore is an entrepôt with no trade barriers. When Singapore separated from Malaysia in 1965, the country changed its development strategy rapidly and totally from import substitution to export development. Here, the government has played a more important role than Hong Kong in export promotion, mostly in institutional support and by providing tax incentives for export-oriented foreign direct investment (Ng and Yang, chapter 8).

While both Hong Kong and Singapore practiced free trade and pursued open industrialization from the very beginning in the early or mid-60's, the other two Asian NIEs took a different path. The success of the export-led development of Taiwan and South Korea is now well known, but both countries pursued an import substitution strategy for some time and struggled hard to change to an outward-looking development strategy. From about 1950 to 1965, Taiwan and South Korea were underdeveloped economies that experienced serious balance of payments problems and relied heavily on import controls as well as external aid. While import controls helped the development of import-substituting industries, the overvalued currency in each country seriously hindered the development of exports, particularly manufactured exports. When import substitution had progressed to a level that limited latitude for further substitution while inflation and high costs spread under import controls, both governments realized that exports had to be promoted to restore external balance. Such a change of policy focus profoundly affected vested-interest groups. Both governments had to overcome political and administrative difficulties in order to change policy successfully.

The new policy measures aimed basically at providing export incentives, which consisted mainly of preferential fiscal and financial schemes. Among them were income tax reduction or exemption for export industries; drawback (refund) of duties on imported inputs for manufacturing exports; low-interest credit for export industries and export traders; and favorable foreign exchange allocation to, and foreign exchange earnings retention by, export industries.

The extent of export incentives given by a government is implicitly related to its currency's exchange rate and the degree of protection given to import substitution. If the exchange rate is realistic, there is little need for export incentives to offset the disincentive caused by any currency overvaluation. The more realistic the exchange rate, the less need there is for import controls and high tariffs to protect domestic industries. Similarly, where import controls and tariffs are less extensive, there is less need for export incentives to maintain a rational allocation of resources between import substitution and export industries. During their early stage of export expansion, both Taiwan and South Korea struggled to devalue their currencies step by step and gradually reduce the degree and scope of export incentives and import controls and tariffs. These policies, combined with deliberate promotion, helped manufactured exports expand and also attracted foreign direct investment. As their economies and exports grew and manufactured exports were upgraded, their balance of payments problems were solved, and both countries entered a new stage of trade liberalization.

Fiscal and financial incentives for exports work quite well through the price mechanism in the essentially market economies of Taiwan and South Korea, but they are inadequate for developing economies, and export promotion institutions are therefore necessary. The role played by the general trading companies in Japan's history of export promotion is an obvious example. Each of the Asian

NIEs established trade promotion organizations early on, some organized by their governments, some organized jointly with the private sector, and some as trade associations. On the whole, they have been quite successful. (For more details on export incentives and trade promotion measures of the NIEs, see Rhee, chapter 3.)

The ASEAN–4, and China even more so, still rely heavily on policy incentives to get their open-industrialization strategies on the right track. In this regard, they are emulating the earlier experiences of Taiwan and South Korea. Among these countries, Thailand appears to be moving ahead of the others (Tables 1.1 and 1.2). In the late 1950s, after the failure of state manufacturing enterprises, Thailand began to reduce the government's "direct involvement in the manufacturing sector and switched instead to playing a supporting role to private enterprises through the granting of investment incentives and the provision of public infrastructure" (Tambunlertchai, chapter 9). However, the emphasis at that time was still on the promotion of import-substituting industries. Compared with the NIEs, Thailand was rather late in switching from a strategy of closed industrialization to open industrialization, largely because its natural-resource-based primary exports had earned needed foreign exchange, so there was no urgency to promote manufactured exports. However, its experience was similar to those of Taiwan and South Korea although perhaps less drastic. Thailand gradually realized "that the scope of further import substitution is limited, as growth of many such industries slowed down due to a saturated domestic market. Furthermore, it was realized that the high protection afforded industries under the import-substitution policy was creating economic inefficiency, a heavy reliance on imported inputs, and the concentration of industrial activities around Bangkok" (Tambunlertchai, chapter 9). The success of the NIEs gave the Thai policymakers confidence, and they encountered little resistance from vested-interest groups to reorienting policy direction toward export promotion.

Beginning in the early 1970s, Thailand revised its investment promotion law to give incentives to the producers of industrial exports. The major measures were quite similar to those adopted in Taiwan and South Korea during their early stage of export promotion, including duty drawback on imported inputs, duty and tax exemptions for imported machinery and equipment, income tax holidays for a period of five to eight years, and preferential interest rates for short-term loans for manufacturing exports (Tambunlertchai, chapter 9). However, these incentives have been modest, as Thailand's exchange rate has generally been quite realistic, following a policy dating back to the early postwar years (see Yang 1957).

The story was similar in Malaysia. From 1958 to 1968, import substitution under the Pioneer Industries Ordinance was the focus of industrial development. In 1968, with the introduction of the Investment Act, industrial export promotion was stressed. This lasted until 1980, when a second round of import substitution in heavy industries was initiated (see Chan and Yang, chapter 10).

Indonesia's industrialization started much later because it took a long time for the country to achieve political stability as well as economic rehabilitation and stabilization after the end of World War II. Serious efforts to establish import-substituting industries in manufacture of final consumer goods were initiated only after 1967. From 1973 to 1981, the oil boom overshadowed industrial development. Buoyed by windfall oil revenues, Indonesia felt no urgent need to promote non-oil exports. Also, the nominal devaluation of its currency was insufficient to offset the effects of inflation, and therefore not as favorable to exports as it should be. Meanwhile, the main emphasis of the trade policy was still import substitution, which expanded further to include intermediate and capital goods. Thus, even with the introduction of the duty drawback scheme, manufactured exports declined. The rapid decline of oil prices in 1986 eventually forced Indonesia to change to a policy of promoting non-oil exports, particularly manufactured goods, with a meaningful currency devaluation. As a result, non-oil exports increased more than 30 percent in 1987 and 1988. The devaluation also allowed Indonesia to reduce protection and deregulate some areas. Duty drawback measures and customs administration were reformed and improved; nontariff trade barriers were removed and replaced by tariffs; and investment and capacity licensing requirements were substantially reduced and streamlined (see Pangestu, chapter 11). However, as a latecomer to production of manufactured exports, Indonesia still produces largely resource-based or labor-intensive light industrial goods. Its manufactures share of total exports is far below that of the other eight countries under study.

The Philippines has pursued a closed-industrialization policy for too long, and its transformation to open industrialization is still incomplete. The country continued its postwar currency overvaluation and maintained exchange and import controls for too long, despite objective observers' advice to move the exchange rate toward more realistic levels and encourage manufactured exports (Yang 1981) as early as 1956, almost a decade before Taiwan and South Korea shifted from import substitution to export expansion. The Philippines decontrolled foreign exchange and imports and devaluated its peso in 1965, at more or less the same time that Taiwan and South Korea changed their policy direction.

Since then, nontraditional manufactured exports in the Philippines have increased tremendously: Their share of total exports shot up from 1.2 percent in 1960 to 36.4 percent in 1980 (Alburo, chapter 12). However, the political instability of the 1980s led to the economy's stagnation, with GDP growth averaging 1.1 percent per year and manufactured sector growth averaging 0.4 percent per year (Tables 1.1 and 1.2). Although substantial traditional manufacturing industries (mostly simple processing of local raw materials) give manufacturing exports a higher share of total exports in the Philippines than in the other three ASEAN countries, industrialization is rather shallow. The development of manufactured exports has been overly concentrated on a few products, chiefly electronic components, garments, and handicrafts. Electronic components involve primarily the assembly or packaging of imported inputs. Garments, handicrafts, and most other exports, such as footwear, furniture, and food products, are labor intensive and require few skills. In 1982, about 78 percent of nontraditional Philippines exports were in the low-capital, low-skill category. All this raises the question of "whether this development of manufactured exports has resulted in a broad-based growth" (Alburo, chapter 12). Alburo observes that these trends have "occurred on the top of the existing protectionist regime" and that "what is needed is a full departure from the country's past import-substitution era."

Thus, in the Philippines and Indonesia, and to a lesser extent in Thailand and Malaysia, policy has turned to open industrialization but import substitution under protection remains a problem. To achieve export expansion and structural upgrading in the future, the ASEAN–4 need further rationalization of the incentive regime and effective protection, as well as maintenance of realistic exchange rates. Here useful lessons can be learned from the experiences of Taiwan and South Korea.

Strategy and Incentives: The Second Round

Under their open-industrialization strategies, the NIEs succeeded initially in developing light and consumer goods industries by the early 1970s. To varying degrees, the ASEAN–4 followed this pattern in the mid-1980s.

When development of light and consumer goods industries reaches a certain stage, demand for intermediate and capital goods as inputs to these industries becomes sizable. The country then faces a choice between continuing to import such inputs or producing them internally. Production of intermediate and capital goods is generally large-scale. It may, therefore, not be feasible for countries with a small domestic market to develop such industries. Industrial leaders like England in the nineteenth century and the United States in the twentieth century, intermediate and capital goods industries developed along with the light and consumer goods industries. But latecomers may be unable to accomplish the same thing without government assistance. Even the United States and Germany, for instance, in their early stages of development during the late nineteenth century, employed protection against such advanced economies as England. In the early period of Japan's industrialization during the late nineteenth and early twentieth centuries, development of the shipbuilding, steel, and chemical industries was initiated and subsidized largely by the government (Orchard 1930). Japan's policies were adopted partly for military reasons.

Taiwan and South Korea first faced the problem of developing intermediate and capital goods industries in the 1970s, while Malaysia and Indonesia followed suit in the 1980s (for China the experience came in the 1950s for different reasons, see below). In South Korea there was pronounced government intervention to achieve second-round import substitution in the heavy and chemical industries (HCI), partly for defense reasons.

Some economists maintain that this excessive government intervention caused a misallocation of resources, and South Korea's economy would have been better off without industrial targeting. As Yoo (chapter 7) points out, in the 1960s (the first round of its industrialization) South Korea's main policy emphasis was to encourage private sector exports through a variety of incentives. Such an incentive regime was intended basically to offset the bias against exports that was generated by protection and currency overvaluation, and did not discriminate among industries and firms: Whoever had the comparative advantage could move ahead.

The 1970s strategy of advancing the industrial structure through protected development, however, was targeted at specific industries, such as HCI, or even specific firms. Indeed, it constituted a second round of import substitution, with incentive measures similar to those used in the first round. They included: (1) fiscal inducements such as tax holidays, special depreciation allowance of fixed assets, and temporary investment tax credits; (2) preferential allocation of investment funds through a special government fund; (3) credit privileges, which are the most powerful measures, including preferential low-interest loans by the banks under government direction; and (4) import controls on HCI products by returning some HCI items to the "negative (controlled) list," which requires prior government approval for competing imports. According to Yoo, this incentive regime was very powerful in the environment of a more realistic exchange rate level. But the protected development of HCI resulted in a substantial misallocation of resources, as reflected in the low rate of capital efficiency and employment creation.

However, this analysis raises some questions. First, if external shocks are taken into account, the difference between capital efficiency in HCI and non-HCI sectors may not be so great. The second oil shock and the subsequent world recession adversely affected South Korea's light industry exports from 1979 to 1983. Worker layoffs might have produced a higher capital-to-labor ratio instead of an operational inefficiency of capital. Second, while phasing-out of export incentives to light industries may have contributed to their low profit rate, it was desirable because the time had come for such industries to be competitive in the world market without incentives. The end of export incentives for the non-HCI industries partly financed the new incentives given to the HCI industries, thereby lightening the government's fiscal burden. Third, the program emphasized that HCI industries should be able to export in the future, so export incentives were given in due course.

The most important aspect of this strategy was its dynamic nature. By targeting HCI development with strong incentives, South Korea might have suffered inefficiency in the intermediate term by some misallocation of resources, but it apparently gained by establishing the early primacy of HCI and exports. South Korea has already exceeded Taiwan in HCI exports. Had South Korea not adopted its deliberate policy, it might have taken fifteen instead of ten years to achieve its present position. Moreover, the success of the second round of manu-factured export expansion enabled South Korea to eventually reduce protection, engage in trade liberalization, and proceed even further in financial market liber-alization.

Nevertheless, I agree with Dr. Yoo that the social cost of South Korea's strategy of deliberate development of HCI should not be ignored. One important cost was the inflation associated with the excessive financing of HCI industries in the 1970s. Another is the concentration of economic power resulting from the monopoly created by the HCI incentive policy, which may be at the root of today's labor and student unrest. Giving preference to individual firms rather than to all industries is not a good national policy. These are valuable lessons for development newcomers.

Malaysia began to develop heavy industries in its public sector and initiated a second round of import substitution in 1980. This second round was in "the capital and technology sector, whose development is influenced by the South Korea model" (Chan and Yang, chapter 10). As in South Korea: (1) the emphasis was on encouraging the private sector through investment incentives and protec-tion; and (2) the second-round import substitution was accompanied by a second-round export expansion. Also as in South Korea, a coherent industrial program—the Industrial Master Plan formulated for 1986 to 1995—targeted the priority development of thirteen subsectors. Among other goals, the investment incentives aimed to attract multinational corporations (MNCs) to invest in the free-trade zones, particularly in technological, capital-intensive, and export-oriented fields. In 1990, the machinery and equipment share of Malaysia's total exports increased to 27 percent, the highest proportion among the ASEAN–4.

Indonesia also embarked on second round import substitution in intermediate and capital goods industries, in the late 1970s. Since it did not achieve much in the first round of industrialization and manufactured export expansion, in light and consumer products, the industrial foundation was poor. Also, little serious effort was made in exports of machinery and equipment which accounted for only 2 percent of total exports in 1991 (Table 1.3). The shift toward the develop-ment of intermediate and capital goods industries was perhaps premature.

Based on the generally successful experiences of the above-mentioned East Asian economies in trade and industrialization, we can draw the following conclusions:

Import substitution and export expansion are not necessarily mutually exclu-sive. Only after some manufacturing industries have been established under pro-tection and developed by import substitution can an economy produce manufactured goods that can gradually become competitive for export. The questions in this learning-by-doing process are how and how soon countries can bring their infant industries to maturity and do away with protection. Normally, when light industrial import substitution has run its course, protection should be reduced and exports expanded. The sooner the government recognizes this turn-ing point and changes its policy direction, the earlier and larger will be the gain to the economy. Also, the more solidly the development of manufacturing industries is based on existing and potential comparative advantage, the easier the endeavor will be.

The success of a development strategy led by light industrial exports might lead some to think that the outward-looking approach should be the goal from the beginning and throughout. But in fact, an underdeveloped country has to begin its industrialization with some import substitution. As South Korea's experience suggests, a country needs import substitution, even after it succeeds in exporting light and consumer goods, and it needs to develop further intermediate and heavy industries. However, the conditions for success of the second stage of import substitution remain the same: (1) to base the development of the selected industries on existing and potential comparative advantage, and (2) in due course to terminate protection and turn to exports.

Thus, import substitution and export orientation are a sequence with some overlap, not an either/or choice forever. In this sequential process, the government's most important role is to provide adequate incentives, recognize the changing situation, judge the arrival of the turning point, change the strategy on a timely basis, and eventually remove protection. Of course, the incentive regime should always be rational and made simple, the criteria clear, and the implementation easy, particularly when the bureaucracy is not very capable or honest.

It is difficult to predict whether there will be a third stage of industrialization involving new changes in trade policy. In manufactured exports, technology-intensive and high-value-added products have become increasingly important. The governments of Singapore, Taiwan, and South Korea, in particular, have started to promote research and development by establishing technology towns, institutes, and councils, and by encouraging technology transfers from the MNCs. Under its traditional nonintervention policy, the government of Hong Kong showed "lack of positive support to industry in terms of manpower development and promotion of basic and applied research. But it has changed recently" (Chen and Li, chapter 5). Singapore's manufactured exports already largely consist of technology-intensive products and are somewhat leveling off. It has decided to develop financial and information services, in addition to further upgrading its manufacturing industry to a higher degree of technology orientation. Many other industrializing economies in the region however may not possess the comparative advantage of such service industry as Singapore.

The Case of China: A Socialist Trade System
Under Reform

China differs fundamentally from the other East Asian industrializing economies. The communist regime had more or less completed its socialization of the economy in 1956. Following the Soviet model, its central planning included foreign trade. The planned import requirements of all government agencies in charge of various sectors of the economy were summed to arrive at total import demand. Total export goals were set to earn enough foreign exchange to pay for total imports, thus maintaining a balance in the current account of international payments. Merchandise exports were surpluses from the various production sectors whose output exceeded domestic demand. Both import and export trade were carried out by the various state trading companies under the direction of the Foreign Trade Ministry. The exportable surpluses were procured at domestic controlled prices and sold abroad at world market prices. At a given exchange rate, the trading companies might have earned profits on certain export commodities and incurred losses on others, depending on whether the unit domestic procurement cost per unit of foreign exchange earned was higher or lower than the official exchange rate. The state tried to fix the official exchange rate at a level where total profits could offset the total loss, thereby leaving that part of the state's finance in balance.

Similarly, on the import side, the domestic prices of planned imports were fixed according to plan priorities and social considerations. Changes in world market prices and the exchange rate had no direct effect on the local prices of imports. Again, any net profit or loss was borne by the state trading companies, which, in turn, passed it on to the trade ministry and, finally, to the state budget.

Such a closed, planned economic and trading system cuts off the connection between domestic and world market prices. In the late 1950s, again following Soviet strategy, China embarked on rapid industrialization by giving priority to the development of heavy industries. The theory was that heavy industries had to be developed to supply machinery to the light industries so that they too could be developed. This domestic supply side or forward linkage approach with no exports in sight was in direct contrast to the all demand side (domestic and foreign demand) backward linkage approach of the other East Asian countries/areas. Thus, for the next thirty years or so, China forced a high rate of investment and high capital-output ratio while providing absolute protection for all industries in import substitution.

After the initial spur to new industries, the economy eventually stagnated, and the level of consumption has remained continuously low. Periodic political and social upheavals, notably the Great Leap Forward and the Cultural Revolution, left people generally dissatisfied.

This state of affairs forced China to initiate economic reform and open its economy to the outside world at the beginning of the 1980s. The foreign trade sector has been in the forefront of reform, conditioned by progress in the basic transformation of the command economy to a market economy. In the first stage of foreign trade reform (roughly, the first half of the 1980s), China experimented with (1) reorganizing the foreign trade administration and trading companies, and (2) decentralizing the conduct of foreign trade to other parts of the central government and to local governments.

Under decentralization, several central ministries in charge of production and many municipal and provincial governments were permitted to have their own trading companies to import and export within their respective jurisdictions, thereby breaking the monopoly of the central government's trading companies. Meanwhile, some large- and middle-size state enterprises were also allowed to engage directly in import and export trade of their inputs and outputs. Enterprises with foreign investment were given more trade autonomy. Under the reorganization, state trading companies were encouraged to conduct planned import and export trade as well as foreign trade business from enterprises and other government agencies. They were also asked to strengthen their connections with foreign markets.

Besides these institutional reforms, some new export promotion policies were introduced—such as a foreign exchange retention scheme, export subsidies, tax concessions, and preferential treatment for processing imported materials and assembling imported components (Xiong et al., chapter 4)—similar to those adopted by other East Asian economies. More favorable preferential treatment in duty and tax concessions, foreign exchange transactions, and so on was given to the special economic zones in south China near Hong Kong, Macao, and Taiwan to attract foreign direct investment and promote exports. Meanwhile, China began to devalue its currency more frequently. But despite these moves toward promoting exports, the planned trading system remained essentially the same: the final profits and losses in foreign trade were still borne by the central government's budget.

In 1988, along with fiscal reform, all local governments and their trading companies were required to make contracts with the central government regarding their export targets, namely, (1) total export earnings, (2) the amount of foreign exchange earnings to be surrendered to the center, and (3) the net loss incurred in export trade. Local branches of central trading companies would be included in the localities' contracts. Generally, 80 percent of the export earnings within the target amount would be surrendered to the central government. Only 20 percent of any earnings exceeding that amount would be surrendered. Any subsidies needed to support this portion of exports should be borne by local governments. Exporters of light industrial goods, handicrafts, and clothing would be responsible for profits and losses. They could retain 80 percent of the foreign exchange earnings but would not receive any government subsidies.

Meanwhile, the scope of planned trade was reduced to: (1) a limited number of large items that are basic essentials and important national needs; (2) exports under foreign quota restrictions; and (3) state trading with socialist countries. The predominant proportion of trade has been conducted through markets with applicable tariffs and licenses, although the number of commodities under import and export license has been reduced. Procurements for export are carried out at market instead of planned prices. Imported items are priced according to the cost-insurance-freight charges plus commissions charged by the trading companies, and the state no longer subsidizes imports. To encourage exports, various taxes (including excise and business taxes) are rebated.

Thus, the second stage of China's foreign trade reform has moved farther away from the central planning–state trading model depicted earlier. However, Chinese policy still mixes planning and market mechanisms, and the overvalued currency (particularly during the 1987–89 inflation), excessive planning, and foreign trade financial losses are still serious problems, although they have largely been passed on to the local governments.

Since the initiation of economic reform and an open policy, China has periodically devalued its exchange rate but always too little and too late. In mid-December 1989 China took a bold step by devaluing 21.2 percent from C¥3.72 per US$1 to C¥4.72 per US$1, which was followed by another devaluation in 1990 to C¥5.3 per US$1. This helped China's exports and reduced foreign trade subsidies significantly. However, while it helped to reduce the government deficit, it increased the money supply and purchasing power of the export sector. The real solution would be: (1) to reduce further and eventually stop export of those commodities whose domestic cost of foreign earnings per dollar exceeds a realistic exchange rate, and (2) to expand the production and export of those commodities whose domestic cost of foreign exchange earnings per dollar is lower than the realistic exchange rate. But without realistic domestic prices, it would be difficult to establish the real domestic cost of exports, which points up the need for price reform. Only with proper cost-price exchange-rate relationships can China minimize both the financial and the economic losses in its export trade and achieve, at least on the export side, more rational allocation of resources in conformity with its comparative advantage.

On the import side, there seems to be no conscious departure from the traditional policy of protecting import substitution. Even more than in the Philippines, with all of China's proclamations of an outward-looking strategy, the various incentives offered to exports have perhaps offset only part of the bias in favor of protecting domestic industries.

Despite all its problems, since the reform, China's merchandise exports increased 11.5 percent per year from 1980 to 1991 (Table 1.2). Manufactured exports increased even more impressively and accounted for 76 percent of total merchandise exports in 1991 (Table 1.3). Despite China's early development of heavy industries, exports of machinery and equipment accounted for only 19 percent of the total in 1991. Exports of textiles and other light, labor-intensive manufactured goods accounted for 57 percent of the total. Exports have increased particularly rapidly in the special economic zones associated with foreign direct investment.

China has tried to export its machinery products but has found that obsolete technology makes them generally not very competitive on world markets. This is why China is eager to upgrade its industrial technology. The country has a wide range of capacity to produce machinery, and the export potential would be substantial if modern technology were applied. However, the inefficiency and lack of competitiveness of Chinese products cannot be corrected without lowering the country's protectionist barriers. (For China's recent development, see also Balassa and Noland, chapter 13.)

Global Adjustments and Regional Cooperation

In an interdependent world, the problems of the expansion of manufactured exports from the East Asian industrializing economies have to be viewed globally.

New Protectionism and Regionalism

The present trade imbalance of the United States and Japan requires large-scale adjustments that will continue to affect countries/areas in East Asia. Similarly, the intensifying regionalism in Europe and North America will tend to redirect international trade and investment, mainly at the expense of East Asian countries. Meanwhile, developed countries are more aware of the increased imports from emerging economies that enter their domestic markets. The more favorable international trade environment that existed for about thirty years before the first oil crisis, through several rounds of multilateral tariff reductions under the General Agreement on Tariffs and Trade (GATT), has begun to fade. Under pressure of persistent budget and trade deficits, the United States has recently changed its trade philosophy from "free trade" to "fair trade," opening the door to protectionism by the industrialized countries. The use of nontariff barriers, bilateral bargaining, and unilateral devices is clearly on the rise (Baldwin 1988; chapter 12). The Asian industrializing economies in particular are hurt by these developments.

As observed by Pearson (chapter 2):

> The remarkable success of East Asian countries in moving up the export ladder comes at a time when the trade system is in considerable disarray, notably the movement away from MFN tariffs to discretionary quantitative restrictions under the guise of "voluntary export restraints" and "orderly marketing agreements." These "gray area" measures, taken by the United States and the European Community, have been directed disproportionately at Asian countries. In addition, the United States has tightened its "unfair" trade provisions in the countervailing duty and antidumping provisions of the 1988 Trade Act and has expanded the list of objectionable practices under Section 301 (see also, Balassa and Noland, chapter 13).

Voluntary export restrictions (VERs), among which the Multifiber Agreement (MFA) is most important, are outside the GATT. The MFA places bilateral quota restrictions on exports of textiles and apparel from each country/area. Moreover, because the quotas are based essentially on historical data instead of current production costs, they tend to "discriminate against recent and low-cost products to the benefit of long-standing and high-cost products" (Balassa and Noland, chapter 13). Although more technologically advanced exporters are given a lower growth factor under the quota system, the differences are so insignificant that earlier exporters enjoy a guaranteed export growth factor, while latecomers (such as the ASEAN countries) face an effective constraint (Chen and Li, chapter 5). Thus the VERs and their rigidity have contributed to the high cost to consumers in the importing developed countries and hindered the exporting developing countries from producing in conformity with their dynamic comparative advantage and efficient allocation of resources. One study has calculated that if such bilateral quotas were removed, export volumes would increase anywhere from 24 percent for Hong Kong to 275 percent for Indonesia (Trela and Whalley 1988, cited by Balassa and Noland in chapter 13, p. 247).

The recent increasing uses of countervailing and antidumping duties have affected the East Asian industrializing economies particularly adversely. For instance, "since 1984, there have been several cases involving either the imposition of anti-dumping duty or countervailing duty by the United States on imports from Thailand. Products affected include textile fabric and garments, steel pipes and tubes, and ball bearings. Although the duties imposed are generally not high, these trade restrictive measures created uncertainties and confusion among Thai exporters" (Tambunlertchai, chapter 9).

A recent GATT report criticized the United States for being overly zealous in using its trade laws to block some imports. Recently, there has been a sharp increase in the number of antidumping actions and high tariffs on a selected group of products, including footwear, textiles, glass, and medical products (*The Washington Post*, March 13, 1992). The East Asian countries/areas are afraid that this may become a convenient method for import-competing industries to harass efficient exporters.

In 1989, the United States also withdrew Generalized System of Preferences (GSP) privileges from the four NIEs and cut eight items of GSP benefits to Thailand. The unilateral decision on graduation and product exclusion created uncertainties among investors in the countries and industries affected.

Taiwan and South Korea, standing near the top of this region's export ladder after Japan, have felt the U.S. pressure for participation in the global adjustment process, particularly in relation to appreciation of their currencies. Taiwan's huge international reserves argue for currency appreciation, even for its own good, to improve its terms of trade and welfare. Moreover, Taiwan needs to catch up on its infrastructure investment, including pollution control, public transport, and so on, by making use of some of its excess foreign exchange reserves directly and indirectly (through increases in general import demand generated by increases in investment). However, the bilaterally negotiated currency appreciation between the United States and Taiwan on one hand and South

Korea on the other, has apparently resulted in unfair treatment of Taiwan, whose appreciation was much greater than Korea's (for the effects on manufactured exports' competitiveness of exchange-rate changes, see Chen, chapter 6). It would be preferable for the United States to negotiate multilaterally with Taiwan and other countries involved.

For a long time, Japan's traditional close-knit industry-trade-government relationship has made it difficult for any imports to penetrate its domestic market. This is equivalent to "hidden protection." Moreover, Japan's overseas investments in emerging East Asian countries without much technology transfer have resulted in constantly increasing demand for Japanese components and parts. Consequently, all these countries suffer huge trade deficits with Japan.

China, which has not yet renewed its membership in GATT, has been hurt particularly by the new protectionism. In 1986, when trade protectionism influenced 31 percent of all manufactured exports from the world developing countries/areas, the corresponding share for China was 49 percent (Xiong et al., chapter 4).

Regional trading blocs also have an adverse impact on manufactured exports from East Asian countries. The unification of the European Community's internal markets will inevitably direct their trade inward. It may even intensify the Community's external protectionism, not only because of demand from the southern European countries but also because there will be heightened competition among enterprises within the member countries, as well as employment pressure. Another fear is that the inclusion of Mexico in the North American Free Trade Agreement will place the industrializing East Asian countries with similar export patterns in an unfavorable competitive position.

The Quest for Regional Cooperation

With the rise in protectionism and regionalism, what should East Asian industrializing economies do? Should they also form a regional trading bloc, and in what way? To what end and with what policies is this feasible? In fact, ASEAN is already a regional organization. ASEAN has established several cooperation arrangements, including: (1) preferential trading arrangements, (2) coordinated establishment of large-scale regional industrial plants, (3) regional joint ventures among private firms, and (4) an ASEAN finance corporation. However, very little progress has been made so far in these areas. In trade, tariff reductions have been rather slow and small with numerous exceptions, so that only 5 percent of intra-ASEAN trade is covered by preferential tariff arrangements. Trade creation has been negligible; intra-ASEAN trade was only 16 percent of member states' trade in 1988. "Perhaps ASEAN's greatest achievement in the economic field has been acting as a pressure group in trade negotiations with industrial countries and in the GATT. ASEAN has been successful in inducing the EC to modify its trade preference system and in inducing Japan to forgo increasing the production of synthetic rubber" (Balassa and Noland, chapter 13).

While the progress of ASEAN in intratrade expansion has been slow, it nevertheless has the potential to play a positive role in rationalizing and harmonizing the rules of trade, taxation, and investment among the member states to achieve greater regional economic integration and a greater market for each of them (see Balassa and Noland, chapter 13).

With this favorable trend, would it be even better to enlarge such regional cooperation? There have been various proposals for greater and different forms of regional cooperation, with varying membership and functions. However, as a condition of success, the member states must have common interests and common goals. One basic consideration would be the importance of trade and investment relations o the member states. Let us examine the case of the East Asia–9 (EA–9), namely, NIEs–4, ASEAN–4, and China.

From 1970 to 1987, exports of EA–9 members to each other increased more rapidly than their exports to the United States, the European Community, and Japan combined: 25.8 times versus 20.2 times. As a result, the intra–EA–9 trade as a percentage of exports to the largest developed areas increased from 37.5 percent in 1970 to 47.9 percent in 1987 (Table 1.5). There are several reasons for the more rapid expansion of this intraregional trade. First, the more rapid GDP growth rate in the region than in the rest of the world means more purchasing power to buy each other's goods. Second, the pursuit of an export-oriented, open-industrialization strategy and the move up the export ladder have resulted in more diversification in production and, therefore, increases of trade with each other. Third, geographic proximity keeps transportation costs low and personal contacts easy. Moreover, cultural closeness makes it easier to conduct trade among these countries. These trends are favorable for further growth of trade in the region.

Accompanying the rapid increase in total intraregional trade are changes in trade structure. These economies, with their differing factor endowments and stages of development, do not necessarily send all their primary exports to developed countries, and their manufactured exports are not always competitive. At different rungs of the export ladder, their exports can be complementary (Xiong et al., chapter 4). Moreover, the subregional division of labor is not only horizontal, it is "also vertical in the sense that the sub process may be passed on to other countries in the production of a particular product" (Chen and Li, chapter 5). Furthermore, with rising labor costs and capital surpluses, Taiwanese and South Korean firms, like Japanese firms, have increased considerably their investment in the ASEAN–4 and on the China mainland. This, in turn creates more trade. Indeed, the manufactured goods share of ASEAN–4 exports to the NIEs is second only to the share exported to the United States. Except for South Korea, intratrade among the NIEs accounts for a higher share of exports than their exports to Japan (Naya, James, and Plummer n.d.:10; Table 1.4).

The natural trend of a rapid increase in intratrade among the EA–9 can be facilitated by regional cooperation in mutual reduction of trade barriers. ASEAN

Table 1.5

Nine East Asian Industrializing Economies' Intra Exports and Exports to Major Developed Areas, 1970 and 1987 (U.S.$ billions)

Direction of Export	1970	1987
A. Exports to:		
United States	29	750
Japan	23	385
European Community	20	320
	72	1,455
B. Exports to Each other:	27	697
B as a percentage of A	37.5	47.9

Source: Kobayashi 1990.
Note: Includes four NIEs, ASEAN-4, and China.

has already started this process. Because the initial common interest in international politics has faded away, ASEAN has made economic cooperation its main focus. This should remove the obstacles to cooperation with the other EA–5. ASEAN, of course, can keep moving toward its goal of subregional economic integration, but this should not prevent its members from enjoying the broader benefits of greater regional cooperation. Greater cooperation among the industrializing countries/areas of the region can be an addition to, rather than a substitute for, ASEAN. The EA–9 group could start with reciprocal reductions of nontariff import restrictions, followed by reciprocal tariff reductions (Xiong et al., chapter 4).

Of course, regional trade cooperation is a complex endeavor. It is necessary to identify precisely the obstacles to intraregional trade; determine priorities for removing such obstacles; assess the gains and losses for each individual member country/area; and equalize the net gains or compensate the less developed countries/areas for their losses. However, once there is agreement on the general principles of regional cooperation, studies of these more specific questions can be initiated to arrive at a more concrete operational framework.

The group involved in greater regional cooperation can also play a stronger role in international trade negotiations with the industrialized countries and GATT, including the Uruguay Round. This group would have common interests in maintaining the multilateral trade system under GATT. It could exercise greater pressure than ASEAN alone in maintaining the openness in manufactured goods trade. In particular, the group should fight to strengthen the safeguard code to ensure that import controls are only temporary and the code's applications are not abused or excessive. It should also fight to outlaw protectionist measures, such as "voluntary" export restrictions, outside the GATT and ban discrimination in the application of trade restraints (Balassa and Noland, chapter

13). The group can even go further to harmonize foreign investment codes to avoid competition in giving excessive preferential treatments to foreign investors.

There has been interest in even wider participation in regional cooperation to include countries in the entire Pacific area, including Japan, Australia, New Zealand, the United States, and Canada. In fact, the Australia-sponsored Asia and Pacific Economic Cooperation (APEC) has already held two meetings. However, this broader membership is too diversified, with conflicting interests. Its common goal is too general to be operative. It could be an Organization of European Cooperation and Development (OECD) type of organization in the Pacific area, serving as a forum to discuss trade and trade-related issues of the region, with the goal of ensuring the openness of the international economic system. But it cannot substitute for a more closely related group that has a more definite common interest. However, there is no reason that the two regional organizations cannot coexist, with even the EA–9 participating in the activities of the Pacific group.

Conclusion

The economic performance of the East Asian developing economies during the past thirty years or so has shown that the rapid expansion of manufacturing production and exports has contributed to the overall rapid growth of GNP and consumption. It has also brought about a shift from resource-based, labor-intensive products to capital- and technology-intensive products, thereby changing the economic structure and upgrading the content of industrialization in the area. The performance of the four NIEs has been particularly remarkable. Singapore, Hong Kong, and Taiwan are already among the world's high-income economies, and South Korea has reached upper-middle-income status.

Structurally, the manufacturing sector's share of GDP generally increased rapidly during this period, reaching a range of 18 percent for Hong Kong to 34 percent for Taiwan in 1990. Manufactured exports increased even faster, with their share of total merchandise exports increasing to over 90 percent for Hong Kong, Taiwan, and South Korea and 62 to 73 percent for the Philippines, Thailand, and Singapore; it was below 50 percent only in Malaysia and Indonesia. Thus, rapid GDP growth has been a result of industrialization, which, in turn, has been led by manufactured exports, a phenomenon of open industrialization.

In manufactured exports a pattern of growth has emerged. Typically, with abundant surplus labor and poor endowment of natural resources, the four NIEs started with labor-intensive industrial production and exports such as textiles, clothing, footwear, and toys. The ASEAN–4, with their respective abundant natural resources, began with processing industries and exports such as plywood, leather goods, jewelry, and handicrafts. However, as their economies grew, surplus labor was absorbed by the rapidly expanding industrial, commercial, and other related activities, and the real wage level rose accordingly. Meanwhile, capital accumulated through increases in business profits and personal income, and real interest rates tended to decline. These factors favored the development of capital-intensive industries such as steel and chemicals. Management and engineering capabilities were built up through learning-by-doing, education, and training. New industries emerged in such subsectors as electrical and other machinery, electronics, and shipbuilding. The four NIEs have led the way, and the ASEAN–4 and China are now following.

This progress, likened to climbing an export ladder, is quantified systematically by Pearson in a matrix of export product similarity indexes. Balassa and Noland project the export structure changes of these economies by using factor endowments of more refined categories. All suggest that a dynamic process of changing comparative advantage has enabled the East Asian industrializing economies to move up the manufactured exports ladder and through successive stages of industrialization. Development efforts are helpful in this process. Foreign trade stimulates improvement and makes more widely available the various factors of production that are the underlying forces in the dynamics of comparative advantage.

The government can play an important role in initiating and speeding up industrialization and expanding exports. Except in Singapore and Hong Kong, which are entrepôt cities, policies of governments in this region have played various key roles. Import controls and tariffs have protected domestic industries initially, bringing many of them into being. In many of these economies, the government itself established new industries. While public enterprises were later found to be inefficient, private enterprises flourished by substituting imports. But when domestic markets were saturated, no room was left for further import substitution. Inflation and high costs spread, and imports of industrial inputs increased with no prospects for improving the balance of payments. Many countries/areas of this region, particularly Taiwan and South Korea, recognized these problems early on and turned to promoting exports. Their governments adopted incentive policies, giving preferential fiscal and financial treatment to export industries and traders. Exchange rates were devalued step by step. All this corrected the bias against exports under the import-substitution regime. Consequently, the country's manufactured exports expanded rapidly, as did its industrial sector and economy as a whole. Countries coming into the game late were left behind. Thailand, China, and Malaysia are currently catching up, while the Philippines and Indonesia are still lagging.

The initial stage of manufactures-led growth or open industrialization was attempted mostly in light consumer goods industries. In relatively large countries/areas, when the economies grew to a certain point, the demand for intermediate and capital goods became large enough to warrant the establishment of industries to manufacture such products. This also became possible because of the accumulation of capital and the availability of more skilled labor, as well as better engineering and management capacities. But to begin the establishment of heavy industries, protection and incentives are also needed. South Korea used such measures during its second round of import substitution in heavy and chemical industries with the eventual aim of exporting these products. The country suffered some short-term misallocation of resources but gained time with its relatively early development of heavy and chemical industries. It finally reduced protection and increased exports of machinery and other capital- and technology-intensive products, marking a return to open industrialization. Thus, South Korea eventually gained a dynamic comparative advantage.

Taiwan achieved some success in moving up the export ladder and expanding its industrial structure with less drastic measures. Meanwhile Malaysia and to a lesser extent, Indonesia are entering this second round of import substitution each intending to follow South Korea's path of eventually building exports.

Considering the whole process of industrialization, one may conclude that the strategies of import substitution and export orientation are not simultaneous static choices but rather a matter of sequence and with some overlap. In this process, the government's most important role is to recognize the changing situation, identify the arrival of the turning points, provide adequate incentives, shift strategy, and reduce protection in due course. Of course, the incentive regime should always be made rational and simple, the criteria clear, and implementation easy. Currently, China, the Philippines and, to some extent, Indonesia are still ambivalent in their trade policies. While they proclaim a policy of promoting export orientation, strong import restrictions and other protective measures still coexist. Initially, in China's socialist economic system, import substitution under protection, and strategy of developing heavy industry hindered its development of efficient enterprises. With reforms in the economy, enterprise, and trade, greater export orientation can be expected, but only when protection for import substitution is considerably reduced can China enjoy the full benefits of open industrialization.

While the East Asian industrializing economies are striving for further manufactured export expansion and open industrialization, new forms of protectionism and trade regionalism are on the increase in the developed countries. The global trading system is moving away from Most Favored Nation (MFN) tariffs to selective quantitative restrictions under the guise of voluntary export restrictions and orderly market agreements. These measures have been directed disproportionately against the manufactured exports of Asian countries/areas. In addition, the United States has tightened its unfair trade provisions in the countervailing duty and antidumping provisions of the 1988 Trade Act and has expanded the list of objectionable practices under Section 301. Generalized System of Preferences (GSP) privileges have also been largely withdrawn from East Asian developing countries/areas.

The unification of the European Community's internal markets will inevitably direct its trade inward and intensify its external protection. The North American Free Trade Agreement will have a similar effect, particularly because it includes

Mexico, a developing country that is similar to the East Asian industrializing countries. Both trends will place the East Asian industrializing economies in an unfavorable competitive position.

With such an international trade environment, it is tempting for the nine East Asian industrializing economies to resort to some form of regional cooperation to promote free trade. First, such regional cooperation would enable them to bargain collectively and, therefore, more forcefully with the industrialized countries to maintain multilateralism with minimum barriers in world trade. Second, it would expand intraregional trade by coordinated acts aiming for mutual reduction of trade barriers.

From a dynamic viewpoint, the economies of these nine East Asian industrializing countries/areas, which are at different stages of development and on different rungs of the export ladder, are sufficiently diversified to suggest continual rapid increases in intraregional trade. The bond of common EA–9 interests in opposing protectionism and countering regionalism is strong enough to prompt initiation of close regional cooperation. The ASEAN can still function as is, but it can also join a new regional trade cooperation organization with similar interests. Efforts for broader Asia and Pacific regional cooperation to include the industrialized countries may encounter interests too diverse to permit any action, but such a group could function as a forum, which the EA–9 could join to pursue its own interests.

References

Baldwin, Robert E. 1988. *Trade Policy in a Changing World.* Chicago: University of Chicago Press.

Council for Economic Planning and Development. 1991. *Taiwan Statistical Data Bank.* Taiwan.

Klause, Lawrence B. 1987. "The Structure of Trade in Manufactured Goods in the East and Southeast Asia Region." In *Trade and Structure Change in Pacific Asia,* eds. Colin I. Bradford, Jr., and William H. Branson. Chicago: University of Chicago Press, pp. 205–226.

Kobayashi, Minoru. 1990. "China and the Development of the West Pacific Economic Zone." *Intertrade* (Beijing) (January): 9–12.

Naya, Seiji; James, William E.; and Plummer, Michael. No date. *Pacific Economic Cooperation in the Global Context.* (Honolulu) East-West Center.

Orchard, John E. 1930. *Japan's Economic Position: The Progress of Industrialization.* New York: Whittlesey House.

Singer, Hans W. 1952. "The Mechanisms of Economic Development." *The Indian Economic Review* (August). pp. 1–18.

Tan, Kong Yam. 1990. "Pattern of Asia Pacific Economic Growth and Implications for China." *Intertrade* (Beijing) (January): 13–16.

Trela, Irene, and John Whalley. 1988. *Do Developing Countries Lose from the MFA?* Cambridge, Massachusetts: National Bureau of Economic Research.

World Bank. 1992, 1993. *World Development Report.* Washington, D.C.

Yang, Shu-Chin. 1957. *A Multiple Exchange Rate System, an Appraisal of Thailand's Experience, 1946–1955*. Madison, Wisconsin: The University of Wisconsin Press.
———. 1964. "Foreign Trade Problems of Economic Development." *Scottish Journal of Political Economy* 11 (June):116–35.
———. 1981. "The Foreign Exchange Problems of the Philippines in the Mid-Fifties." *The Philippine Economic Journal* 20(2): 127–50.
———. 1990. "Reflections on Patterns of Manufactured Export Structural Changes in East Asian Industrializing Economies and Possible Regional Cooperation." *Intertrade* (Beijing) (January): 17–20.

CHAPTER 2

The Asian Export Ladder

CHARLES S. PEARSON*

Introduction

The countries of the Asia-Pacific region exhibit a dynamic process of changing comparative advantage. The essential feature, apart from rapid overall growth of manufactured exports, appears to be the changing structure of manufactured exports. A useful analogy may be countries at different rungs and moving up a product-sophistication "ladder," with labor-intensive, capital-intensive and technology-intensive products at the lower, middle, and upper rungs, respectively. In this view, Japan and the United States compete at the upper rungs, the Asian NIEs (South Korea, Taiwan, Singapore, and Hong Kong) have moved from lower to middle rungs, and ASEAN countries have recently started the climb from the lower rungs. Alternatively, one can view export products as moving down a country "ladder," as, for example, in the shift of labor intensive products from Japan in the 1950s and early 1960s, first to the Asian NIEs and more recently to ASEAN countries.

This process of dynamic change in comparative advantage has profound implications for trade and industrial policy. For Western industrial countries, the source of import competition in traditional manufactures is shifting. Countries at the top of the Asian export ladder, particularly Japan, now challenge the West in emerging high-technology products. For individual Asian exporting countries, the rapidly changing structure of exports suggests competitive pressure by countries at lower rungs of the ladder, but the changing structure also means new export opportunities, as countries at higher rungs vacate export markets. The delayed entrance of the People's Republic of China (PRC) into this process of multiple export catch-up both complicates the policy questions and makes them more interesting.[1]

Moreover, the adjustments required by the changing structure of exports come

* The author is grateful to Mark Ellyne, who assisted in an early version of this study done in 1985, and to Karen Kizer, Jamil Mubarak, and Mitchiko Kinefuchi for research assistance in the current study.

at a time when the international trade system is in considerable disarray. Elements of this disarray include unprecedented external trade surpluses and deficits (United States, Japan, Taiwan, South Korea); a partial abandonment of the principle of nondiscrimination (MFN) and increased recourse to bilateralism; and the aggressive pursuit of "fair trade" as the new cornerstone of United States trade policy.

The first section of this paper examines the process of multiple export catch-up in Asia and proposes a method for measuring this phenomenon. Section two describes this measure, an export similarity (dissimilarity) index, and the data. Section three applies the index to ten Asia-Pacific countries for the 1962–86 period and interprets the results. The final section discusses the implications of the empirical results in light of current trade policy issues.

The Ladder Hypothesis and Multiple Export Catch-up

In its simplest terms, the ladder hypothesis asserts that the Asian exporters of manufactures are rapidly climbing a product-sophistication ladder, as revealed by their export structures, and that export products are shifting down a country ladder. The phenomenon is consistent with both a dynamic version of the Heckscher-Ohlin factor endowment model, in which Asian countries' relative factor endowments of labor, capital, human capital, and technology change quickly, and the product-cycle theory, which predicts movement of production from more advanced to less advanced countries as products mature and become standardized.

Simply ranking countries by per capita income and assigning them rungs on the product-sophistication ladder may not capture reality, however. Two of the countries considered (Hong Kong and Singapore) are city-states, and four (Indonesia, Malaysia, Philippines, and Thailand) are major exporters of natural resources, as, indeed, is the United States. These special features may well affect export structures of manufacturers.

Indeed, the movement up the ladder can be expected to vary in accord with differing factor endowments. We may expect the resource-abundant ASEAN countries to move through a natural resource processing phase that was less strongly observed in Korea and Taiwan, and their movement into capital- and skill-intensive products may be correspondingly delayed.

Moreover, the rungs on the product-sophistication ladder may not be evenly spaced, and a country may have a secure foot on two rungs. Most important, no country maintains a static position on the ladder. Measuring the relative positions of countries over time gives some insight into the time lags between them and whether there is a general tendency toward convergence of export structures.

There is some empirical support for hypothesizing the effects of changing factor endowments on export structure. For example, as early as 1976, Peter Heller explained the changing structure of Japanese exports by changing factor endowments. More recently, Young Sun Lee (1986) investigated the changing export structures of South Korea, Taiwan, and Japan, using data for 1963 to 1977. He found that South Korea and Taiwan, unlike Japan, did not generally export products with high levels of human and physical capital, but that over this period the commodity structure of Korean exports did become more physical- and human-capital intensive, while Taiwan continued to exploit its comparative advantage in labor- or skill-intensive products.

William Cline (1984) found that middle-income developing countries gener- ally have not lost their share of import markets to lower-income developing countries in traditional manufactures, although they have gained import market from industrial countries in nontraditional manufactures exports. Cline's data, however, run only through 1978 and are confined to imports by seven industrial countries. Moreover, his analysis is based on import market shares and the pres- ent study considers export structures.

If true, a multiple catch-up in export structures has direct implications for trade policy. For importers like the United States, the source of competitive pressure in traditional labor-intensive products would shift. But to the extent that imports from one country merely *displace* imports from another, no new domes- tic resource adjustment costs arise. Also, when the United States imposes selec- tive (i.e., discriminatory) trade restraints, as it has done for nonrubber footwear, stainless-steel flatware, color television sets, steel, machine tools, and other products, reallocation of production to countries at lower rungs is accelerated.[2] Finally, following the ladder analogy, the United States and Japan at the top rungs find themselves in direct competition in technologically sophisticated products—supposedly the last bastion, apart from agriculture and certain raw materials, of United States comparative advantage.

Trade policy issues for exporting countries are equally important. The more rapidly Japan yields world markets in capital-intensive products (and yields its domestic market in labor-intensive goods), the more rapidly the more advanced developing countries gain export markets in capital-intensive goods while yield- ing, in turn, world markets in labor-intensive goods to countries newly recruited to exporting manufactures.

The delayed entrance of the People's Republic of China into this dynamic process in the late 1970s poses interesting questions. Where has China settled on the export structure ladder, and how rapidly will it climb? Are Korean and Taiwan export structures sufficiently sophisticated to escape pressure from China from below? Will the entrance of China slow the progress of the ASEAN export- ers? What competitive pressures are countries like the United States likely to experience? Does the sheer size of the Chinese economy and its export potential add a new dimension?[3]

Apart from the entrance of China, other interesting empirical questions arise. Is the manufactures export structure of Japan converging on the export structure of the United States, suggesting increased competition in third-country markets?

How closely are the Asian NIEs tracking the Japanese export model, and are they catching up or converging? How closely are the ASEAN countries tracking the Asian NIE model? Does their continued reliance on natural-resource exports imply that their export structure in manufactures is substantially different from the natural-resource-poor Asian NIEs?

The calculation of export similarity indices offers some insight into these questions. Finger and Kreinin (1979) have developed an export similarity (dissimilarity) index that permits comparison of the commodity composition of exports across countries, over time, and among countries at different points in time. Kellman and Schroder (1983) investigated the structural properties of the index, including stability over time and sensitivity to aggregation bias.[4] We propose to use this tool to investigate the changing structure of manufactures exports in the Asia-Pacific region in the past two and a half decades.

Measurement and Data

An export similarity index can be defined[5]

$$S_{AB} = 100 \sum_{i=1}^{n} (F_{iA}, F_{iB})$$

where S_{AB} is the similarity of product composition of manufactured exports of country A to those of country B (or to those of country A at some different time).

F_{iA} is the share of A's total manufactured exports, accounted for by the export of the ith product.

F_{iB} is the share of B's total manufactured exports, accounted for by the export of the ith product.

$i = 1 \ldots 106$ for three digit SITC.

S_{AB} ranges from 0 (no similarity or total dissimilarity) to 100 (identical commodity pattern).

A priori, one expects S_{AB} to be (relatively) high among countries at a similar stage of industrialization and with similar patterns of comparative advantage. When comparing export structures for a single country over time, a (relatively) low value of S_{AB} indicates rapid structural change in exports. By comparing two countries, each at different time periods, one can investigate how closely one country tracks another, the duration of the lag, and whether there is convergence in export structures.

S_{AB} values may be sensitive to the level of aggregation. Ideally, the level of disaggregation should be sufficiently fine to eliminate intracommodity trade but not so fine as to make superficial product distinctions (e.g., blue shirts versus white shirts). In a test of Mediterranean country trade patterns, Kellman and Schroder find the ranking of export similarities among eleven countries to be statistically significant between the two- and the three-digit SITC levels and between the three- and the four-digit levels but not between the two- and four-digit levels. In this analysis we use the three-digit SITC, which comprises 106 manufactures categories.

Besides domestic sources of change, S_{AB} values might be expected to respond over time to the changing patterns of world demand for particular exports. If S_{AB} calculations over time can be normalized for changes in world demand (import) patterns, the adjusted S_{AB} becomes a better measure of supply shifts in the exporting country. This was done as deemed appropriate in the analytical section.

Finally, when measuring S_{AB} indices for export structures over time (but not across countries), changes in relative prices among export products may be responsible for a low index. For some purposes, a comparison of export values is sufficient, but for other purposes, changes in the relative quantities, by product, may be of greater interest. In principle, S_{AB} can be measured in constant base-year prices, but this requires detailed price indices by SITC product, which are not available for manufactured goods at the necessary level of disaggregation. All calculations in this chapter are in value terms.

The data sources are as follows: OECD *Commodity Trade Statistics*, Series C, Exports, are used for the United States and Japan.[6] All other countries are based on U.N. *Commodity Trade Statistics* except for PRC and Taiwan post-1970, which are not reported by the United Nations. For PRC and Taiwan post-1970, total OECD imports are used in lieu of their actual exports. OECD imports capture 65 to 75 percent of Taiwanese exports of manufactures. To assess the similarity of patterns of Taiwan's global exports to its exports to the OECD, we calculate the correlation coefficient between the two export profiles for 1970 at 0.94. This suggests that OECD import data provide a reasonable source.[7] SITC Revision 2 data were regrouped to Revision 1 categories for 1980 and subsequent years. In general, data were taken from 1962, 1965, five-year intervals through 1980, 1983 (OECD) or 1982 (U.N.), and finally 1986, yielding seven points in time. For this study, manufactures are defined as SITC 5–8. A good case can be made that processed foods could have been considered as manufactures and included. SITC 68, nonferrous metals, could be excluded. Some data problems remain, but they do not appear crippling.

Overview of Export Structures and Empirical Results

Before turning to similarity indices, it is useful to have a broad overview of export structures. Table 2.1 presents the percentage share of each country's total manufactured exports that each two-digit SITC represents in the latest available year (1986). Several features stand out.

First, the natural-resource-rich ASEAN countries (Malaysia, Thailand, Indonesia, Philippines) tend to have relatively large export shares in natural-resource-based manufactures—SITC 63 (wood products), SITC 66 (nonmetallic manufactures) and SITC 68 (nonferrous metals).

Second, the traditional items of textiles (65) and clothing (84) remain important for all developing countries (although in different proportions). Footwear (85) is important for Taiwan and Korea, and to a lesser extent, the PRC and Thailand. For most developing countries the "basket" category (89), which includes musical instruments, toys, sporting goods, and jewelry is also important.

Third, for certain developing countries nontraditional exports, have become important: nonelectrical machinery (71) for Singapore and Taiwan and electrical machinery (72) for all developing countries except Indonesia and the PRC.

Fourth, for the United States, machinery and transport equipment (71, 72, 73) dominate. The same is true for Japan, which also shows relatively high export share for scientific instruments, optical and photographic equipment (86) and the "basket" category (89).

Table 2.2 presents the percentage point *change* in export market shares by two-digit SITC and by country for 1965 to 1986. The most striking changes are:

(1) The United States increased its concentration in its dominant exports (72, 73) and in scientific and controlling instruments, but all changes appear modest.

(2) Among Japanese exports, the textiles (65) share lost 12 percentage points (18 percentage points since 1962), and iron and steel (67) lost 10 percentage points. All machinery and equipment (71, 72, 73), particularly transport equipment, gained a substantial share of Japan's manufactured exports.

(3) Both wood products (63) and textiles (65) lost export market share for South Korea, with gains registered in electrical machinery (72), transportation equipment (73), and footwear (85).

(4) In Taiwan, textiles and wood products lost market share, while nonelectrical machinery, footwear, and miscellaneous manufactures (89) made strong percentage-point gains.

Other patterns of change can be seen by studying the table.

Export Profiles

Table 2.3 presents a triangular matrix of export similarity indices in which eleven countries' 1986 manufactures export profiles are compared.[8] The arrangement, or ordering of countries, was done as follows: The United States was chosen as the "base" country, and the country measured to be most similar to the United States (Japan) was then entered. Next, the country most similar to Japan (South Korea) was chosen, and so on. In this sense, the *ordering* of countries in the matrix was determined by the similarity indices and represents a continuum along a similarity dimension.

Note that by this arrangement rule, the principal diagonal forms a "ridge" of high numbers. If there were perfect symmetry among export profiles, the rows and columns off the principal diagonal would decrease monotonically (indicating decreasing average of elements in the diagonals as one moves away from the principal diagonal).

Table 2.1

Share of Total Manufactured Exports by Two-Digit SITC and by Country, 1986

	SITC Category	Hong Kong	Indo-nesia	Japan	South Korea	Malay-sia	Philip-pines	China	Singa-pore	Taiwan	Thai-land	U.S.
51	Chemical Elements and Compounds	0.0	1.7	1.9	1.1	1.2	4.9	3.5	3.5	0.5	0.9	5.7
52	Chemicals from Coal, Petro., & Nat. Gas	0.0	0.0	0.0	0.0	0.0	0.0	0.0	0.0	0.0	0.0	0.0
53	Dyeing, Tanning Materials	0.1	0.4	0.4	0.2	0.1	0.0	0.3	0.4	0.1	0.2	0.3
54	Pharmaceuticals	0.1	0.6	0.3	0.2	0.4	0.4	1.8	1.0	0.1	0.3	2.2
55	Oils & Perfume Materials	0.3	1.6	0.2	0.1	0.5	0.4	0.6	0.6	0.1	0.3	0.6
56	Fertilizers	0.0	4.3	0.1	0.5	0.4	7.0	0.6	0.2	0.0	0.0	1.3
57	Explosives	0.0	0.0	0.0	0.0	0.0	0.1	1.2	0.0	0.0	0.0	0.1
58	Plastics	0.4	0.1	1.4	1.1	0.4	1.2	0.2	2.5	1.0	1.2	2.4
59	Chemical Materials	0.1	0.2	0.5	0.2	1.3	0.1	1.1	1.5	0.0	0.6	2.3
61	Leather & Leather Manufactures	0.2	0.5	0.1	0.3	0.1	0.2	0.4	0.1	0.5	1.8	0.3
62	Rubber Manufactures N.E.S.	0.0	0.4	1.0	1.8	1.1	0.2	0.0	0.5	1.1	1.5	0.7
63	Wood and Wood Products	0.1	38.2	0.0	0.3	3.8	7.4	0.5	1.5	2.3	2.1	6.4
64	Paper, Paperboard & Manufactures	0.6	1.1	0.6	0.7	0.5	0.1	0.4	1.0	0.3	0.9	1.7
	thereof											
65	Textile Yarn, Fabrics	7.0	9.8	2.7	10.0	3.8	2.6	24.2	3.2	3.1	13.0	1.7
66	Non-Metallic Min. Manufactures, N.E.S.	0.6	2.0	1.2	1.4	1.4	1.1	2.0	0.6	2.1	9.5	1.3
67	Iron and Steel	0.1	2.3	6.3	6.2	1.8	2.0	0.6	1.5	1.1	2.0	0.7
68	Nonferrous Metals	0.2	11.6	0.7	0.4	5.2	12.4	0.8	2.1	0.3	3.6	1.1
69	Manufactures of Metal	2.4	0.1	2.0	4.4	0.9	0.6	3.1	1.9	6.2	1.6	1.8
71	Non-Electrical Machinery	6.4	0.8	20.9	5.1	5.3	0.7	0.8	24.3	11.9	4.6	27.9
72	Electrical Machinery, Apparatus & Appl.	15.6	0.6	16.0	16.5	55.2	21.3	2.4	33.8	17.5	18.1	12.4
73	Transport Equipment	0.1	0.7	29.1	12.5	3.7	0.1	0.2	4.4	2.9	0.6	23.3
81	Sanitary, & Lighting Fixtures & Fittings	0.8	0.0	0.1	0.3	0.3	0.1	0.1	0.1	1.2	0.2	0.1
82	Furniture	0.4	0.7	0.1	0.3	0.3	5.5	0.0	0.7	4.8	1.8	0.5
83	Travel Goods	1.1	0.0	0.1	0.3	0.3	0.7	0.0	0.1	3.1	0.7	0.0
84	Clothing	35.5	17.5	0.4	17.1	7.6	17.9	36.4	5.0	13.7	20.7	0.6
85	Footwear	0.8	0.3	0.0	6.4	0.4	1.9	3.1	0.1	9.9	2.9	0.0
86	Scientific & Controlling Instruments	9.3	1.3	5.3	1.7	1.9	0.3	0.3	3.3	2.3	1.3	6.1
89	Misc. Manufactures	18.0	3.9	8.6	9.4	2.8	9.8	16.2	6.1	13.8	9.3	3.9

Source: United Nations, *Yearbook of International Trade Statistics,* 1986 (New York).

Table 2.2

Percentage-Point Change in Share of Exports by Two-Digit SITC and by Country, 1965–86

SITC	Category	Hong Kong	Indonesia	Japan	South Korea	Malaysia	Philippines	China	Singapore	Taiwan	Thailand	U.S.
51	Chemical Elements and Compounds	-0.1	1.7	-1.2	1.0	1.0	0.2	-4.9	1.5	-3.5	0.9	-0.1
52	Chemicals from Coal, Petro., & Nat. Gas	0.0	0.0	0.0	0.0	0.0	0.0	0.0	-0.4	-0.1	0.0	-0.1
53	Dyeing, Tanning Materials	-0.3	0.2	-0.1	0.2	-0.4	0.0	-0.3	-0.4	-0.1	0.2	-0.2
54	Pharmaceuticals	-0.3	0.6	-0.2	0.2	-0.3	-2.2	1.4	-1.0	-0.1	-0.1	0.7
55	Oils & Perfume Materials	0.2	0.2	0.0	0.1	-2.0	0.4	-4.4	-1.4	-3.9	-1.1	-0.1
56	Fertilizers	0.0	4.3	-1.1	0.5	0.4	7.0	0.0	-1.8	-1.9	0.0	0.4
57	Explosives	0.0	0.0	-0.1	1.1	0.3	0.1	1.2	-0.3	-0.6	0.0	-0.1
58	Plastics	0.3	0.1	0.2	0.2	1.2	1.0	-0.3	1.7	0.0	1.2	0.0
59	Chemical Materials	0.1	0.0	0.0	0.3	0.3	0.2	-0.3	-0.1	0.5	0.2	0.4
61	Leather & Leather Manufactures	0.1	0.5	-0.2	0.9	-0.8	1.0	-4.5	-0.2	0.3	1.1	-0.1
62	Rubber Manufactures N.E.S.	0.0	0.0	-0.5	0.3	-0.8	0.2	0.0	-1.0	0.3	1.5	-0.3
63	Wood and Wood Products	-0.2	-94.6	-1.2	-16.9	3.4	-67.6	-0.2	0.4	-12.6	1.4	0.0
64	Paper, Paperboard & Manufactures thereof	0.5	38.2	-0.3	0.5	0.2	0.1	-0.3	-0.7	-1.3	-0.4	-0.5
65	Textile Yarn, Fabrics	-10.8	1.1	-11.9	-14.9	2.6	-9.9	-2.2	-12.2	-22.5	7.0	-1.3
66	Non-Metallic Min. Manufactures, N.E.S.	-0.2	9.1	-2.2	-1.1	0.4	1.1	-0.2	-3.9	-4.0	-9.0	-0.5
67	Iron and Steel	-0.8	2.0	-10.3	-5.8	1.3	2.0	-18.3	-4.1	-2.6	1.7	-2.9
68	Nonferrous Metals	0.0	2.3	-0.9	-2.4	-76.3	12.4	-18.4	0.5	-2.4	-59.6	-2.1
69	Manufactures of Metal	-1.0	9.4	-1.9	2.4	0.3	-0.2	2.7	-4.3	3.5	1.1	-1.4
71	Non-Electrical Machinery	5.8	-0.2	12.9	2.9	3.0	0.7	0.4	12.5	9.8	4.6	-1.2
72	Electrical Machinery, Apparatus & Appl.	9.3	0.8	6.1	14.7	54.5	21.3	1.9	28.3	11.4	17.1	2.5
73	Transport Equipment	-0.4	0.6	13.1	11.5	0.5	0.1	0.2	-12.4	1.9	0.8	4.1
81	Sanitary, & Lighting Fixtures & Fittings	-1.6	0.7	-0.2	-0.1	0.0	0.1	0.1	-0.4	1.1	0.2	-0.2
82	Furniture	-0.6	0.3	-0.1	0.3	-0.1	4.4	0.1	-0.1	4.6	1.8	0.2
83	Travel Goods	0.1	0.0	-0.3	2.0	0.0	0.7	0.0	-0.5	2.9	0.7	0.0
84	Clothing	-2.0	17.5	-3.3	-2.4	7.3	16.4	29.7	-0.5	2.6	18.1	-0.4
85	Footwear	-2.4	0.3	-1.0	2.5	-0.3	1.9	3.1	-0.9	8.6	2.9	0.1
86	Scientific & Controlling Instruments	8.5	1.3	2.0	1.3	1.8	0.3	-0.3	1.2	2.1	1.3	2.4
89	Misc. Manufactures	-4.2	3.6	2.4	1.0	2.0	7.9	13.0	0.1	6.2	6.3	0.0

Source: United Nations, *Yearbook of International Trade Statistics*, 1965 and 1986 issue (New York).

Table 2.3

Export Similarity Matrix, 1986

	U.S.	Japan	Korea	Taiwan	Hong Kong	China	Thailand	Philippines	Malaysia	Indonesia	Avg. of Elements in Diagonal	Singapore
U.S.	100	62	36.3	37.7	26.7	18.3	26.7	24.1	32.9	15.8		57.0
Japan		100	49.5	42.1	31.2	14.2	28.1	18.2	37.0	13.6	15.8	55.9
Korea			100	62.1	53.4	41.9	52.1	39.6	43.5	35.6	23.2	49.1
Taiwan				100	57.5	40.4	48.3	41.5	40.3	26.0	32.2	49.8
Hong Kong					100	59.1	48.2	33.6	33.8	33.0	28.6	40.4
China						100	45.3	39.8	23.4	34.8	31.9	23.1
Thailand							100	41.8	36.7	38.3	33.9	39.6
Philippines								100	36.1	36.1	36.3	22.7
Malaysia									100	29.7	46.7	59.5
Indonesia										100	49.2	36.8

The table tells two interesting stories. First, the ten countries can indeed be arrayed along a similarity/dissimilarity dimension, with the resulting pattern very close to the "ideal" pattern of decreasing rows and columns. The uniformity is seen in the column reporting the average of the diagonal elements, which starts at the ridge value of 100, decreases to 49.2, 46.7 . . . 15.8.[9] This suggests that there are regularities in export structures that make comparative work interesting for economic analytical purposes.

Second, and more interesting, the *arrangement* of countries in the matrix according to export similarity indices confirms *a priori* expectations that it is useful to group countries' export profiles. The advanced industrial countries—United States and Japan—are similar. Next to them on the export similarity continuum are the Asian NIEs—Korea, Taiwan and Hong Kong—which form a group.[10] The PRC fits itself between the Asian NIEs and the resource-rich ASEAN countries—Thailand, Indonesia, Malaysia, Philippines. The four ASEAN countries show similarities, among themselves, although they are somewhat less strong than the similarities among the Asian NIEs. Only Singapore is an exception.

A second question of interest is the extent to which the eleven countries have experienced shifts in the commodity composition of their manufactures exports over time. If the ladder analogy is correct, one expects to see significant changes in the composition of exports at the country level.

Table 2.4 reports the extent of similarity (dissimilarity) between each country's export profile in the base year (1965) and the current year (1986). The table shows that the United States, followed by Hong Kong and Japan, has experienced the least change (greatest stability) in its export structures. In contrast, all of the remaining developing countries have experienced substantial changes in the composition of their manufactures exports.[11] Among the developing countries, Hong Kong has stayed closest to its original export products. A check of the export share data at the two-digit level confirms this: clothing (84) and miscellaneous manufactures (89) accounted for 56 percent of Hong Kong exports in 1962 and 56 percent in 1982. By 1986 they still accounted for 54 percent.

Table 2.5A reports the export similarity matrix between the United States and Japan for six time periods. The table allows comparison of the Japanese export profile in any year with the United States in that year or any other year.[12]

The hypothesis of a convergence, or "catching up" of Japan to the United States in export structures can be tested by examining the elements of the principal diagonal. An increasing trend left to right indicates convergence. The statistics show convergence, from 44.5 in 1961 to 62 in 1986. Assuming that all other factors are equal, this convergence suggests greater competition between the two countries in third-country markets. Interpreted somewhat differently, the row for 1986 shows that over time the Japanese export structure is becoming increasingly similar to that of the United States. Interestingly, the reverse is not true.

Table 2.4

Comparing Export Structures over Time, by Country, 1986 over 1965

Country	Export Similarity Index 1986 (with 1965 =100)
U.S.	76.6
Hong Kong	65.6
Japan	51.3
China	49.5
Korea	44.4
Singapore	43.3
Taiwan	36.3
Thailand	26.5
Malaysia	15.5
Philippines	13.9
Indonesia	4.4

Reading vertically for column 1986, United States exports became more similar to 1986 Japanese exports between 1961 and 1970, but the index has been essentially stable since then.

Table 2.5A also provides evidence concerning Japan's "lag" of the United States export profile and the duration of the lag. If, for example, Japanese export structure lagged United States export structure by eight years, we would expect the United States 1975–Japan 1983 index to be high. In fact, the index is at its maximum in precisely this cell (62.8), but the variation within the column is small. By 1986 the lag apparently disappeared, and we can draw no strong conclusions.

Table 2.5B confirms these results by presenting the matrix of correlation coefficients between the United States and Japan at different time periods. Again, the principal diagonal shows a strongly increasing trend, suggesting convergence. The evidence for lag is eleven years (that is, Japan 1986, United States 1975:76), but it is not strong. To summarize, Tables 5A and B provide confirmation of the view that Japan is converging on the United States export structure, suggesting increased competition between the two in third-country markets.[13]

Table 2.6A examines the extent to which South Korea is following the Japanese export structure "model" and, if so, the duration of the lag and whether it is becoming shorter. Turning first to the principal diagonal, there is evidence of a convergence, from a similarity index of 33.7 in 1962 to an index of 56.5 in 1986. However, the increase is not uniform over time, reaching a local maximum in 1965 before resuming steady growth between 1970 and 1986. Elements along the principal diagonals reveal convergence toward a moving target—as shown in earlier tables, the Japanese export structure itself has changed considerably over the period.

South Korea in 1986 most closely resembles Japan in 1965 and 1970, suggesting a lag of fifteen to twenty years. The resemblance, with indices of 62.7

Table 2.5A

Export Similarity Matrix, United States–Japan, 1961–86
Japan (with U.S. = 100)

Japan U.S.	1961	1965	1970	1975	1980	1983	1986
1961	44.5	48.3	54.9	54.5	55.8	56.2	54.5
1965	42.2	47.8	56.2	56.7	60.8	59.6	59.7
1970	40.0	45.0	54.8	56.0	60.5	61.0	62.2
1975	41.0	45.6	53.1	58.2	61.7	62.8	62.1
1980	39.6	44.2	51.6	52.4	54.8	57.5	58.7
1983	37.9	42.6	51.2	51.7	54.9	57.7	60.4
1986	N/A	42.0	50.5	53.0	55.9	58.9	62.0

Table 2.5B

Export Structure Correlation Coefficient Matrix, United States–Japan, 1965–86

Japan U.S.	1965	1970	1975	1980	1983	1986
1965	0.33	0.52	0.59	0.71	0.73	0.72
1970	0.30	0.51	0.57	0.68	0.72	0.73
1975	0.31	0.51	0.60	0.73	0.76	0.76
1980	0.26	0.45	0.50	0.59	0.66	0.67
1983	0.25	0.45	0.49	0.57	0.67	0.70
1986	0.23	0.44	0.49	0.61	0.67	0.72

and 62.3, is quite high (by Table 2.3 standards) and suggests some South Korean tracking of the Japanese export structure model but not slavish repetition. The hypothesis of a lag of fifteen to twenty years is given some support when we note that South Korea in 1982 was most similar to Japan in 1962 and 1965 (62.9 and 63.7). The correlation matrix for the same countries and years, along with reports in Table 2.6B, shows South Korea in 1986 and 1982 most like Japan in the 1965–70 period, tending to confirm the lag of fifteen to twenty years.

The export share data themselves offer some explanation. South Korea and Japan had similar export shares for SITC textiles (65) in 1962: 23.3 percent and, 21.4 percent, respectively. By 1982, these shares had fallen to 12.2 percent in South Korea and 3.7 percent in Japan; by 1986 they had dropped to 10 percent in South Korea and 2.7 percent in Japan. Thus, Japan's ability to shed textile exports rapidly accounts for some increased *dissimilarity*. Also, transport equipment (73) increased to 12.5 percent in South Korea but grew even more rapidly to 29.1 percent in Japan. Thus, South Korea's "target" was itself moving rapidly, thereby increasing dissimilarity. Finally, clothing and footwear (84 and 85) in-

Table 2.6A

Export Similarity Matrix, Japan–South Korea, 1962–86
South Korea (with Japan = 100)

Japan	South Korea 1962	1965	1970	1975	1980	1982	1986
1962	33.7	48.6	37.3	52.5	64.0	62.9	N/A
1965	26.8	41.2	33.4	49.5	61.9	63.7	62.7
1970	21.8	35.7	26.9	45.9	57.0	59.3	62.3
1975	17.8	25.2	20.7	36.4	50.0	52.2	58.3
1980	15.2	22.6	19.9	37.1	48.7	46.9	58.7
1982	14.4	21.0	20.3	36.9	46.5	45.0	58.4
1986	11.9	17.1	18.3	33.6	39.1	38.5	56.5

Table 2.6B

Export Structure Correlation Coefficient Matrix, Japan–South Korea,
1965–86

Japan	South Korea 1965	1970	1975	1980	1982	1986
1965	0.4	0.23	0.38	0.53	0.58	0.59
1970	0.26	0.12	0.26	0.42	0.45	0.56
1975	0.08	−0.01	0.11	0.23	0.31	0.41
1980	0.04	−0.03	0.03	0.11	0.14	0.32
1982	0.03	−0.01	0.06	0.14	0.15	0.38
1986	N/A	−0.02	0.04	0.09	0.10	0.34

creased export market share in South Korea through 1982 but were never large in Japan. Thus, despite rapid South Korean growth in the machinery and equipment categories, the evidence that its export structure is more similar to Japan today than in the past is not overwhelming. In terms of the ladder analogy, South Korea has not fully "caught up" because it is still stuck to some extent on the clothing/footwear rung, while Japan has climbed to higher rungs.

Table 2.7A presents similar data comparing Taiwan and Japan. Examining the principal diagonal, there is no evidence of a convergence, nor can we find any strong evidence in the column for 1986 of a lag between Taiwan and Japan in export structures. For one reason, clothing and footwear actually increased their share of Taiwan's exports during the period from 1965 to 1986, but they have never been important export products for Japan. Our finding, that South Korea has followed the Japanese export structure model and Taiwan has not, is consistent with Young Sun Lee's conclusion that South Korea's policy of industrial deepening has led to exports becoming more physical- and human-capital inten-

Table 2.7A

Export Similarity Matrix, Taiwan–Japan, 1962–86
Taiwan (with Japan = 100)

Japan \ Taiwan	1962	1965	1970	1975	1980	1982	1986
1962	37.1	48.3	55.2	42.8	45.3	45.7	N/A
1965	30.8	42.3	47.6	39.2	41.8	42.8	42.4
1970	23.4	35.4	43.8	39.5	41.5	44.1	43.5
1975	19.1	29.3	34.7	31.2	33.3	35.1	34.5
1980	16.7	27.3	34.8	33.3	36.4	38.6	38.5
1982	15.2	26.1	33.2	32.6	35.7	39.6	40.1
1986	12.7	24.0	30.4	30.3	35.5	37.8	42.0

Table 2.7B

Export Structure Correlation Coefficient Matrix, Taiwan–Japan, 1965–86

Japan \ Taiwan	1965	1970	1975	1980	1983	1986
1965	0.25	0.38	0.32	0.31	0.31	0.28
1970	0.12	0.31	0.27	0.28	0.30	0.28
1975	N/A	0.12	0.09	0.11	0.12	0.11
1980	−0.02	0.1	0.07	0.09	0.11	0.11
1983	−0.03	0.11	0.10	0.11	0.15	0.16
1986	−0.04	0.09	0.08	0.10	0.13	0.18

sive, whereas Taiwan continued to exploit its comparative advantage in labor- and skill-intensive products.

In a further effort to understand the extent to which South Korea and Taiwan follow the Japanese model, we compared their 1982 export structures with hypothetical export structures for Japan in 1970 and 1975. The hypothetical structures were calculated by adjusting Japan's 1970 and 1975 export structures to 1982 world import patterns, allowing comparisons of 1982 South Korean and Taiwanese export profiles with the Japanese export profiles that would have obtained in 1970 and 1975 if Japan had faced 1982 world import demand patterns. The results are quite similar to those reported in Tables 2.6A and 2.7A, suggesting that changing patterns of world demand are not responsible for dissimilarities between South Korea and Taiwan in 1986, and Japan in 1970 and 1975.

The final question is whether ASEAN countries are following the Asian NIEs export structure model and, if so, the length of the lag and whether there is convergence. Table 2.8 presents the evidence for ASEAN and Asian NIEs as grouped. The principal diagonal shows definite convergence from 1965 to 1986. The highest similarity indices, as for example between ASEAN in 1986 and the

Table 2.8

Export Similarity Matrix, Asian NIEs–ASEAN, 1962–86
ASEAN Grouped (with Asian NIEs = 100)

NIEs \ ASEAN	1962	1965	1970	1975	1980	1982	1986
1962	31.5	25.0	34.7	41.1	48.8	54.6	56.5
1965	31.2	24.4	33.1	40.7	50.1	54.8	58.2
1970	25.9	20.6	27.2	39.3	53.1	56.7	60.3
1975	27.5	21.3	27.9	40.7	54.9	57.5	62.3
1980	20.6	16.6	21.5	37.9	51.6	55.1	59.3
1982	20.5	15.8	20.7	37.7	50.9	54.7	58.7
1986	18.9	13.7	17.7	35.7	49.3	53.2	57.5

Note: Export shares by three-digit SITC were obtained as the simple averages of the shares for the individual countries in each group.

Asian NIEs in 1975 (62.3), suggest that there is some tracking of the Asian NIEs model but less strongly than South Korea follows Japan. The apparent lag is about ten years, but the variations in column 1986 are small. On the other hand, the table strongly suggests that over time the similarity between ASEAN and NIEs export structures has become considerably greater (31.5 in 1962 versus 57.5 in 1986). Both groups are changing their export structures in a fashion that increases commodity overlap and presumably increases competitive pressures. The PRC has settled in at a point between the two groups (Table 2.3) and thus may exert pressure on other exporting countries from "above" and "below" and may itself be subject to a similar squeeze.

Conclusions and Implications for Trade Policy

One way to test the ladder analogy is to measure countries' shares of world trade by commodity. This approach may be misleading however, if one country's total exports grow more rapidly than another's. An alternative, used in this chapter, is to measure the share of a commodity in a single country's manufactures exports.

Summary data at the two-digit SITC level for the most recent year show the continued importance of natural-resource-based manufactures for ASEAN countries and the importance of traditional manufactures for all the developing countries, although nontraditional manufactures have also become important for the Asian NIEs and Malaysia. The United States import structure has changed least, while the Hong Kong structure also has been surprisingly stable.

Export similarity indices and correlation matrices confirm that it is useful to group the eleven countries by export structures, and the groupings conform to expectations. There is some evidence that Japan's export structure is converging on the United States' and that South Korea is tracking the Japanese model, but the target itself is moving. ASEAN countries appear to be tracking and converging on Asian NIEs, with increasing commodity overlap.

The PRC appears to fit between the ASEAN countries and the Asian NIEs, which suggests competitive pressure by the PRC on both groups, with China itself the object of a "squeeze."

We have not yet calculated the factor intensity of exports, which is necessary for a full test of the ladder hypothesis; we will do so in subsequent research. It appears, however, that traditional and presumably labor-intensive manufactures have moved up only modestly on the product ladder. Put somewhat differently, the Asian NIEs have moved up the product ladder slowly, maintaining a position on the "traditional products" rung while also securing a position in nontraditional manufactures at higher rungs. One explanation for the slow movement may be that countries have become adept at upgrading to higher-value-added products within the same product category, thus increasing the skill and capital intensity of what appear to be traditional manufactures.

The remarkable changes in export structure as Asian countries move up the export ladder come at a time when the trade system is in considerable disarray. One obvious change in the trade system is the movement away from MFN tariffs to selective (i.e., discretionary) quantitative restrictions under the guise of "voluntary export restraints" and "orderly marketing agreements." These "gray area" measures, taken by the United States and the European Community, have been directed disproportionately at Asian countries. In addition, the United States has tightened its "unfair" trade provisions in the countervailing duty and antidumping provisions of the 1988 Trade Act and has expanded the list of objectionable practices under Section 301 to include such ill-defined concepts as export targeting.

There is a connection between rapid changes in export structure and these trade policy measures, all of which are country-specific and hence discriminatory. Established trade patterns require little adjustment and generate minimal objections in importing countries. Disruptions to the status quo, however, are resisted more fiercely. The status quo is upset by the earlier emergence of Japan as a major world exporter of manufactures, with the challenge to Europe and the United States posed by its export volume, its 1980s trade surplus, and, as demonstrated in this chapter, its convergence on the United States export structure. All these changes have contributed to numerous trade actions directed against Japan. The perception and, to some extent the reality, that Asian NIEs are following the Japanese model has drawn the attention of trade policymakers in Europe and the United States. Thus the NIEs, too, are drawing trade-restrictive measures by the United States and Europe, as well as strong pressure to liberalize their own import markets. Even the ASEAN countries are beginning to draw protective measures, as for example, the United States' recent partial removal of GSP preferences from Thailand for alleged inadequate protection of intellectual property rights. This process may accelerate as Japanese foreign investment in Southeast Asia's new export-oriented industries grows.

The use of discriminatory measures (that is, selective measures) is inherently inefficient and in some instances ineffective. Restricting one country's exports shifts import demand to other suppliers. The analysis of changing export structures presented here shows that this process of dynamic comparative advantage is widespread in Asia—restricting a product from country Y simply accelerates the emergence of country Z as a competitor. It would be preferable for importing countries to implement better macro policies and better micro adjustment policies to eliminate large external imbalance and to respond to changes in comparative advantages.

The analysis presented here, however, also has a strong positive conclusion for Asian exporters. Most have shown great ability in moving up the product-sophistication ladder and, by implication, upgrading the composition of their more traditional manufactures (for example, clothing). They have accomplished this in spite of rising trade barriers. In the ladder analogy, countries may face a competitive push from below, but increases in markets for more sophisticated products are opening at higher rungs. The United States and Japan today stand on the top rungs of the ladder, but new rungs are added continually, and the two leaders need not be forced off what is, in effect, a constantly growing ladder.

Notes

1. The term *multiple export catch-up* is borrowed from the apt description of Toshio Watanabe (1984).
2. The United States imposed a tariff-quota on stainless-steel flatware in 1959. As the dominant (quasi-monopolist) supplier, Japan restricted exports to within quota limits, but by 1965–66 Korea and Taiwan were significant exporters despite ad valorem equivalent over quota rates of 60–115 percent. See Pearson (1979). The United States imposed quotas under an OMA on Japanese exports of color television sets in 1977. Production shifted to Taiwan and Korea, and trade restrictions were subsequently imposed against the new suppliers. U.S. OMAs with Taiwan and Korea on nonrubber footwear imposed in 1977 shifted production to Thailand, Philippines, and Hong Kong, among others.
3. Korea, Taiwan, Malaysia, and Singapore reportedly have been concerned with increased competition with PRC (*Far Eastern Economic Review*, February 28, 1985, p. 94). For analysis of PRC's prospective effects on U.S. imports and employment, see James Tsao (1985).
4. Pomfret (1979) has used the index to evaluate effects of the entrance of Greece and Turkey to the EC on other Mediterranean countries. Pearson and Ellyne (1984) have used the index to compare import surge profiles among countries.
5. The export similarity index also can be used to compare geographic patterns of trade among countries.
6. Except for 1986, which used United Nations data. A comparison of U.N. and OECD data for 1983 for Japan and the United States produced virtually identical similarity indices, suggesting that the change in the data source is of no consequence.
7. Correlation coefficients in earlier years tended to be lower.
8. The matrix is symmetrical around the principal diagonal. Singapore's export profile resembles both the United States and Japan (57.0, 55.9) and Malaysia (59.5). Its inclusion in the triangular matrix would lead the ranking of countries down "false" paths.

9. There is no necessary reason for the data to produce this pattern. Had Singapore been included, the smooth "slopes" off the ridge would have been marred by transverse and parallel ravines and spines.

10. Singapore is the maverick.

11. The index for several developing countries may reflect minimal exports of manufactures in the base year. For example, 1962 U.N. data for Indonesia show 85 percent of Indonesian manufactures exports in SITC 53, 54, and 55 (dyeing and tanning materials, pharmaceuticals, essential oils and perfumes).

12. Note the matrix is no longer symmetrical along the principal diagonal and cannot be reported in a triangular array.

13. See Lawrence Krause (1982) for analysis of U.S.–Japanese competition in Southeast Asia.

References

Cline, William. 1984. *Exports of Manufactures from Developing Countries*. Washington, D.C.: Brookings Institution.

Finger, Michael, and Kreinin, M.E. 1979. "A Measure of Export Similarity and Its Possible Uses." *Economic Journal* 89 (December).

Heller, Peter. 1976. "Factor Endowment Change and Comparative Advantage: The Case of Japan." *Review of Economics and Statistics* (August).

Kellman, Mitchell, and Schroder, Tim. 1983. "The Export Similarity Index: Some Structural Tests." *Economic Journal* 93 (March).

Krause, Lawrence. 1982. *U.S. Economic Policy Toward the Association of Southeast Asian Nations*. Washington, D.C.: Brookings Institution.

Lee, Young Sun. 1986. "Changing Export Patterns in Korea, Taiwan and Japan." *Weltwirtschaftliches Archive* 122 (1).

Pearson, Charles. 1979. "Protection by Tariff Quota: Case Study of Stainless Steel Flatware." *Journal of World Trade Law* 13, no. 4 (July/August).

Pearson, Charles, and Ellyne, Mark. 1984. *Import Surges: The Role of Japan and the Developing Countries*. Washington, D.C.: U.S.–Japan Studies Center, SAIS, Johns Hopkins University.

Pomfret, Richard. 1979. "The Import of EEC Enlargement on Non-Member Mediterranean Countries' Exports to the EEC." *Economic Journal* (December).

Tsao, James. 1985. "China's Economic Development Strategies and Their Effects on U.S. Trade." U.S. International Trade Commission Publication 1645, February.

Watanabe, Toshio. 1984. "Multiple Catch-up in Asia: Industrialization in Asian Developing Countries." *Speaking of Japan* 5, no. 46 (October).

CHAPTER 3

Managing Entry into International Markets: Lessons from the East Asian Experience

Yung Whee Rhee

Few would dispute that outward-oriented development strategies are the key to efficient industrial development, which in turn is vital for increasing income, reducing debt, and creating dynamics for growth in the developing countries of the world. However, how to initiate outward-oriented industrial development, particularly in developing countries with unfavorable start-up conditions, is unclear. The success stories of the newly industrializing economies (NIEs) of East Asia are well known, but practical and specific lessons from their success in world markets need to be articulated, particularly for the countries that lack initially favorable conditions for entry into those markets. This chapter provides an overview of such lessons.

The East Asian NIEs covered in this discussion are Hong Kong, Singapore, the Republic of Korea (South Korea, hereafter referred to as Korea), and Taiwan. References to Japan's experience at the early stage of its export development are included in relevant sections.

Initial Conditions in Developing Countries and Relevant Lessons in International Competitiveness

Many developing countries are at a significant competitive disadvantage because their firms lack the information and know-how to compete in these markets; their internal policy environments fail to ensure that their firms will have equal footing with foreign competitors; and their institutions and infrastructure are inadequate to support export and related trade and production activities.

Lack of Capacity to Export. Firms in developing countries do not have the capacity to enter world markets largely because exporters and their agents are still in their infancy. They do not have the technical, marketing, and managerial know-how critical to starting up the manufacture of exportable industrial goods

53

or the ability to package the technical, marketing, and managerial know-how with domestic resources and external resources.[1] Nor do they have adequate access to information and links to the world markets for manufactured goods.

Unfavorable Policies. Several policy factors are responsible for the failure to ensure exporters equal footing with foreign competitors: unrealistic real exchange rates; inadequate and difficult access to short-term trade financing at world market or domestic market interest rates; restricted access to raw materials and intermediate inputs (and capital goods) at world market prices; and difficult access to investment licensing for the creation of export production capacity, as well as to investment financing. A fundamental objective of the export incentives of the East Asian NIEs has been to ensure equal footing with foreign competitors to resolve the first three of these problems.

Insufficient Infrastructure. The insufficient institutional and physical infrastructure for supporting export and associated trade activities again reflects the infancy of export development. The lack of funds and human resources to deal with externalities and economies of scale are also hindrances. Developing countries need to sequence the necessary policy reforms and infrastructure buildup efficiently, because their limited resources and other factors tend to constrain institutional and policy change.

Relevant Lessons. A frequent question is whether the East Asian experience can be replicated (or emulated) in countries with markedly different initial conditions. Most observers of the East Asian NIEs during the 1950s noted their limited capacities and adverse conditions, which were not unlike the elements that affect the performance of developing countries today. Thus, some lessons for the current situation can be gleaned from the main factors that have contributed to the success of the East Asian NIE performance in initiating outward-oriented strategies. An assessment of policies, institutions, and economic agents critical for entry into the manufactured exports market can lead to an understanding of the basic practical mechanisms for facilitating that entry. Consequently, the emphasis in this discussion is on the East Asian experience in the 1960s and 1970s.

Combining Foreign and Domestic Factors

In the 1960s, the four East Asian NIEs—South Korea, Hong Kong, Singapore, and Taiwan—established outward-oriented development strategies based on manufactured exports. Each developed its capacity to enter the world markets in a different manner, particularly in combining foreign and domestic factors.

Hong Kong and Singapore

The outward orientation of Hong Kong and Singapore, two resource-poor city economies, evolved from their status as regional entrepôts under British colonial rule (Hong Kong serving China, and Singapore, the Southeast Asian region) in the nineteenth century. In the early 1950s, Hong Kong adopted an export strategy for light manufactured goods, since its entrepôt trade with China had ended. Singapore developed an export strategy in the mid-1960s after becoming independent from Malaysia.

Two types of catalysts initiated the export of light manufactured goods from Hong Kong. One was the Chinese businessmen who in the late 1940s fled to Hong Kong from Shanghai, the industrial center on the China coast. These businessmen brought along skilled workers and textile machinery and initiated textile production with refugee workers, who thus formed technical cadres. Generous bank loans (capital was abundant, with heavy inflows from abroad) allowed them to increase the number of spindles from 8,000 units in 1948 to 210,000 units in 1951 and to raise employment in manufacturing from 47,000 workers in 1947 to 177,000 in 1959.

The second catalytic group consisted of the British and Chinese merchant houses of Hong Kong, with their long-standing international commercial ties. They provided Hong Kong textile products with access to markets in the United Kingdom and later in the United States. Other multinational companies (MNCs) from the United States, Europe, and Japan rushed to form joint ventures or subcontracting arrangements with the numerous small Hong Kong firms. In turn, the many small Hong Kong trading companies, having learned the skills and networks of the British and Chinese merchant houses, developed a strong capacity to channel the manufactured products of their small producers into external markets.

In the mid-1960s Singapore switched its development strategy from import substitution to export orientation. The government acted on the belief that financial stringency and economic realities required that experienced foreign companies be induced to come to Singapore and develop manufactured exports. This would be more expeditious than waiting for the slow buildup of local capital and capabilities (Geiger and Geiger 1975). The government thus encouraged direct foreign investment (DFI) and joint ventures and used government funds to acquire minority equity interests in new enterprises and to provide loans. The Singapore Economic Development Board was the catalyst in attracting foreign firms into export activities by offering various incentives and an attractive industrial environment. Although MNCs have been the main agents for Singapore's outward-oriented strategy, the government has continually attempted to ensure that local firms play an effective complementary role.

Taiwan and Korea

Taiwan and Korea experienced similar major external and internal events in the twentieth century before initiating outward-oriented development strategies. Both were under Japanese colonial rule from the first half of the century until the end of World War II (Taiwan for fifty years, Korea for thirty-five years). Both were involved in military confrontations (Taiwan had Kuomingtang confronting the mainland since 1949, and Korea the war from 1950 to 1953). In addition, both initiated outward-oriented development strategies in the late 1950s or early 1960s (the so-called 19 Point Reforms in Taiwan in 1959 and the policy reforms of the Park Chung Hee regime in Korea in early 1960).

In Taiwan, the entrepreneurs who initiated exports of manufactured goods were: (1) merchants and industrialists who had fled the mainland; (2) expatriate Chinese who set up factories in Taiwan; and (3) native Taiwanese, who learned how to conduct business from the Japanese during the occupation or from the first Chinese entrepreneurs. Once Taiwan's reputation for manufactured exports was established, MNCs from the United States, Europe, and Japan became extensively involved in exporting from Taiwan through subcontracts with small- and medium-sized local firms on an original equipment manufacture (OEM) basis. Although the role of foreign trading companies was dominant in marketing the manufactured exports, the small Taiwanese trading companies also became important as they learned trading skills and how to use the network (Chang 1987).

At the end of World War II, Korea was left with industrial facilities, entrepreneurs who had been exposed to Japanese technological organization and management, and a large, educated work force familiar with manufacturing (Jones and Sakong 1980). After Korea's independence in 1948, after three years of a U.S. military regime, and even after the Korean War, the country's close ties with the United States were an important source of modern industrial skills (including organizational and managerial skills). When the government adopted an outward-oriented development strategy in the early 1960s, Korea's *chaebol* (conglomerates) played a role in initiating the export industry by expanding their manufacturing facilities and upgrading localized production skills with the assistance of domestic bank and foreign loans.[2] Export marketing by foreign trading companies and buyers supported the chaebols' efforts.

Some of these conglomerates became general trading companies (GTCs). Having learned overseas marketing from the foreign trading companies, GTCs became actively involved in channeling the exports of small and medium producers. Even in the early 1960s, Korea's outward-oriented strategy enabled large private firms to use their capacity to package the critical factors needed to enter world markets and to acquire the additional foreign know-how for upgrading and diversifying export products and markets. These large firms relied on foreign buyers, foreign trading companies, foreign machine suppliers, skilled Korean workers returning from overseas, and technical or marketing agreements with foreign firms to acquire the factors needed to enter the world markets at an early stage (Rhee, Ross-Larson, and Purcell 1984).

Japan

Japan's leadership in outward-oriented development strategies in East Asia is rooted in its experience as the first Asian economy exposed to Western industrialization. The Meiji Restoration of 1868 paved the way for opening Japan to Western know-how and to foreign trade. In the first decade of Meiji rule, Western companies built textile, cement, and other factories in Japan to Western specifications; Western personnel supervised their operation until the Japanese were able to replace them. Private Japanese enterprises later took over these factories (Woronoff 1986: 29). From this experience, Japan developed a capability for borrowing foreign technology (Peck 1976: 527).

Also beginning in the Meiji period, the government encouraged Japanese companies to replace the foreign trading companies. To do so, Japanese trading companies had to overcome local ignorance of foreign markets and languages, but the Japanese were spurred on by a desire to participate in the world economy. Some of the trading companies grew into *zaibatsu* (large family-controlled business groups), the origin of Japan's GTCs, which were catalysts in Japan's outward-oriented strategy (Krause and Sekiguchi 1976). The GTCs' role in providing an "invisible link" between large modern factories and smaller subcontractors has been as critical as their role as catalysts in penetrating overseas markets and transferring foreign know-how (Yoshino and Lifson 1986).

Lessons for Developing Countries

Beginning with the European Industrial Revolution, the East Asian economies depended on Western elements to initiate their industrial development and trade in manufactured goods. Table 3.1 summarizes the primary foreign and domestic elements that were critical in initiating outward-oriented development strategies. The East Asian experience provides some lessons for developing countries regarding the ideal combination of foreign and domestic elements needed to enter the world markets for manufactured goods.

Capacity to Package. The most important element in an outward-oriented strategy is the capacity to use both local and external resources to package the technical, marketing, and managerial know-how for entry into world markets. This capacity can be acquired only through a long association with foreign and local companies that already embody this capacity (that is, through on-the-job training and learning by doing). Japan acquired its capacity from Western companies; Korea and, to some extent, Taiwan initially acquired theirs (in light manufacturing) from Japan during the colonial periods (Westphal, Rhee, and Pursell 1981). Hong Kong and, to an extent, Taiwan benefited from the inflow of Chinese businessmen who had acquired their capacities through association with foreign managers and skilled workers. Singapore, needing rapid capital and ca-

Table 3.1

Foreign and Domestic Elements That Were Critical in Initiating Manufactured Exports In East Asian NIEs

Key Elements	Hong Kong (Early 1950s)	Singapore (Mid–1960s)	Taiwan (Late 1950s)	Korea (Early 1960s)
A. Technical know-how	F (L)	F	L, F (L)	L
B. Marketing know-how	L	F	F	F
C. Managerial know-how	F(L), L	F	L, F(L)	L
D. Capital	F, Local	F	Local	F
E. Access to overseas markets	L	F	F	F
F. Capacity to package (A), (B) and (C) with (D) and (E)	L, F(L)	F	F(L)	L

Note: F = foreign source; L = localized source; and F (L) = localized foreign source.

pacity accumulation, relied exclusively on MNCs to package the critical elements for its export-oriented strategy. Most developing countries with unfavorable initial conditions may be similar to Singapore in that direct foreign investment would be an expeditious way to obtain foreign "packages" at the early stages of their export development.

Foreign Assistance with Missing Elements. This capacity to package critical factors is lacking in most developing countries at the early stages of export development. Thus, for them, the lesson from Singapore is important. Other East Asian economies, with built-in resources, used foreign and local know-how to package the elements they needed to enter world markets. Korea relied on local technical and managerial know-how to manufacture light industrial items for export but used foreign sources for marketing know-how and access to the world markets. Korea also sought foreign loans to finance production and investments for exports. Hong Kong relied on local marketing know-how and access to world markets, which it had gained through its entrepôt trade experience. At an early stage, it also used skilled immigrant personnel to gain the technical and managerial know-how for manufacturing exports. Taiwan, like Korea, relied on foreign sources for initiating external marketing, and it followed both Korea and Hong Kong in employing local technical and managerial know-how.

Table 3.2

Overview of Methods of Achieving Free-Trade Status of East Asian NIEs

Schemes	Hong Kong	Singapore	Taiwan	Korea
Free trade	Free trade from 1950s	Free trade after 1967		
Free trade zone (FTZ)	Commercial FTZ until 1950	Commercial FTZ until 1960s	3 FTZs (1966, 1970, 1971)	2 FTZs 1970, 1971)
Bonded manufacturing warehouse (BMW)			336 BMWs (in 1981)	218 BMWs (in 1981)
Automatic import license and duty exemption		Used before 1967	60 percent used duty exemption (in 1981)	Used before mid-1970
Automatic import license and duty drawback		Used before 1967	40 percent used duty draw-back (in 1981)	Used after mid-1970

Ensuring Free-Trade Status for Export Activities

An important means of eliminating the disadvantages of exporters in developing countries is to guarantee unrestricted access to the imported inputs that generate export value added at world market prices. Imports would be free of import and foreign exchange restrictions as well as tariffs and indirect taxes. Indirect tax exemptions for exports achieve a neutral status with respect to indirect taxes for domestic sales under the destination principle, as well as free-trade status. (Ensuring free-trade status for direct and indirect export activities is acceptable to the GATT and to importing economies.) In addition, free-trade status for exports is a first step in completely liberalizing imports for the domestic market.

The five main methods of achieving free-trade status for export activities are: (1) free trade, (2) free trade zones, (3) bonded manufacturing warehouses, (4) automatic import license and duty exemptions, and (5) automatic import license and duty drawbacks. Table 3.2 provides a comparative overview of the methods of achieving free-trade status in the East Asian NIEs.

Free Trade

Free-trade status for exporters is ensured if a country adopts a free-trade policy for the entire economy. Given the small size of their domestic markets, extensive involvement in entrepôt trade, and specialization in the final stage of production. Hong Kong and Singapore were ideally equipped for free trade in virtually all commodities, including imported inputs used for manufacturing exports. Until 1967, however, Singapore had a policy of temporary limitation (i.e., tariff and import restrictions) of imports sold domestically. Given the prevalence of the tariff redundancy observed in 1967, it also appears that Singapore used an outward-orientation strategy to build up its internationally competitive industries before it had completely eliminated its domestic market protection (Tan and Hock 1982).

Free-Trade Zone

A free-trade zone (FTZ) is a special industrial area located physically or administratively outside a country's customs barrier and devoted to the production of exports. Transactions in FTZs are not subject to import restrictions and tariffs and therefore escape the delays and administrative costs often associated with the duty exemptions or drawback systems applied to firms outside FTZs. FTZs usually offer fully serviced land and facilities, with easy access to ports and industrial plants. Good physical trade infrastructure (such as ports, transports, and communication) is a precondition for any export including FTZ exports. FTZs are to attract foreign investment in their export industries. They usually offer additional incentives, such as income tax holidays and unrestricted transfer of profits.

Hong Kong and Singapore. Commercial FTZs have been in existence in Singapore since 1819 and in Hong Kong since 1842. When Hong Kong and Singapore adopted their export-oriented development policies in the 1950s and 1960s, they expanded their commercial FTZs into countrywide industrial FTZs.

Taiwan. The Kaohsiung FTZ, established in 1966 in southern Taiwan, was the world's first FTZ for manufacturing. The Nantze and Taichung FTZs were established in 1970 and 1971, respectively. In 1987, 254 enterprises were located in the FTZs, and they employed approximately 94,500 people. In the mid-1980s, FTZ employment was 4.8 percent of the economy's total manufacturing employment. Total exports from the zone in 1987 were US$2.4 billion, approximately 6.4 percent of Taiwan's total exports (ILO/UNCTAD 1988).

Korea. Korea established two FTZs in the early 1970s as a part of its outward-oriented industrial development strategy (Masan in 1971 and Iri in 1975). As of 1980, the zones had ninety-four enterprises, seventy-two of which were foreign-owned operations and twenty-eight joint ventures. Employment in the zones in 1987 was close to 39,000. However, employment in the FTZs has never accounted for much more than 1 percent of Korea's total manufacturing employment. Exports from the zone in 1986 were US$460 million, or 2.8 percent of Korea's total exports.

Although the Korean FTZs have not accounted for a substantial part of employment and exports, it is believed that Korea benefited substantially from backward linkages with FTZ operations. For example, the exports from the Masan FTZ had more than 50 percent local content. Besides the two FTZs designed to attract foreign investments, by the mid-1980s more than 3,000 export manufacturing factories were located in the twenty-four export-processing estates designed to provide infrastructure primarily for domestic firms (ILO/UNCTAD 1988).

Bonded Manufacturing Warehouse System

To allow companies outside the FTZs to bypass certain customs procedures when they import inputs needed for producing exports, the East Asian NIEs established bonded manufacturing warehouse (BMW) systems. The usual requirements for licensing BMWs are as follows:

(1) The firm's factories must engage exclusively in manufacturing commodities for export.

(2) The firm's factories must have separate warehouses approved by customs for the storage of imported inputs and finished commodities.

(3) Customs officers must be stationed at the BMWs to inspect the imported inputs and finished outputs.

In 1981, Taiwan had 336 and Korea 218 BMWs, which accounted for about 14 percent and 12 percent of total exports and about 10 percent and 6 percent of total imports, respectively (Ministry of Finance, the Republic of Korea 1982).

Automatic Import License and Duty / Indirect Tax Exemption

To provide free-trade status for exporters outside the FTZs and the BMW system, automatic import licensing and exemption from foreign exchange restrictions (i.e., automatic access to the foreign exchange needed to pay for imports for exports) need to precede the duty (and indirect tax) exemptions (sometimes called temporary import) or drawback (sometimes called refunds). A duty (and indirect tax) exemption system exempts exporters from paying duties (and indirect taxes) on imports used for export production.[3]

Korea. Korea used a duty and indirect tax-exemption system until the mid-1970s. It had two successful aspects. First, it ensured unrestricted choice between imported and domestically produced inputs, while treating indirect exporters the same as direct exporters in ensuring access to duty-free imports (and other export incentives). This policy extended free-trade status to indirect exporters and resulted in efficient backward linkages. Second, administrative efficiency was achieved through two major instruments: (1) pretabulated and published physical input-output coefficients; and (2) the use of trade-financing procedures and documents for duty-free imports.

Although Korea changed formally to the duty-drawback system in the mid-1970s, it supplemented this in the 1980s with an innovative duty-exemption system—the imported input stock accounting book method (see below)—mainly in the case of selected qualified exporters. This innovation was based on lessons learned from the experience of Taiwan (Ministry of Finance, the Republic of Korea 1982).

Taiwan. The duty-exemption system of Taiwan uses import and export entry accounting to estimate outstanding duties associated with unfulfilled exports only at the end of certain periods. This system requires effective monitoring of the maximum ceiling on input stocks imported duty-free. As in Korea, successful implementation of the Taiwan system depended, in part, on the effective use of pretabulated input coefficients. About 80 percent of the duty-free imports in 1975 depended on the duty-exemption system. Because of the parallel implementation of the duty-drawback system, the share of duty exemptions declined to about 60 percent in 1981.

Duty-Drawback System

In a duty-drawback system, exporters located outside FTZs or BMWs obtain refunds of the duties (and indirect taxes) they have paid on imported inputs after they complete the exports. There are two ways of making the refunds. Under the individual drawback systems, duties (and indirect taxes) paid by firms are refunded on a case-by-case basis; this system operates much like a system of exemptions. Under a fixed drawback system, the estimated duties (and indirect taxes) that enter into the cost of producing export commodities are refunded according to a preset schedule. Just as in the case of duty exemptions, without the automatic import licensing and automatic allocation of foreign exchange needed to import inputs for export production, a duty-drawback system would fail to provide free-trade status in a developing country with import and foreign exchange restrictions.

Korea. Korea switched from a duty-exemption system to a duty-drawback system in the middle of 1975 because of worsening balance of payments problems after the first oil crisis. The government intended to institute a fixed drawback system, which might have meant a less than free-trade status for many exporters. When exporters were increasingly concerned about the possibility of losing equal footing with foreign competitors, the government instead introduced a duty-deferred payment system that was equivalent to an exemption system for many exporters. It then modified the fixed drawback system by combining it with an individual drawback system (only about 20 percent of Korean exports were subject to the fixed drawback system in 1980).

While maintaining the duty-deferred payment system, the Korean government in 1981 implemented a new drawback schedule that combined the advantages of both fixed and individual drawbacks: Wherever major imported items were involved, the highest priority was to provide free-trade status through individual drawbacks; in the case of miscellaneous imported items, the highest priority was administrative simplicity through fixed drawbacks. Subsequently, a two-step drawback payment system was implemented that provided immediate drawback payments after the exports were completed, based on rough estimates, followed by careful accounting within a three-month period. Korea has also made continuing efforts to streamline the administration of the input coefficients.

Taiwan. Taiwan uses a drawback system mainly with exporters who are not qualified to use the duty-exemption system. About 40 percent of the duty-free imports in 1981 involved the duty-drawback system. Basically, Taiwan has a fixed drawback system. However, exporters who can document that they actually paid duties exceeding more than 10 percent of the drawback amount shown in the published schedule can use the individual drawback system. There are two types of fixed drawback schedules: One specifies the drawback amount (money value) per unit (i.e., physical quantity) of a designated export item; the other specifies the drawback amount as a certain percentage of the money value of a designated export item. The former (i.e., the quantity-based system) is generally used for export items that do not need a large number of diversified imported inputs; the latter (i.e., the money value–based system) is generally used for export items that need numerous imported inputs. These fixed drawback schedules are published periodically. The input-coefficient data are critical bases of the schedules.

Lessons for Developing Countries

Achieving free trade by eliminating the restrictions and duties (and indirect taxes) on all imports is a desirable and rational long-term objective for developing countries. However, often it cannot be achieved unless pursued gradually, since the initial conditions in these countries are unfavorable. If adopted quickly, free trade would allow imports to displace much domestic production, including infant industries that could otherwise become competitive.

If not fully "compensated for" by exchange rate and associated real sector adjustments, immediate across-the-board import liberalization also increases the balance of payments deficits, worsening the already heavy external debt burden. Often the political and social reaction to very rapid or ill-considered across-the-board import liberalization has resulted in a regression to import and foreign exchange controls.

Nevertheless, developing countries should immediately implement the measures designed to guarantee free-trade status for all activities that generate export value added. Such measures are acceptable under the GATT rules, and they are one of the minimum conditions for providing exporters equal footing with foreign competitors. They also constitute a first step in gradually implementing complete import liberalization.

FTZs. FTZs can be very effective in the early stages of an export drive as a means of attracting foreign investors and demonstrating the country's export potential, especially in countries that lack the capacity to package the critical elements needed to initiate an outward-oriented development strategy. However, the development of infrastructure, formulation of appropriate incentives, and other elements of the work environment must be well-managed. It should be noted that where outward development strategies have been sustained and reinforced, as in the East Asian NIEs, the relative importance of FTZ exports has tended to decline as exports of other domestic industries have expanded under free-trade status.

BMWs. A bonded manufactured warehouse system is quite advantageous for well-established large firms that produce exports only. It is particularly desirable for such products as electronics, which require numerous imported inputs, because it reduces the administrative burden of estimating and monitoring input coefficients. These are the most critical data in determining the effectiveness of a duty-exemption or drawback system. However, BMWs are impractical for small producers and indirect exporters, as well as for producers selling in both the export and the domestic markets.

Duty Exemptions. For countries in the early stage of exporting, a duty-exemption system is preferable to a duty-drawback system for several reasons. First, although both systems impose a similar administrative burden in terms of the need for input coefficients and other data, the duty-exemption system does not burden exporters with the working capital requirements and interest rates associated with the duty-drawback system. Second, both systems require automatic import licensing and free access to foreign exchange for imported inputs if the government wants to guarantee free-trade status (that is, the duty-drawback system cannot succeed unless all the administrative arrangements needed for "temporary imports" are in place). The reason is that the potential costs for exporters stemming from a failure to resolve the restriction on imports and foreign exchange would be much higher than those stemming from the failure to resolve the duties and indirect tax burdens for exporters in countries with a highly distorted import regime. Third, the duty-exemption system seems to carry less risk than the duty-drawback system does in terms of potential export subsidy charges by importing economies.

The East Asian experience provides a number of lessons concerning the effective implementation of a duty-exemption system:

(1) The success of a duty-exemption system depends on speedy processing based on a transparent, nondiscretionary, and simple formula prepared in ad-

vance. The formula does not come from a magic equation but from systematic and careful advance estimation of input coefficients by the government. The administrative costs of such estimates are, however, much smaller than those exporters and the government face under the ad hoc approaches many developing countries have been relying on, which fail to ensure speedy processing to provide free-trade status.

(2) Administrative efficiency can be achieved with duty exemptions by using the trade-financing disbursement/liquidation mechanisms and instruments.

(3) Indirect exporters and direct exporters should be treated equally in providing free-trade status.

(4) Capital goods should be included in the duty-exemption system at an early stage of export development, even if domestic capital good industries are competing with imports.

(5) The imported input stock accounting book method should be allowed for well-established exporters.

(6) The administrative burden of the duty-exemption system can be reduced by eliminating all redundant import and foreign exchange restrictions and tariffs and gradually lowering protections.

Duty Drawbacks. The parallel use of a duty-drawback system is desirable in developing countries to allow firms that did not foresee exporting when they imported inputs to enjoy a free-trade status while they were exporting. Under a fixed drawback system, the option of an individual drawback is needed to safeguard exports from an excessive sacrifice of free-trade status that may stem from the fixed drawback.

Ensuring Easy Access to Trade Financing

To ensure easy access to trade financing, policymakers must first understand the role of trade financing in the economy (for a detailed discussion, see Rhee 1989).

The Role of Trade Financing

Exporters cannot respond to goods orders unless they have ensured access to trade financing.[4] Access to trade financing based on export orders and bills of completed exports is critical to realizing a supply response. Preshipment export finance is needed to pay for imports of foreign raw materials and intermediate inputs, domestic raw materials and intermediate inputs, domestic value-added components (wages, interest, and rents) needed for export production, and inventories of finished commodities to be exported.

Normally granted on export orders and provided for less than ninety days, preshipment financing is particularly important in countries that have underdeveloped money markets and segmented bank-lending markets. Export orders cannot be filled—and existing export opportunities cannot be realized—unless exporters can meet their import, domestic purchase, production, and inventory-financing needs before shipment.

Short-term postshipment export finance is needed to finance export sales on credit. Normally it is granted for up to 180 days on an accepted bill (an unconditional promise that a bank or importer will make payment for the export commodities received by a definite date). Medium- and long-term postshipment export financing, which finances export sales (mostly of heavy industry products) on credit exceeding 180 days, is not as important at the early stage of export development in most developing economies. To highlight the lessons on trade financing from the East Asian experience, the focus here is on short-term preshipment trade finance and short-term postshipment export finance.

Methods of Trade Financing

There are four methods of financing trade: company credit, bank credit, bank loans, and self-financing. In addressing the issues related to financing under the different methods, it is important to distinguish clearly between bank lending and bank credit and between bank credit and company credit. When a bank provides a "loan," it lends actual money. When it creates a banker's acceptance (BA)—its unconditional promise to pay a certain sum of money at a definite date to the bearer—it lends "credit." The bank creates a BA strictly on the basis of the expected revenue from a particular trade transaction: traders meet their trade-financing needs through the BA discount market, part of the money market. Company credits involve selling and buying between affiliated companies or between trading companies and suppliers "on credit." The most elementary method is self-financing from retained earnings.

Choosing among these methods and enacting appropriate measures to resolve access problems depend, among other factors, on the stage of development of the banking industry and the money market, the structure of trading companies and export manufacturers, and the percentage of trade financing to be met by retained earnings.

Intra-MNC Credit-Based Trade Financing

As shown in Table 3.3, Singapore has been the only East Asian NIE to use intra-MNC credit-based trade financing extensively. At the same time, the Singapore government has not neglected the complementary role that bank loans can play. It introduced a preshipment and short-term postshipment financing system known as "the rediscounting scheme for pre-export and export bills of exchange" in 1975. Administered by the Monetary Authority of Singapore, it has complemented the intra-foreign MNC credit-based financing system, particularly in meeting the financing needs of local companies. Further, the Export Credit Insur-

Table 3.3

Comparative Overview of the Primary Trade Financing System of the East Asian Economies

Primary Trade-Financing System	Preshipment Export Finance	Short-Term Postshipment Export Finance	Medium & Long-Term Postshipment Export Finance	Exporter Nonperformance Risk Handling		Overseas Buyer Nonpayment Risk Handling	
				Internalize by Firm or Bank	PEFG[a]	Internalize by Firm or Bank	ECI/G[b]
Intra-MNC credit-based	Singapore	Singapore	Singapore	Singapore		Singapore	
Interfirm credit-based	Hong Kong Taiwan	Hong Kong Taiwan		Hong Kong		Hong Kong Taiwan	
Bank credit-based	Hong Kong	Hong Kong		Hong Kong		Hong Kong	
Bank loan-system supported by the government	Korea Singapore Taiwan	Korea Singapore Taiwan	Korea Taiwan		Korea Singapore Taiwan		Korea Singapore Taiwan
Self financing	Taiwan						

[a]PEFG = preshipment export finance guarantee.
[b]ECI/G = export credit insurance and guarantee.

ance Corporation of Singapore Ltd. has supplemented the intra-MNC risk taking related to overseas buyer nonpayment. In 1985 it introduced a preshipment export finance guarantee to ensure local companies access to preshipment financing. In 1986 the Economic Development Board introduced the Small Industries Finance and Guarantee Schemes.[5]

Interfirm Credit-Based Trade Financing

Japan's GTCs ensured access to trade financing for small producers, a role the commercial banks would not undertake because of their aversion to risk. Because they knew the small firms, the GTCs were able to internalize risk taking. Moreover, the GTCs themselves were able to tap into major financing resources because of their close banking ties and because most GTC credit to small, input- or output-supplying indirect exporters was tied to specific trade transactions. Often the credit to indirect exporters was in the form of imported raw materials on credit or advance payments for indirect export items, all provided before the GTCs received payment from overseas buyers. The GTCs also provided loan guarantees for small producers, so that they could gain direct access to bank loans. In short, Japan's GTCs provided a typical form of interfirm credit-based trade financing.

Many developing economies have attempted to establish Japanese-type GTCs in the hope of providing a similar "invisible link" in expanding exports. Except for the Korean trading companies, most such attempts have not been successful, as the companies have lacked the human and financial resources to carry out their diverse tasks. Moreover, in many cases domestic policy has not fully supported an outward-oriented strategy, and cultural factors have not been conducive to large GTCs (Ozawa 1987). Even Korea's GTCs, which have been successful in providing marketing and technical services to small indirect exporters, have not been active in credit-based trade financing. The reason is that Korea's GTCs have been closely tied to the conglomerates, which have abundant human resources, but they and the conglomerates have had to rely on banks and foreign borrowing for their own capital.

Among the East Asian NIEs, Hong Kong and Taiwan have relied most on interfirm financing to meet the trade-financing needs of numerous small manufacturers of exports (Table 3.3). The small manufacturers have had to act as indirect exporters, relying on trading companies for direct exporting and company credit-based trade financing for imported inputs, even though the numerous Hong Kong and Taiwan trading companies also have been small.

Trade Financing Based on Bank Credit

The origin of the trade-financing market was the discount market for trade bills in England (a trade bill of exchange or draft is the seller's unconditional written demand for payment).[6] Hong Kong is the only developing economy whose trade financing evolved as it did in England: from trade development to merchant banking to BA financing. In Hong Kong, in the early 1800s, bill discounting, tightly linked with the economy's entrepôt trade, became the bread and butter of the large agency houses and the British and European merchant banks, known as "eastern exchange banks."

The main reason for establishing the Hong Kong and Shanghai Banking Corporation, a Shanghai bank with Hong Kong interests, was the comparative lack of enthusiasm among the exchange banks for intra-China coastal business. The corporation also became heavily involved in financing the entrepôt trade, as was the case with its Anglo-Indian counterparts (Ghose 1987). The bills and BA outstanding domestic export ratio ranged from 8 percent to about 14 percent during 1980–85, the implication being that trade financing based on bank credit probably met about one- to two-thirds of the trade-financing needs, assuming four or five annual turnovers.

Although Hong Kong's BA-based trade financing may have evolved relative to other developing economies, after 150 years of experience it has not reached maturity. One reason is the absence of an active secondary market, a major obstacle to the development of money market instruments. This problem is largely the result of the fact that Hong Kong does not have a central bank that could provide direction and serve as "lender of last resort" through a rediscount window. The Hong Kong Shanghai Bank, which acts informally as a central bank, may not need a discount market or commercial paper for its own banking business. Since a secondary market would help its competitors, it has not worked to develop one (Skully 1976). In 1985, the Bank of China advocated establishing a government-sponsored discount window in Hong Kong to revitalize the secondary money market and to resolve the cash-flow problems of local banks (Ghose 1987).

Trade Financing Based on Bank Loans

Exporters in most developing economies cannot meet their trade financing needs through bank credit or company credit, because they lack modern banks and trading companies that can internalize the risk taking. Therefore, the immediate objective of ensuring access to trade financing for all exporters with direct and indirect export orders must be met through bank loans.

Basic Instruments. The bank loan financing system is based on a trio of instruments and institutions: (1) transaction-based, self-liquidating mechanisms for trade financing (including rediscount mechanisms of the central bank); (2) institutions that can deal with exporters' nonperformance risk (i.e., preshipment export finance guarantees [PEFG]); and (3) institutions that can deal with overseas buyers' nonpayment risk (i.e., export credit insurance and guarantees [ECI/G]).

Hong Kong and Singapore. Hong Kong's primary trade-financing system is characterized by a mixture of bank and interfirm credit-based mechanisms. The only way in which the government has been directly involved has been to provide ECI/G to complement firms' and banks' internal handling of the risk of overseas buyers' nonpayment (Table 3.3). In contrast, Singapore's primary trade-financing system is intrafirm credit within large MNCs. However, given a parallel need to develop backward linkages with local enterprises, the trade-financing needs of these firms have been met by the bank loan system supported by the Singapore government. The system includes a PEFG and ECI/G that supplement the MNCs' internal handling of exporter nonperformance risk and overseas buyer nonpayment risk (Table 3.3).

Taiwan. Among the East Asian NIEs, Taiwan has relied on the most diverse sources of trade financing, excluding trade financing based on bank credit (Table 3.3). Bank loan-based trade financing supported by the central bank has supplemented local and foreign company credit-based trade financing, commercial loan-based trade financing of multinational banks, and self-financing (Chiu 1981; Biggs 1988).

Japan. A pillar of the Japanese government's first postwar economic plan was its carefully created export policies and export institutions. The trade-financing system of the Bank of Japan was one of the critical components of these export policies. In the absence of a well-developed money market, the Bank of Japan implemented a preshipment export finance rediscount system, the Export Advance Bill System. Until the value of exports exceeded $1 billion, the system met more than half of the preshipment export financing needs. Even though the outstanding loan amounts declined after 1970, as exporters turned to other financing modes, certain exporters still use the system. The short-term postshipment financing schemes used until the early 1970s were the Export Usance Bill System, Loan Facilities for Export Time Bills, and the Foreign Exchange Bill Purchase System. The import financing schemes were the Import Settlement Bill System, the Import Financing Loan, and Import Usance Facilities.

Korea. Korea's trade-financing system is composed of: (1) the Bank of Korea's trade transaction-based, self-liquidating trade-financing disbursement/liquidation mechanisms (together with its rediscount system); (2) the Korea Credit Guarantee Funds' PEFG; and (3) the Korea Export-Import Bank's ECI/G. The Bank of Korea's trade-financing mechanisms have been a particularly shining example of successful trade financing based on bank loans. They have made a more important contribution to the effective implementation of the outward-oriented development strategy than any other export policy instrument.

Self-Financing

Traders meet some part of their trade-financing needs with their own funds. In fact, the trade-financing system based on bank loans discussed above normally finances only 85 percent to 90 percent of the value of trade transactions. The remaining 10 to 15 percent is self-financed. For exporters who are denied access to trade loans because they fail to supply collateral, and in the absence of a modernized export financing system, the only way to fill export orders is to rely on self-financing. However, no developing economy has succeeded in expanding its trade when it is based mainly on self-financing. The only developing economy in which some exporters have relied significantly on self-financing appears to be Taiwan. Many small- and medium-size export manufacturers were able to use their high retained earnings to supplement trade financing based on company credit and bank loans because of the unusually high savings rate in Taiwan. This stemmed from the cultural heritage and favorable macroeconomic policies (Chiu 1981; Biggs 1988).

Lessons for Developing Countries

The export success of the East Asian economies has been facilitated by speedy and undisrupted access to trade financing for all (direct and indirect) exporters based on confirmed export orders or accepted bills of completed exports. Developing countries should attempt to develop all four methods of trade financing: company credit, bank credit, bank loans, self-financing—and combinations of these. Although the complementarity among these methods has to be maintained, most developing countries must—in the absence of modern domestic banks and trading companies that can internalize risk taking—start with foreign bank credit, foreign company credit or intra-MNC credit, and bank loan finance. The East Asian experience regarding bank loan trade financing yields a number of lessons for developing countries.

Importance of Access to Trade Financing. For success in exports, short-term preshipment and postshipment export financing is much more important than investment and general working capital financing and longer-term postshipment financing. Short-term trade financing based solely on confirmed export letters of credit (L/Cs) and other export orders, and associated import or domestic trade and production transactions must be available if the export potential of a developing country is to be exploited. In turn, the traditional analyses that assume the only role of trade financing is to provide an interest subsidy fail to capture the true objective of trade financing based on bank loans as demonstrated by the East Asian experience. For example, Korea and Taiwan could have achieved their export successes without export loan interest rate preferences (which were estimated to be 4.5 percent of Korea's export value in 1968 and 0.2 percent of Taiwan's export value in 1976) even when the interest rate preferences were the most extensive in these economies. However, Korea (and to some degree Taiwan) could not have achieved a similar success without the bank loan mechanisms that ensured easy access to trade financing based on export orders.

Modern trade finance consists of various mechanisms: bank credit instruments such as L/Cs, domestic L/Cs, and BAs; export and associated import and domestic purchase transaction-based, self-liquidating trade loan disbursement/liquidation mechanisms; lender-of-last-resort facilities of central banks; institutions that deal with exporter nonperformance risk; and institutions that deal with overseas buyer nonpayment risk. Developing countries should give high priority to the first three of these mechanisms.   Properly developed, a modern trade-financing system composed of these mechanisms, which charges international or domestic market interest rates and covers all trade transactions, is completely different from the so-called sectorally targeted credit-rationing mechanisms.

In fact, these three mechanisms are the first steps in developing the truly market-based (i.e., money market–based) trade-financing mechanisms. In turn, developing countries should implement a system of accepted export bill discounting (at world market rates) backed by central bank rediscounting for short-term postshipment financing, even in the absence of a money market. Further, trade transactions related to domestic sales should be treated the same as those related to exports, in having access to the lender-of-last-resort facilities of central banks, as long as the domestic sales accompany the first two mechanisms, as that would eliminate the risk of loan misuse and cover a significant part of the supplier nonperformance risk.

As for the establishment of institutions to deal with exporter nonperformance risk and overseas buyer nonpayment risk, developing countries need to wait until the social gains associated with the additional exports stemming from a PEFG and/or an ECI/G outweigh the social costs of operating these schemes. In addition, the operational effectiveness of and effective learning-by-doing in such institutions are critical for their success. Actual beneficiaries of those schemes must cover the full costs of operating them in a multiyear framework.

Foreign Currency Loan Scheme. When the domestic financial market is segmented and the foreign exchange rate does not always reflect opportunity costs, and when external borrowing plays a large role in financing development, the best way to ensure efficient management of foreign exchange is to denominate all loans tied to the use of foreign exchange reserves in foreign currency and to charge an international market interest rate plus some margin. Foreign currency loans for imported inputs for export production must be included in this category.

In the East Asian NIEs that have established correct priorities in foreign exchange management, nothing has received higher priority than the allocation of foreign exchange for importing the inputs needed for exports that earn additional foreign exchange. If foreign exchange holdings are scarce, external financing to create a foreign exchange revolving fund should receive priority. Between 1979 and 1983, Costa Rica, Mexico, Guyana, Jamaica, Zimbabwe, and Yugoslavia, with the assistance of the World Bank, all established foreign exchange revolving funds for foreign currency loans.

The "foreign exchange retention scheme" used in some developing economies as a means of ensuring access to imported inputs is not a rational system, because current foreign exchange needs usually do not match the past export performance of dynamic export industries.

Efficient Administrative Tool for Export Incentives. Modern trade loan disbursement/liquidation mechanisms that extensively use L/Cs, domestic L/Cs, and BAs also serve as efficient mechanisms for administering such export incentives as duty-free indirect tax-free, and restriction-free imports and indirect tax exemptions for all exporters. In turn, such instruments as domestic L/Cs are very effective in extending export incentives—including trade financing, duty-free imports, and indirect tax exemptions—to indirect exporters. Such extensions of export incentives are critical in developing backward linkages and local trading companies in developing countries.

Maintaining a Realistic Exchange Rate

As I have pointed out elsewhere (Rhee 1985), the exchange rate is the most important variable affecting the returns exporters realize in local currency for the foreign exchange they earn through export value added. The determination of the real exchange rate depends on a country's foreign exchange management regime and its stabilization policies. In turn, its approach to foreign exchange management cannot be separated from financial market development and the payment and trade regimes. Table 3.4 provides an overview of foreign exchange and payment systems in the East Asian NIEs in the 1970s. A developing country pursuing an outward-oriented development strategy can and should maintain a realistic exchange rate whatever its regime of foreign exchange management. One criterion distinguishing the different types of foreign exchange regimes is whether the regime is based on a free foreign exchange market.

A Foreign Exchange Regime Based on a Free Market

Currency Convertibility. An economy cannot have a free foreign exchange market unless the domestic currency is convertible (Article VIII of the IMF's Articles of Agreement defines current account convertibility). Japan did not formally achieve convertibility until 1964, while Hong Kong implemented Article VIII in 1961 and Singapore in 1968.

Financial Markets. The financial structure is the focus of analysis in choosing a foreign exchange regime (Branson 1983). A free foreign exchange market requires mature financial markets and institutions integrated with the international financial markets. Early British connections and exposure to international trade-

Table 3.4

Overview of Foreign Exchange and Payment Systems of East Asian NIEs in the 1970s

	Hong Kong		Singapore		Korea		Taiwan	
	1970	1979	1970	1979	1970	1979	1970	1978
Currency convertibility								
Article VIII status	X	X	X	X				
Article XIV status					X	X	X	X
Exchange rate flexibility								
Par value	X		X				X	
Pegged rate (U.S. dollars)					X	X		X
Composite currency rate				X				
Floating rate		X						
Payment restriction								
On current account			X		X		X	X
On capital account			X		X	X	X	X
Surrender requirement for export proceeds			X		X	X	X	X

Source: International Monetary Fund (1970, 1979, and 1980).

related activities gave Hong Kong and Singapore ample opportunities to develop Western-style financial and trade-related institutions. Because they were entrepôt trade centers, their financial institutions developed around international trade. As early as the 1850s, more than ten foreign banks representing British, Dutch, French, and American interests were operating in Singapore and Penang. Within a century the financial institutions and markets of Hong Kong and Singapore had developed into international financial centers (Geiger and Geiger 1975). In 1980, Hong Kong had fourteen licensed banks with 1,123 branches operating within the territory, or about one branch for every 4,000 people, a ratio exceeding that of many developed countries. However, Korea's and Taiwan's financial markets and institutions were not well developed when they initiated their outward-oriented development strategies in the 1960s.

Hong Kong. Hong Kong's foreign exchange market became active after Hong Kong was excluded from the sterling zone in 1972. The government ended the pegging of the Hong Kong dollar to the U.S. dollar in 1974. Since that time, the Hong Kong dollar has floated according to market conditions. However, the government has been active in the foreign exchange markets through its commercial bankers, to the extent that portfolio management of the Exchange Fund requires and to the extent that the timing of transactions can be varied with a view to their impact on the exchange rate of the Hong Kong dollar. In short, Hong Kong's foreign exchange regime has helped it maintain its competitive position as a major exporter of manufactured goods.

Singapore. Even though Singapore conformed to the IMF's convertibility requirements in November 1968, it maintained control over foreign exchange transactions, including restrictions on borrowing or depositing by Singapore residents in foreign currencies, particularly Asian currency units. Singapore's foreign exchange market became much more active after the Singapore dollar began to float in 1973. Its foreign exchange regime is a successful example of an integrated strategy of monetary and exchange rate policies for a small open economy (McKinnon 1982).

The centerpiece of Singapore's domestic monetary policy in the 1970s was the stabilization of its exchange rate with respect to the U.S. dollar. Singapore's monetary base was largely endogenized to maintain an orderly foreign exchange market. Instead of setting firm internal rules for rates of monetary growth, Singapore allowed the monetary base to reflect foreign exchange intervention. This policy maintained the stability of the exchange rate even though the money supply fluctuated widely in the short run. Such short-run fluctuations did not, however, endanger price stability in Singapore's open economy, in which domestic prices were completely dominated by imports and exports.

Managed Foreign Exchange Regimes

As already indicated, underdeveloped financial markets and financial institutions were among the main reasons Korea and Taiwan adopted managed foreign exchange regimes in the 1960s and 1970s instead of relying on a free foreign exchange market. Although they pursued financial maturity and rational trade regimes, the transitional status of foreign exchange management was inevitable in these economies. Financial immaturity and repression also are closely related to trade regimes. Capital constraints stemming from financial market fragmentation explain the persistent use of import and payment restrictions for infant industry support in developing countries (McKinnon 1971, 1979).

Unlike Hong Kong and Singapore, Korea and Taiwan did not have an early opportunity to develop financial institutions specializing in trade financing and foreign exchange transactions. Nor did they have the opportunity to develop modern financial markets and institutions during the Japanese colonial period. Even Japan's financial markets were noncompetitive and segmented, unlike the Western industrial economies at a similar stage of development (Wallich and Wallich 1976). Consequently, managed foreign exchange regimes in the 1960s and 1970s were integral to their managed financial systems.

The influence of the commercial banks and nonbank customers in creating a unified market for foreign exchange, either spot or forward, is not as great under a managed foreign exchange regime as it is under a free-market regime. Instead, the central bank has the most influence. In other words, the role of the government in maintaining a realistic exchange rate is more critical under a managed foreign exchange regime than under a free foreign exchange market.

In contrast to other developing economies, Korea and Taiwan succeeded in maintaining realistic and unified real exchange rates in the 1960s and 1970s, through their managed foreign exchange regimes, while continuing to build financial maturity. Judging from the success of Korea's outward-looking development strategy, which involved heavy external borrowing, the country's managed foreign exchange system helped prevent capital flight, allowed selectivity in capital inflows, used a foreign currency loan scheme for exchange reserves, and maintained stability in the real exchange rate or effective real exchange rate.

The successful macroeconomic stabilization policies in Korea and Taiwan, as well as in Hong Kong and Singapore, also helped these NIEs maintain realistic and unified *real* exchange rates while initiating their outward-oriented strategies. The average annual inflation rate in Hong Kong and Singapore in the 1960s was a mere 1 to 2 percent, and Taiwan's rate during the same period was less than 5 percent. Korea's rate during that period was more than 10 percent, in part because of the large devaluations carried out in the early 1960s as part of the stabilization policy.

Lessons for Developing Countries

Achieving a free foreign exchange market is a desirable and rational long-term objective for developing countries. While they pursue policies for building conditions in the financial markets and the trade regimes needed to have a free foreign exchange market, they should also try to achieve a realistic and unified real exchange rate without delay. This is possible even under a managed foreign exchange regime. In achieving this objective, macroeconomic stabilization should precede any other measures.[8]

Building Institutional and Physical Infrastructure

Because of externalities and scale economies in infrastructure investments and the imperfect nature of information in the world markets, the physical infrastructure (ports, transport, and communication) and institutional infrastructure needed for trade-oriented development have to be built through a joint effort of the public and private sectors.

Physical Infrastructure

When the East Asian NIEs initiated their outward-oriented development strategies in the 1950s and 1960s, a basic physical infrastructure was in place—left over from the entrepôt trade of Hong Kong and Singapore, and from Japanese colonial rule in Korea and Taiwan. Subsequently, the NIEs devoted considerable resources to infrastructure investments (e.g., the Hong Kong government constructed a major port for container shipping in the early 1970s).

Although all of Hong Kong and Singapore can be considered FTZs, the government-run Hong Kong Industrial Estates Corporation and Singapore's Jurong Town Corporation have developed industrial estates specifically to lease ready-built factory units at rents that would recover the full costs. These zones have been important in attracting foreign companies for export activities. Similarly, the three FTZs in Taiwan and two in Korea, established by the public sector, played an important role in attracting direct foreign investment to these economies in their early stages of export development. Industrial estates, export processing zones, and science parks have provided the additional infrastructure needed to upgrade, diversify, and expand industrial exports.

Institutional Infrastructure

It is equally important, however, to have an effective institutional infrastructure that is able to deal with imperfect information and imperfect competition in the world markets. Here, institutional infrastructure has a broad meaning, encompassing all the public and private organizations and agents that are development players.[9]

Export Marketing Institutions. As previously suggested in Table 3.1, in the 1950s and 1960s the East Asian NIEs generally relied on foreign trading companies for overseas marketing know-how and for providing access to world markets (except Hong Kong, which relied on local resources, namely, the British and Chinese merchant houses). As these economies pursued more aggressive strategies for penetrating and exploring external markets, they established public or semipublic marketing promotion institutions. Table 3.5 provides an overview of the export marketing institutions of the East Asian NIEs. However, their role has been coordination, information-gathering, and dissemination rather than direct marketing.

Trading Companies. Korea appears to be the only developing economy that has succeeded in emulating large, Japanese-type private GTCs based on existing conglomerates. Singapore's GTC, INTRACO, is a public corporation. The trading companies in Hong Kong and Taiwan comprise many small businesses. In recent years, about 50,000 Hong Kong manufacturers have employed close to one million workers (fewer than twenty-nine workers per firm). With more than 90 percent of Hong Kong's products being exported, more than 90 percent of its firms employ fewer than ten workers. In Taiwan, 99 percent of the more than 120,000 manufacturing firms are small- and medium-sized operations (Medium and Small Business Administration 1987).

Table 3.5

Comparative Overview of the Primary Export Marketing Institutions of East Asian NIEs

Institutional Role	Hong Kong	Singapore	Korea	Taiwan
Institutional support	Hong Kong Trade Development Council (established in 1966)	Singapore Trade Development Board (established in 1983)	Korea Trade Promotion Corporation (established in 1962)	China External Trade Development Council (established in 1970)
Export marketing channels	Merchant houses; small trading firms	MNCs; INTRACO	Korean general trading companies	Japanese general trading companies; small trading companies

These small manufacturers are indirect exporters relying on trading companies for direct exports and imports of raw materials. The numerous Hong Kong and Taiwan trading companies supporting these small manufacturers are also small. More than 90 percent of the 28,000 trading enterprises in Hong Kong employ fewer than twenty people. The large trading companies in Hong Kong that employ more than 100 people account for only 1.3 percent of the total trading establishments (Chan 1987: 65). The more than 50,000 registered trading companies in Taiwan are all small- and medium-sized, except for several big trading companies being promoted by the authorities without much success (Chan 1987).

What have been the underlying factors enabling the small trading companies of Hong Kong and Taiwan to succeed in linking small producers to overseas markets? How have they been able to collect overseas information, provide the necessary financing, and take considerable risks? Why has the size of Hong Kong and Taiwan trading companies differed so markedly from that of Japan's and Korea's GTCs, which have exploited economies of scale in overseas market intelligence, sales, and distribution and have been able to tap the resources of the conglomerates?

The relationships between small traders and small manufacturers in Hong Kong and Taiwan have worked well because of the strong trust developed through close personal contacts, the flexibility and efficiency of small producers in meeting small orders and changing their product composition, the lower management and operating costs of smaller trading companies, and the smaller resource requirements for intrafirm credit-based trade financing. These advantages have outweighed scale and financing limitations. Trust and flexibility among family-related businessmen are also traditions in the Chinese culture. The vitality and prevalence of small- and medium-sized trading companies might also be related to a cultural preference for owning a business rather than being employed in a big corporation.

Business-Government Partnerships. The East Asian culture and other unique institutional underpinnings have forged effective partnerships between the business communities and governments (frequently characterized as Japan Inc., Singapore Inc., and the like), while basically private firms of the East Asian NIEs have carried out manufactured export production and overseas sales.[10] This relationship has been markedly different from the more typical characterization of private versus public sector, or market versus intervention dichotomy, and has been vital to successful implementation of the outward-oriented development strategies in the East Asian NIEs.

Lessons for Developing Countries

Conditions in most developing countries offer neither the physical infrastructure found in the East Asian NIEs in the 1960s nor the investment resources to create it. Consequently, the concentrated development of infrastructure in a few FTZs is a key strategy these countries can use to attract direct foreign investment. The experience of Hong Kong and Singapore in developing industrial estates and factory units with proper cost-recovery leasing policies is valuable in light of the capital shortages of developing countries and the fact that subsidized rents alone would never induce such investment. Furthermore, the experience of some Latin American FTZs (e.g., in Costa Rica and the Dominican Republic) that have relied on private enterprises and capital (domestic or MNC) for establishing FTZs also is valuable.

Imperfect information about external markets and technology as well as economies of scale and external economies in overseas marketing justify institutional support for export marketing. However, the creation of a trade promotion agency in a developing country does not guarantee the level of success experienced by the East Asian NIEs. Efforts to improve the efficiency of such an organization are needed as well. For example, the Hong Kong Trade Development Council deliberately limited the share of expenses for personnel (to 30 percent) to prevent overstaffing; its investment was directed toward more trade services. The Singapore Trade Development Board was created (in 1983) by reforming the trade promotion function of previous agencies. The role of a trade promotion agency as central coordinator of the promotion activities of chambers of commerce, industry associations, trading companies, and export manufacturers is even more important than its information-gathering and disseminating functions.

A lesson for developing countries is that each culture has a unique institutional infrastructure that can become a foundation for effectively implementing an outward-oriented development strategy provided deliberate efforts are made to capitalize on the positive aspects. For example, Korea capitalized on the pragmatism of Korean shamanism. Research is needed to find, for example, the types of trading companies suitable for different cultures.

Conclusions

The emphasis in this chapter has been on the lessons from the East Asian NIEs that are relevant to developing countries today. These countries should pay particular attention to the NIEs' process of initiating outward-oriented development in the 1950s, 1960s, and 1970s. Of course, the task may be more difficult for developing countries, given their initial conditions and current world market environments. Such difficulties should not prevent them from pursuing an outward-oriented strategy, however. The strategy can initiate dynamic development in an outward-oriented direction, expand imports, and provide a more competitive domestic industrial base. The sequencing of the reforms related to policies and institutions and infrastructure building in the East Asian NIEs should be of special interest.

Initiation of Development. A developing country with unfavorable initial conditions, as explained earlier, needs to bring in foreign parties and partners who can package the critical foreign and domestic elements needed to enter the world markets and establish the minimum policy and infrastructure environments that put domestic firms on an equal footing with their foreign competitors.

Diffusion of Development. Acquiring the capacity to enter the world markets by working with MNCs is a first step in gaining the industrial competence needed to sustain an outward-oriented development strategy. Development initiated through collaborative efforts with MNCs needs to be transmitted efficiently to other domestic firms and throughout the economy by taking advantage of the tremendous externalities that come from international contacts and competition.

Sequencing of Reforms. Given its significant policy distortions, the underdevelopment of its institutions (including markets), and its insufficient infrastructure, a developing country can seldom afford to wait until perfect, rational policy, institutional, and infrastructure environments exist before promoting outward-oriented development. It first must establish an "equal footing policy" and institutional and infrastructure arrangements. These not only are necessary conditions for encouraging foreign firms to participate and for initiating development in an outward-oriented direction, but they also can be the first steps in establishing perfectly rational policies, mature institutions, and rich infrastructure.

Upgrading the capabilities of institutions (such as banks, trading companies, and government agencies) that implement the policies that provide equal footing with foreign competitors will stimulate the government's willingness to extend export policy regimes to nonexport activities.

The East Asian experience suggests that developing countries would have a better chance of succeeding in their export policy reforms (that is, free-trade status, easy access to trade financing, realistic and unitary real exchange rates, and so on) and of extending them to the whole economy if these reforms were sequenced in parallel with the increasing industrial and institutional competence gained through world market competition.

Notes

1. For empirical evidence on the capacity to package the elements needed to enter the world markets in eleven non-East Asian NIEs, see Rhee and Belot (1989).

2. Localized technology means technology that originally came from foreign sources but has been well absorbed by local firms with or without some modifications. See Rhee, Ross-Larson, Pursell (1984), p. 42.

3. The duty exemption systems in the East Asian NIEs are mainly related to imports of raw materials and intermediate inputs. However, even those East Asian NIEs that later adopted the policies to promote domestic capital goods industries in the 1970s and 1980s had implemented the policies to provide free-trade status for capital goods imports at the early stages of export development in the 1950s and 1960s.

4. Cooper (1987) noted the important consensus reached at the IMF–World Bank Symposium on Growth-Oriented Adjustment Programs: In sequencing policy reforms aimed at resuming sustained growth, developing countries need to assign a high priority to measures that ensure rational regimes for export activities, whatever other economic measures are taken. He noted that "this conference has relied mainly on generalities. There have been few concrete suggestions ... the really constructive work involves getting down to operational details." In addressing the issue of ensuring equal footing with foreign competitors in access to trade financing and to inputs at world market prices (in compliance with GATT rules), as well as maintaining realistic exchange rates—the three most important components of a rational regime for exporting—this discussion focuses on specific operational lessons from the East Asian experience.

5. This was in response to an assessment in the 1986 report of the Economic Committee, entitled *The Singapore Economy: New Directions*, which stated that "local companies, particularly the small ones, lack access to capital" (Ministry of Trade and Industry, Republic of Singapore 1986: 36).

6. In England, bill discounting was the original function of commercial banks before they engaged in providing overdrafts and loans.

7. Developing these three mechanisms is not so different from the British government's efforts in the nineteenth century (in establishing the bill of exchange rediscounting of the Bank of England and enacting the Bill of Exchange Act of 1882) and the BA rediscounting of the U.S. Federal Reserve Board.

8. See Cooper (1987), Lin (1987), Ozawa (1989), and Sachs (1987) on the East Asian experience regarding the sequencing of liberalization in the various markets. The experience indicates that the precondition for liberalization was macroeconomic stabilization.

9. Arrow (1974) and Stiglitz (1989) argue that the inequality in economic development stems largely from the differences in organizations and institutions that deal with imperfect and costly information.

10. President Park used Korea's "monthly trade promotion meetings" effectively to enhance public awareness of the outward-oriented development strategy at Korea's early stage of export development. This measure was a uniquely Korean adaptation of Japan's

model, transposed to Korea's cultural background and temperament. The other East Asian NIEs also used their unique institutional mechanisms to induce collective efforts to implement their outward-oriented strategies.

References

Arrow, Kenneth. 1974. "Limited Knowledge and Economic Analysis." *American Economic Review* 64, no. 1 (March): 1–10.

Biggs, Tyler. 1988. *Financing the Emergence of Small and Medium Enterprise in Taiwan: Financial Mobilization and the Flow of Domestic Credit to the Private Sector.* Washington, D.C.: U.S. Agency for International Development, August.

Branson, William. 1983. *Economic Structure and Policy for External Balance.* International Monetary Fund Staff Paper 30, no. 1 (March).

Chan, Kung Wai-Ying. 1987. "A Laissez Faire Approach to Trade in Hong Kong: Positive Non-Interventionism." In *Role of General Trading Firms in Trade and Development,* ed., Terutomo Ozawa. Tokyo: Asian Productivity Center.

Chang, Victor. 1987. "Big Trading Companies in the Republic of China." In *Role of General Trading Firms in Trade and Development,* ed., Terutomo Ozawa. Tokyo: Asian Productivity Center.

Chiu, Paul C. H. 1981. *Performance of Financial Institutions in Taiwan.* Taipei: Institute of Economics, Academia Sinica.

Cooper, Richard N. 1987. "Discussions." In *Growth-Oriented Adjustment Programs,* eds., Vittorio Corbo, Morris Goldstein, and Moshin Khan. Washington, D.C.: International Monetary Fund and the World Bank.

Geiger, Theodore, and Geiger, France M. 1975. *The Development Progress of Hong Kong and Singapore.* New York: Macmillan.

Ghose, T. K. 1987. *The Banking System of Hong Kong.* Singapore: Butterworths.

ILO/UNCTAD. 1988. *The Economic and Social Effects of Multinational Enterprises in Export Processing Zones.* Geneva.

International Monetary Fund. 1970. *22nd Annual Report on Exchange Restrictions.* Washington, D.C.

————.1979. *Exchange Arrangements and Exchange Restrictions,* Washington, D.C.

————.1980. *Exchange Arrangements and Exchange Restrictions.* Washington, D.C.

Jones, Leroy, and Sakong, Il. 1980. *Government, Business and Entrepreneurship in Economic Development: The Korean Case.* Cambridge, Mass.: Harvard University Press.

Kim, Kyong-Dong. 1988. "The Distinctive Features of South Korea's Development." *In Search of an East Asian Development Model,* eds., Peter L. Berger and Hsin-Huang Michael Hsiao. New Brunswick, N. J.: Transaction Books.

Krause, Lawrence B., and Sekiguchi, Sueo. 1976. "Japan and the World Economy." In *Asia's New Giant: How the Japanese Economy Works,* eds., Hugh Patrick and Henry Rosovsky. Washington, D.C.: Brookings Institution.

Lin, Ching-Yuan. 1987. *Policy Reforms, International Competitiveness and Export Performance: Chile and Argentina versus The Republic of Korea and Taiwan, Province of China.* Washington, D.C.: International Monetary Fund.

McKinnon, Ronald. 1971. "On Misunderstanding the Capital Constraints in LDCs: The Consequences for Trade Policy." In *Trade Balance of Payments and Growth: Papers in International Economics in Honor of Charles Kindleberger,* eds., Jagdish Bhagwati, Ronald Jones, Robert Mundell, and Jacoslav Vanek. New York: North-Holland.

————.1979. "Foreign Trade Regimes and Economic Development: A Review Article." *Journal of International Economics,* Vol. 9, pp. 429–52.

————.1982. "Offshore Markets in Foreign Currencies and National Monetary Control:

Britain, Singapore, and the United States." In *The International Monetary System: A Time of Turbulance*, eds., Jacob Dreyer, Gattfried Haberler, and Thomas Willett. Washington, D.C.: American Enterprise Institute for Public Policy Research.

Medium and Small Business Administration. 1987. *Statistics of Small and Medium Business in Taiwan*. Taipei, August.

Ministry of Finance, the Republic of Korea. 1982. *Trade Promotion System of Taiwan*. Seoul, September.

Ministry of Trade and Industry, Republic of Singapore. 1986. *Report of the Economic Committee—The Singapore Economy: New Directions*. Singapore, February.

Ozawa, Terutomo. 1987. *Role of General Trading Firms in Trade and Development*. Tokyo: Asian Productivity Center.

————.1989. *Laying the Foundation for Competitiveness: Policy Sequencing in Japan and Possible Application in Developing Countries*. Washington, D.C.: World Bank.

Peck, Merton. 1976. "Technology." In *Asia's New Giant: How the Japanese Economy Works*, eds., Hugh Patrick and Henry Rosovsky. Washington, D.C.: Brookings Institution.

Rhee, Yung Whee. 1985. *Instruments for Export Policy and Administration: Lessons from the East Asia Experience*. World Bank Staff Working Paper 725. Washington, D.C.: World Bank.

————.1989. *Trade Financing for Developing Countries*. Policy and Research Series, no. 5. Washington, D.C.: World Bank. Photocopy.

Rhee, Yung Whee, and Belot, Therese. 1989. *Export Catalysts in Low-Income Countries: A Review of Eleven Success Stories*. World Bank Discussion Paper, no. 72. Washington, D.C.: World Bank.

Rhee, Yung Whee; Ross-Larson, Bruce; and Pursell, Garry. 1984. *Korea's Competitive Edge: Managing the Entry into World Markets*. Baltimore, Md.: Johns Hopkins University Press.

Sachs, Jeffrey. 1987. "Trade and Exchange Rate Policies in Growth-Oriented Adjustment Programs." In *Growth-Oriented Adjustment Programs*, eds., Vittorio Corbo, Morris Goldstein, and Moshin Khan. Washington, D.C.: International Monetary Fund and World Bank.

Skully, Michael T. 1976. *Merchant Banking in the Far East*. London: Baker Research Unit.

Stiglitz, Joseph. 1989. "Markets, Market Failures, and Development." *The American Economic Review: Papers and Proceedings of the 101th Annual Meeting of the American Economic Association*. May.

Tan, Augustine H. H., and Hock, Ow Chin. 1982. "Singapore." In *Development Strategies in Semi-Industrial Economies*, eds., Bela Balassa et al. Baltimore, Md.: Johns Hopkins University Press.

Wallich, Henry, and Wallich, Mable I. 1976. "Banking and Finance." In *Asia's New Giant: How the Japanese Economy Works,* eds., Hugh Patrick and Henry Rosovsky. Washington, D.C.: Brookings Institution.

Westphal, Larry; Rhee, Yung Whee; and Pursell, Garry. 1981. *Korean Industrial Competence: Where It Came From*. World Bank Staff Working Paper 469. Washington, D.C.: World Bank.

Wong, Siu-lun. 1988. "The Applicability of Asian Family Values to Other Sociocultural Settings." In *In Search of an East Asian Development Model*, eds., Peter L. Berger and Hsin-Huang Michael Hsiao. New Brunswick, N. J.: Transaction Books.

Woronoff, Jon. 1986 *Asia's "Miracle" Economies*. New York: M.E. Sharpe.

Yoshino, Michael Y., and Lifson, Thomas B. 1986. *The Invisible Link: Japan's Sogo Shosa and the Organization of Trade*. Cambridge, Mass.: MIT Press.

CHAPTER 4

China's Manufactured Exports and Possible Regional Cooperation

XIONG XINGMEI, LIN YUHUA, WANG RUI, ZHU TONG, AND WU XIAOTIAN

After World War II, especially since the 1960s, scientific and technological revolutions have promoted world industrial production and international trade. The trade value of manufactured goods as a proportion of total world trade value has increased from around 50 percent in the early 1960s to about 70 percent in 1988 (GATT 1987–88). Within manufactured exports, the capital- and technology-intensive products have expanded more rapidly. The developing countries in the East Asia region, particularly the newly industrialized economies (NIEs), have followed the trend with distinction. They have upgraded their industrial structures, and manufactured goods have taken an increasingly important place in the commodity composition of international trade.

China is a developing country with the largest population in the world. It has gained substantially in economic development over the past four decades and contributed to the expansion of international trade in recent years. With the economic structural readjustment, radical changes have taken place in the commodity composition of China's exports. Forty years ago China exported mainly primary products, but now it exports mainly manufactured goods. The expansion of manufactured exports is bringing in more foreign exchange, generating more employment, raising productivity, and promoting the growth of the entire economy. Therefore, methods to further expand the export of manufactured goods are of great importance to China's economic development.

In this chapter we will analyze first the experience of China's export of manufactured goods and discuss the problems encountered. Then we will explore the possibility for regional cooperation in manufactured exports. (For

We would like to express our gratitude to Mr. Xu Ming for preparing the first three statistical tables and to Dr. Shu-Chin Yang and Mr. Zhang Peiji for their valuable comments and suggestions on the first draft, as well as to Dr. Yang for his revisions after the seminar.

Table 4.1

China: Gross Value and Shares of Industrial and Agricultural Production (at current prices, RMB billion yuan)

Year	Gross Value of Industrial & Agricultural Production	Gross Value of Agricultural Production		Gross Value of Industrial Production	
		Gross Value	Share (%)	Gross Value	Share (%)
1952	81.0	46.1	56.9	34.9	43.1
1953	96.0	51.0	53.1	45.0	46.9
1958	164.9	56.6	34.3	108.3	65.7
1965	223.5	83.3	37.3	140.2	62.7
1966	253.4	91.0	35.9	162.4	64.1
1979	637.9	168.8	26.6	468.1	73.4
1980	707.8	192.3	27.2	515.5	72.8
1981	758.1	218.1	28.8	540.0	71.2
1985	1,333.7	362.0	27.1	971.7	72.9
1986	1,520.7	401.3	26.4	1,119.4	73.6
1987	1,848.9	467.6	25.3	1,381.3	74.7
1988	2,371.8	561.8	23.7	1,810.0	76.3

Sources: State Bureau of Statistics, *China's Statistical Yearbook* (Beijing), 1988, 44–47. *Guan Ming Daily* (Beijing), March 1, 1989.

broader issues and more recent developments, see Yang, chapter 1; and Balassa and Noland, chapter 13; parts on China.)

Performance of China's Manufactured Exports

In the early 1950s, China was an economically backward country with a low level of industrial production. In 1953, industrial output value accounted for about 46.9 percent of the total of agriculture and industrial output value (see Table 4.1), and manufactured goods constituted only about 20.6 percent of total exports (see Table 4.2).

The rehabilitation of the national economy in the early 1950s and the successful fulfillment of the First Five-Year Plan (1953–57) laid the foundation for China's industrialization. This was followed by the implementation of the Second Five-Year Plan (1958–62), which emphasized the development of heavy industries. The subsequent three-year period (1963–65) of economic readjustment slowed China's economic growth, although industrial growth on the whole was still quite rapid. Between 1953 and 1965, the proportion of the total industrial output value to the gross value of industrial and agricultural production rose from 46.9 percent to 62.7 percent (see Table 4.1). The manufactured goods share of total exports increased from 20.6 percent to 48.8 percent during the same period. Of the manufactured exports, textiles and light industrial products ex-

Table 4.2

Composition of China's Manufactured Exports (as percentage of total export value)

Year	Total Manufactured Goods	Heavy Industrial & Chemical Products	Chemical Products Only	Manufactured Goods by Raw Materials	Machinery and Transport Equipment	Textiles & Light Industrial Products
1953	20.6	8.3	0.7	7.6	—	12.3
1957	36.4	10.1	1.3	8.7	0.1	26.3
1965	48.8	17.8	2.4	7.9	7.5	31.0
1966	39.7	11.7	2.0	6.6	3.1	28.0
1970	46.5	12.8	2.9	6.8	3.1	33.7
1975	43.6	12.5	3.0	6.1	3.4	31.1
1976	45.4	11.8	2.9	5.4	3.5	33.6
1980	46.6[a]	12.9	3.4	4.8	4.7	33.7
1981	50.4[a]	18.2	3.4	6.3	8.5	32.2
1985	45.8[a]	13.9	2.3	3.1	8.5	31.9
1986	56.3[a]	20.4	3.0	4.0	13.4	35.9
1987	61.2[a]	20.9	2.9	4.8	13.2	40.3

Source: Ministry of Foreign Economic Relations and Trade (MOFERT), *Almanac of China's Foreign Economic Relations* (Beijing), 1988.

Notes: The figures are all from the Statistics of the Ministry of Foreign Economic Relations and Trade and are different from the statistics of the customs due to differences in calculation, coverage, and time periods. Due to commodity classification problems, the subsector figures add up to more than the figures for the total manufactured goods percentages.

[a]The customs statistics resulted in the following shares (%): 1980 49.8, 1981 53.3, 1985 49.3, 1986 63.4, 1987 66.5, 1988 69.6.

panded remarkably. Their proportion of China's total commodity exports climbed from 12.3 percent in 1953 to 31 percent in 1965, while the proportion of heavy and chemical industrial products rose from 8.3 percent to 17.8 percent during the same period. During the chaotic decade (1966–1976), the national economy was seriously damaged, and there was no significant change in the export commodity composition (see Table 4.2).

After 1978, the state implemented a policy of invigorating the domestic economy and opening to the outside world. It introduced comprehensive reforms of the economic and foreign trade systems, thus accelerating economic growth and foreign trade. In 1988, the total export value reached US$47.54 billion, nearly five times the 1978 level. From 1978 to 1988, there were ups and downs in the proportion of manufactured goods to total commodity exports. Between 1978 and 1983, this proportion rose, but afterward, due to the rapid increase in the export of oil products, the proportion of primary products rose while that of manufactured goods fell correspondingly. In 1986, China's oil exports decreased because the world oil prices fell and the country made an effort to support OPEC's move to stabilize these prices. At the same time, China proceeded with more flexible trade practices, such as processing with imported materials, processing according to imported samples or designs, assembling with imported parts, and compensating foreign investment with export goods. As a result, manufactured exports expanded. Their share of total merchandise exports increased rapidly, reaching 61.2 percent in 1987 (66.5 percent according to customs statistics), not too far below the world average (see Table 4.2).

The expansion of China's manufactured exports has the following features:

(1) The change from exporting mainly primary products to exporting mainly manufactured goods is closely linked to the reform of China's economic and foreign trade systems, the "open policy," the readjustment of the industrial structure, and active participation in world economic growth and the international division of labor.

(2) In the mix of the manufactured exports, the majority were low-grade, labor-intensive products with extensive raw materials content and low value added. Although heavy industry was developed earlier in China, the export of machinery and electrical products has been expanding slowly, and the export value has been low, averaging only US$430 million annually from 1970 to 1978. During the Sixth Five-Year Plan period (1981–85), the export value of machinery and electrical products grew more rapidly: from US$1.68 billion in 1985 to a peak of US$6.15 billion in 1988. They accounted for 12.9 percent of China's total goods export value but only 0.5 percent of the world's total export value of machinery and electrical products.

(3) There has been a significant change in the geographic direction of China's manufactured exports. In the 1950s China's manufactured goods were exported mainly to the Soviet Union and Eastern European markets; from the late 1950s manufactured exports were gradually shifted to the Western countries and the developing countries/areas. Of the manufactured goods exported in 1986, 62 percent went to the developing countries/areas. Hong Kong is the most important market for China's manufactured exports and re-exports. In 1987, 44.1 percent of the manufactured goods were exported to Hong Kong, 10.1 percent to the European Community (twelve countries), 8.6 percent to the United States, and 8.4 percent to Japan.

China's Efforts to Expand Manufactured Exports

China's efforts to expand manufactured exports are manifested mainly in the following areas:

(1) Establishment of a strong industrial foundation. From 1953, the first year of the First Five-Year Plan, to 1965, China expanded its industrial capacity and technological base substantially, with the establishment of many new industries.

Consequently, the gross value of industrial production at current prices more than tripled during 1953–65; when the retail price level increased only 16 percent. It reached RMB140 billion yuan in 1965, equivalent to US$57 billion at the official exchange rate. This development enhanced China's capacity for the expansion of manufactured exports. From 1953 to 1965, the export value of textiles jumped from US$62 million to US$449 million, with its proportion of total merchandise export value rising from 6 percent to 20 percent. The export value of light industrial prouucts other than textiles climbed from US$213 million to US$520 million, with its proportion of total merchandise export value rising from 20.8 percent to 23.4 percent (World Bank 1988; Ministry of Foreign Economic Relations and Trade [MOFERT]). Imports of advanced technology and equipment have modernized many industries in China. For example, the vinylon plant introduced from Japan has filled a gap in China's chemical fiber production. Also, as early as the 1950s, China imported large paper-making machines from the Soviet Union, Finland, and Austria; in the 1960s it imported equipment for the clock and watch industry from Switzerland and industrial facilities for the leather, glass, and sewing machine industries from the Federal Republic of Germany, Italy, and Czechoslovakia. All this has contributed to the establishment of a strong foundation for industrial production and exports, particularly in the light industry sector.

To speed up industrial modernization, more advanced foreign technology has been imported since 1978. From 1979 to 1987, 2,922 items of advanced technologies were imported, with a total value of US$16.8 billion. These advanced technologies and installations were allotted to such industrial departments as metallurgical, light industry, textiles, machinery, electronics, and ship-building; thus, many existing large factories were renovated and expanded and new large enterprises were established. In addition, China strengthened the technical transformation and equipment renewal of medium-sized and small enterprises. More than 200,000 projects were completed and put into operation, expanding further the production capacity of the processing and manufacturing industries. Between 1979 and 1988, the total value of industrial production at current prices leapt from RMB468 billion yuan (US$280 billion at the official exchange rate) to RMB1,810 billion yuan (US$832 billion at the official exchange rate), with the output value of textile and light industries jumping from RMB204 billion yuan (US$122 billion at the official exchange rate) to RMB895 billion yuan (US$412 billion at the official exchange rate), thereby expanding the sources of supply for export.

(2) Deepened reform of the foreign trade system. China's former foreign trade system was a highly centralized state monopoly management system that had played an important role under the historical conditions prevailing before it launched economic reform in 1979. But later the defects of this system gradually emerged; its excessive and rigid control became unsuited to the changing world market. The earlier guiding principle for foreign trade had stressed that import

and export trade was aimed at exchanging production surplus among countries, satisfying each other's needs, and filling the gap between domestic supply and demand. Since 1978, China has implemented the open policy, emphasizing active participation in the international division of labor as a means to promote economic development. Thus, the government has implemented a series of measures for reforming the old foreign trade system. The guidelines have been clearly defined: enterprises are to be responsible for their own profits and losses; government is not to interfere in management; foreign trade is to be integrated with production operation; and a trade dealer system is to be instituted.

(3) Development of Outward-Oriented Coastal Regions. In early 1988, China announced the strategy of outward-oriented economic development in the coastal regions. By giving full play to the advantage of China's abundant labor supply and low labor cost, as well as relatively strong processing capacity, the outward-oriented processing industries have developed by importing raw materials from abroad and exporting finished goods. This policy has contributed to an impressive increase in China's manufactured exports.

(4) Adoption of the Following Export Incentive Measures:

• Export tax reimbursement and preferential loans. The categories of taxes for reimbursement to the manufacture exporters include the product tax (or value-added tax) and the business tax. In addition, customs has lowered export tariffs and gradually reduced or canceled the adjustable corporate tax on export-oriented enterprises. To reduce costs, the state has also provided low-interest preferential loans for foreign trade and export-oriented enterprises.

• Instituting a reward system. Foreign trade and export-oriented enterprises that have provided manufactured goods for export are given a prescribed bonus in accordance with their actual volume of exports or the domestic procurement value of exports. The money is used for workers' bonuses and operation of workers' welfare undertakings. As an incentive, workers' compensation is linked to the enterprise's fulfillment of export targets.

• Retaining foreign exchange. For a long time, China's foreign exchange has been under the state's unified management. The foreign exchange earned by export enterprises was handed over to the state, and foreign exchange needed by enterprises was allocated under the state's plan. There was no connection between the sources and uses of foreign exchange. To encourage the earning of foreign exchange, the foreign exchange allotments to central and local governments as well as export enterprises have been reallocated. Of the foreign exchange earned through export, local government and export-production enterprises can each retain at least 12.5 percent, while the rest is surrendered to the state. Export-production enterprises and localities can use the retained foreign exchange to import needed materials. To a large extent, this provides an incentive to enterprises to produce for export and to localities to guarantee the supply of materials that supports the expansion of exports.

• Setting up foreign exchange centers. For a long time, China has exercised strict control over foreign exchange; settlement of exchange was made by the state. The determination of exchange rates was divorced from the relation between market supply and demand. In order to adjust the production enterprises' surpluses and deficiencies of foreign exchange funds, the state set up the first foreign exchange center in Shenzhen in 1986. After several years of experimentation, twenty additional centers were set up across the country. Foreign exchange retained by enterprises, foreign exchange invested by foreign businesses, and donated foreign exchange can all be sold at the foreign exchange centers. At these centers production enterprises can buy the foreign exchange needed to import equipment, raw and semifinished materials, and components and parts. The exchange rate at the center is determined according to market supply of and demand for foreign exchange. In this way, enterprises can quickly obtain the foreign exchange funds they need for production. Statistics show that in 1988, the nation's volume of transactions of foreign exchange at the centers reached US$6.264 billion, constituting one-third of the nation's total value of retained foreign exchange and 18 percent of the foreign exchange used for imports during the same period (*People's Daily*, February 14, 1989).

• Adjusting exchange rate to promote export. For a long time, the overvaluation of the renminbi (RMB) has hampered export. During the mid-1980s, China readjusted the exchange rate of the renminbi versus the U.S. dollar three times. In January 1985 the exchange rate was RMB2.8 yuan to US$1; in October of the same year it was devalued to 3.2 yuan to US$1; in June 1986 it was further adjusted to 3.7 yuan to US$1. In December 1989 it was again devalued to RMB4.7 and further to RMB 5.3 = US$1 in 1990. This gradually increased the competitiveness of China's exports. Apart from the official exchange rate, there is the rather flexible exchange rate at the foreign exchange centers, which, to a certain extent, has helped to balance the demand and supply.

• Attraction of foreign investment. A large portion of the production equipment and technology of China's industries is already obsolete and backward. It needs to be updated, renewed, and replaced. While this will help to improve the quality of existing products, new investment in modern equipment is also needed to produce a greater variety of new products with ready markets abroad. All this would require a large amount of investment, particularly foreign investment, which can bring in modern equipment, new technology, and efficient management. To attract foreign investors, the government has adopted a number of measures to improve the investment environment. From 1979 to 1988, it enacted and implemented over 400 sets of laws and regulations on economic relations with foreign countries and signed investment protection agreements with twenty-three countries and agreements on avoidance of double taxation with twenty-one countries. These laws and regulations stipulate that foreign investors are given the following preferential treatments: reduction of or exemption from corporate taxes; reduction of the service charge; reduction of the fees for the use of sites; and priority for the supply of electricity, transport, and communications facilities needed for production. During this period, China approved the establishment of more than 15,900 foreign-funded enterprises with a contract value amounting to US$25 billion and the value of actual investment reaching US$9 billion *(International Business News,* January 24, 1989). Customs statistics show that the export value of solely foreign-owned enterprises, Sino-foreign joint ventures, and Sino-foreign cooperative businesses (hereinafter referred to as "the three types of foreign-funded enterprises") amounted to US$2.416 billion in 1988, accounting for 5.1 percent of China's total merchandise export value. The overwhelming majority of such exports were manufactured goods, which accounted for 7.3 percent of total manufactured export value. Machinery and electrical products made up 50 percent of all such export commodities, while textiles and clothing constituted about 25 percent. Moreover, the advanced technology and management expertise introduced by these foreign investments have set examples for the Chinese industrial enterprises to emulate in improving their efficiency.

Problems of China's Manufactured Exports

To expand manufactured exports, China obviously needs to improve its industrial sector and trade-related activities considerably. But the country also requires a relatively favorable trade environment, ready markets, and fair trade practices from its trading partners. In these respects, China is faced with many problems, which are discussed below:

(1) The growing international trade protectionism. Compared with conditions in the 1960s, the international trade environment has undergone great changes in recent years. In the 1960s, free trade prevailed; there were fewer trade barriers, and the international trade environment was generally favorable. Now protectionism has stiffened, and new trade barriers have emerged one after another. In the past, the tariff barrier was the chief protective device adopted among the developed countries. Now, although tariffs are no longer the principal protective measure, the tariff structure is still unfavorable to the developing countries. The average customs tariff on the developed countries' imports of industrial goods has been reduced substantially after several rounds of multilateral trade negotiations under the auspices of GATT. However, the developed countries' tariff peaks and escalations are aimed mainly at goods produced at comparatively higher processing stages by the developing countries, such as textiles, clothing, certain petrochemical products, footwear, and leather. The tariff level on these commodities far exceeds the average level of 6–7 percent. For example, tariff rates on 33 percent of European Community imports and 17 percent of U.S. and Japanese imports exceed 10 percent (Boonekamp 1989:15). With the rise in the processing level of products, the nominal tariff has been raised steadily, with the result that the developed countries' effective protective rates on such products far exceeds their nominal rate (World Bank 1987:139).

Moreover, the past two decades have found the developed countries adopting more and more nontariff barriers. These usually include import quotas; voluntary export restrictions; tariff quotas; discriminatory and nondiscriminatory import licensing; antidumping investigations; strict technology, hygiene and health standards; and strict product origin standards. Statistics show that in 1987, 25 percent of the developed countries' imports from the developing countries and 21 percent of the latter's imports from the developed countries were affected by nontariff barriers (Boonekamp 1989:17; World Bank 1987). Discriminatory automatic export restrictive measures increased from 50 in 1978 to 135 in 1987 and further to 260 in 1988, of which 123 were aimed at restricting exports of the developing countries (see Laird and Yeats 1989:13). In 1966, among all imports of the developed countries, nearly 17 percent of the SITC four-digit products were subject to nontariff barriers. By 1986 the number of products subject to such barriers had doubled, with particularly severe restrictions on nonstaple foods, agricultural raw materials, textile fiber, animal and vegetable oil, textiles, and clothing. The manufactured goods subject to such barriers broadened from 5 percent in 1966 to 51 percent in 1986. The notable products subject to such nontariff barriers were textiles, clothing, metals, machinery, and transport equipment (Boonekamp 1989:17). In 1986 world trade, the percentages of commodities subject to the developed countries' nontariff barriers were as follows: iron and steel, 61.1 percent; textiles, 42.5 percent; clothing, 71.1 percent; and footwear, 21.1 percent. Among commodities subject to restriction, manufactured goods as a whole not including chemicals constituted 20.2 percent (UNCTAD 1988:6).

The intensified international trade protectionism is seriously hindering expansion of China's manufactured exports. In 1986 the proportion of China's total exports affected by trade protectionism was 28.9 percent; the manufactured goods share was 49 percent. Among the world's export commodities, 20.3 percent were affected by protectionism; and 20.5 percent for manufactured exports. For the developing countries/areas the proportion of commodities affected by protectionism was 17.5 percent for all exports and 31 percent for manufactured exports (calculated according to UNCTAD data). Obviously, China's manufactured exports suffer more from trade protectionist influence than do those of the developing countries in general.

(2) The lower-grade mix of China's manufactured exports. Most of China's manufactured exports are medium- and low-grade labor-intensive products. Textiles and clothing are China's largest category of export commodities, accounting for 25 percent of total goods export value in 1988. In this category, textiles constituted 57 percent and clothing, 43 percent. Among the textiles, most are materials, such as cotton yarn, blended yarn, cotton cloth, and terylene cotton fabric. In the clothing category, most are low-priced lounge suits, jackets, shirts, underwear, pajamas, and children's clothes. Very few are fashionable clothes with higher value added.

The second largest category of China's manufactured exports is light industrial goods, which made up 20 percent of the total merchandise export value in 1988. Major commodities include bicycles, sewing machines, trunks and bags, toys, electric fans, enamelware, glassware, table sets, thermoflasks, sanitary fittings, and other ordinary articles of daily use. The quality and design of these products have been improved steadily, but on the whole progress is slow, lagging far behind competitors in varieties, multiple functions, and automation. Some are produced by crude techniques, packaged poorly, delivered late, serviced poorly after the sale, or sold at a low price. China's commodities are basically still in a backward state of using first-class raw materials in production, yielding second-class finished products that are put in third-class packaging and sold at fourth-class prices.

Today, in world manufactured export trade, machinery and electrical products have become major items. In 1987 the export value of the world's machinery and electrical products reached US$978 billion, accounting for 39 percent of the world's total export value (GATT 1987–88:Table AB3). China's exports of machinery and electronic products, however, have long been stagnant. In 1988 export value of those products was US$6 billion, accounting for only 13 percent of China's total export value. The production and designing capacity of China's machinery and electronic sector lags far behind that of the developed countries and NIEs.

To expand China's manufactured exports, the urgent task is to improve design, raise the quality of products, and optimize the mix. Also, China needs to do the following: constantly improve the operation and management of its industrial enterprises; improve sales methods; guarantee the quality and quantity of goods as well as their timely delivery; further enhance its reputation in trade; and strengthen its cooperation and coordination with other countries/areas.

(3) High cost of manufacturing. The cost of manufacturing China's exports is relatively high because of inflation, currency overvaluation, and structural problems. In recent years, inflation has caused dramatic increases in manufacturing costs and weakened the competitiveness of China's manufactured goods on the world market. Some manufactured exports have become unprofitable at the existing exchange rate, while their sales on the home market were more lucrative. After the devaluation in June 1986, domestic prices increased considerably, and soon the currency became overvalued again. (The exchange rate of the RMB was devalued on December 16, 1989, from Y3.72 to U.S.$1 to Y4.72 to U.S.$1.) Furthermore, the strains on the energy supply and communication and transport services limited the supply of manufactured goods available for export.

(4) Lack of complementary measures. After the reforms of the foreign trade system and enterprise management, other complementary measures were not adopted accordingly. Since the management of foreign trade was delegated to the lower administrative levels in 1979, China has set up many foreign trade companies and expanded sales channels. More foreign trade companies in different

departments at various administrative levels began to scramble for markets for exports of manufactured goods and strived to win more clients. They rushed to purchase goods at high prices on the home markets and competed to sell them at reduced prices abroad to earn foreign exchange. These acts disrupted the market and affected the orderly development of China's manufactured exports. Furthermore, some companies were not well informed, lacked experience, and failed to deliver the goods on schedule, thereby tarnishing China's export reputation.

Possibilities for Regional Cooperation

China has a vast territory, rich resources and a large population, but its per-capita resources and income are low. It is handicapped by lack of capital and advanced technology. Its industrial processing capacity is large and diversified, but the supply of raw and semifinished materials is inadequate. Its labor is cheap, but productivity is low; and its level of operation and management efficiency is low. While domestic reform is absolutely necessary, external cooperation with other developing countries, particularly East Asian developing countries/areas, could help boost China's manufactured exports in various ways. Although China may be competing with them in some respects, in other respects their economies and China's complement each other. Because of its geographic proximity, East Asia is the principal region to which China has exported its manufactured goods. On the other hand, with their rapid growth of manufactured exports, many of those countries/areas are also constantly searching for markets abroad. As trade of manufactured goods within the region continues to increase rapidly, cooperation in the form of lower trade barriers will go a long way to facilitate such trade expansion and enable the trading partners to enjoy their comparative advantage. Moreover, to increase exports of manufactured goods to third markets, China and other East Asian countries have common interests in fighting against the growing protectionism exercised by the rich countries and could join hands in international negotiations.

China's relations with East Asian countries/areas in manufactured exports involve both competitive and complementary elements. However, complementarity and competition are neither mutually exclusive nor static. Competition can lead to the readjustment of trade and production structures of the countries/areas that are involved, thereby forming new complementarity among them. Complementarity promotes growth in the trade of the countries/areas involved as well as progress in their industrialization, thereby leading to a new state of competition on a higher level. In the future, China and East Asian developing countries/areas must strengthen their cooperation and properly handle competition, helping to expand each other's manufactured exports.

In China's manufactures trade with various East Asian countries/areas, the nature and extent of competition and complementarity are not the same. Therefore we shall classify them in two groups, the NIEs and the ASEANS, in discussing possible cooperation. Then we will discuss possible cooperation of East Asian industrializing countries in trade issues *vis-à-vis* the developed countries.

China and the NIEs

Compared with the NIEs, China's manufactured exports are at a low stage of development. China's manufactured exports constitute a clearly lower proportion of its total value of merchandise export than is the case in the NIEs. In 1986, this share was 56 percent for China, compared with slightly over 90 percent for Taiwan, South Korea, and Hong Kong and 68 percent for Singapore (see World Bank 1988: 248–49). Differences in development levels are the main determinant of the complementary and competitive characteristics of China's relations with the NIEs in manufactured exports. Judging from the mix of export commodities, the complementary aspect of China's relations with NIEs is obvious. China's manufactured exports currently are still traditional labor-intensive commodities, such as textiles and clothing, in which it has comparative advantage, and the proportion of textiles and clothing in its total merchandise export value is on the rise; whereas in the late 1970s and early 1980s, the NIEs had switched to the export of capital- and technology-intensive products with higher value added. Except in Hong Kong, the clothing and textiles proportion of total merchandise export value is declining (see Table 4.3). However, the proportion of China's clothing exports to world clothing exports is still lower than that of the NIEs. In fact, in the export of such products, China's comparative advantage lies in low labor costs, whereas the NIEs' comparative advantage lies in quality, design and product variety, production technology, and marketing techniques.

As for markets, China's manufactured goods, which are of low-grade, are exported mostly to Hong Kong and developing countries; whereas the exports of the NIEs are aimed mainly at the markets of the developed countries. In 1986, manufactured exports to industrial countries with market economies as a percentage of total exports were 32 percent for China, 78 percent for Taiwan, 75 percent for South Korea, 60 percent for Hong Kong, and 55 percent for Singapore. On the other hand, the proportion of manufactured exports to the developing countries was 62 percent for China, 19 percent for Taiwan, 20 percent for South Korea, 38 percent for Hong Kong, and 40 percent for Singapore (World Bank 1988:248–49). This trend lessens the severity of competition between China and the NIEs.

On the import side, for China, large quantities of capital- and technology-intensive products are imported from developed countries, the import cost is high, and the technology may not necessarily be appropriate. China could switch to importing some of these products from the NIEs, with lower costs and technology more suited to China's condition as a developing country. In this way, China would provide a market for the NIEs' exports of engineered products. Because China has the advantage of low production costs for labor-intensive products, the NIEs are experiencing increasing difficulties in their competition

Table 4.3

China and Three NIEs: The Proportion of Textile and Clothing Exports to Total Value of Merchandise Exports and to the Total Value of the World's Same Category of Exports (percent)

Exports	China	Hong Kong[a]	Taiwan	South Korea
Textiles:				
Proportion to the export value of world's same kind of exports: 1987	7	7	5	5
Proportion to total export value of the country/area:				
1980	14	9	9	12.5
1987	14.5	11.5	7.5	8.5
Clothing:				
Proportion of the export value of world's same kind of exports: 1987	4.5	13	6	9
Proportion to total export value of the country/area:				
1980	9	25	12.5	17
1987	9.5	22	9.5	16

Source: GATT, *International Trade, 1987–1988*, Geneva.
[a]Including re-exports.

with this country. The NIEs could shift production of such products to areas where labor is cheap and speed up the replacement of exports with direct investment in labor-intensive industries overseas. China's "open policy" provides preferential treatment for foreign capital and technology imports, thus the NIEs' investments in China would be profitable. Currently, many entrepreneurs from Hong Kong and Taiwan have come to China's mainland to invest and set up factories, engage in cooperative production, develop processing with materials supplied by the investor, and conduct compensatory trade in the form of payment for equipment investment with product to be exported. Such ventures have played an important role in developing China's manufactured exports. China is willing to open its markets to the NIEs' capital- and technology-intensive products and welcomes the NIEs' direct investment in the development of labor-intensive industries in China. This is the natural path for cooperation between both sides in exporting manufactured products, an objective that should be actively promoted by all concerned.

China and the ASEAN Countries

The ASEAN countries follow a basically export-oriented development strategy. The proportion of manufactured exports to total export value in these countries has increased considerably for more than a decade (GATT 1987–88). Among them, Singapore is obviously at a higher stage of development, and its economy is essentially complementary to that of China. But China's export trade is to a certain extent competitive with Indonesia, the Philippines, and Thailand, mainly in the area of labor-intensive manufactured goods. However, the ASEAN countries differ in the development patterns of their manufactured exports and their competition with China. For Thailand and the Philippines, the growth of labor-intensive manufactured exports is most striking. This growth is not confined to textiles and clothing, it is also taking place in "miscellaneous manufactured products." The proportion of Thailand's miscellaneous manufactured exports (SITC 8, principally labor-intensive products) to their total manufactured export goods was 11.6 percent in 1970, 25.6 percent in 1975, and 33.4 percent in 1982. Textiles and clothing exports increased rapidly, rising from an insignificant amount in 1965 to 15 percent of total manufactured exports in 1986. The situation was similar in the Philippines, where the proportion of sundry manufactured exports to total manufactured exports rose from 11.2 percent in the 1970s to 52.1 percent in 1982. The proportion of its textiles and clothing exports to total manufactured exports was less than 1 percent in 1965 but reached 7 percent in 1986.

As textiles, clothing, and other labor-intensive products are also important among China's manufactured exports, competition is unavoidable. But the labor-intensive exports of the ASEAN countries still enjoy greater comparative advantage than those of China. According to Xie's analysis, in 1982 labor-intensive products accounted for 66.7 percent of the total value of Thailand's manufactured exports to China but only 24.1 percent of Thailand's imports of manufactured goods from China. Similarly, labor-intensive products made up 16.8 percent of the total value of Philippine manufactured exports to China but only 3.1 percent of its imports of manufactured goods from China (ibid.).

Competition between China and Malaysia and Indonesia, on the other hand, is currently not very extensive. Among Malaysia's manufactured exports, machinery and transport equipment have increased most rapidly. The proportion of these exports to the total value of Malaysia's manufactured exports climbed from 2 percent in 1965 to 26 percent in 1986. This was related mainly to the development of Malaysia's export-processing zones. In China, the export of machinery and transport equipment has just begun to expand. Among the ASEAN nations, Indonesia's progress in export substitution is the slowest. Its manufactured exports are mainly natural-resource-based, particularly in timber. They do not conflict with China's comparative advantage, which lies in the export of labor-intensive products. However, China now attaches great importance to developing its exports of machinery and transport equipment, and Indonesia also intends to speed up its industrialization process. Therefore, competition is developing between China and Malaysia and Indonesia.

On the whole, on the supply side, at least for the foreseeable future, China apparently holds the upper hand in labor costs, while the ASEAN countries (excluding Singapore) abound in natural resources. Future development of manufactured exports in these obvious directions would be mutually beneficial. Meanwhile, China has established a comparatively complete industrial structure and has a fairly solid industrial foundation with the potential for developing technology-intensive products. Its future manufactured exports could be more diversified.

On the market side, the ASEAN nations' manufactured exports are concentrated among the developed countries. In 1986, the proportion of ASEAN's manufactured exports to the developed countries to its total manufactured exports was 24 percent for the Philippines, 60 percent for Thailand, 50 percent for Indonesia, and 69 percent for Malaysia (World Bank 1988:248–49). In the face of the slow economic growth of the industrialized countries and their adoption of new protectionist measures, the ASEAN countries need to find markets in the developing countries. Geographically, China is close to these ASEAN countries, and China's economy, with its large market, is growing rapidly. Cooperation with China would, therefore, have far-reaching effects on the expansion of ASEAN's manufactured exports.

Cooperation between China and the ASEAN countries in manufactured exports could begin in two areas. First, China and the ASEAN countries could coordinate their trade policies and foreign exchange controls. At present, tariff, quotas, and licensing are still widely used by the ASEAN countries in manufactured imports. Because of foreign exchange scarcity, Chinese authorities also control and regulate imports of manufactured goods in accord with the country's domestic economic policy. Second, cooperation between China and the ASEAN countries could start with discussion of unclogging trade channels in order to facilitate circulation of goods and services and reduce distribution costs.

East Asian Developing Countries versus the Developed Countries

The trade-protective measures adopted by the developed countries have significantly offset, or even more than offset, the benefits of the lower average tariff rates enjoyed by the developing countries. Estimates suggest that even if the industrial countries cancel all their tariffs, the developing countries' total exports will increase by only around 5 percent. But assuming that the elasticity of supply is infinitely large, cancellation of all the restrictions on imports from the developing countries would cause the developing countries' exports of textiles and clothing (which are under the restrictions of the Multi-fiber Agreements) to increase by 125 percent, iron and steel products by 60 percent, and footwear by 85 percent (Boonekamp 1989:17). Among the developing countries, East Asia is one of the principal suppliers of textiles, clothing, footwear, iron and steel, electronics, and other products. Thus it is one of the principal victims of the developed countries' trade-protective measures.

Moreover, the recent shifts toward bilateral negotiations and regional trade groups are increasingly eroding the multilateral principle of international trade. Owing to the country's huge trade deficit, U.S. trade policy has gradually deviated from GATT's nondiscriminatory treatment principle and has moved toward bilateralism, as shown by Congressional enactment of the Comprehensive Trade Bill in August 1988. The United States may, therefore, conduct more antidumping investigations, levy an antidumping tax, cancel quota stipulation, and resort to various other methods to obstruct the exports of East Asian countries/areas to the United States unilaterally or bilaterally. This is particularly true for exports of textiles, clothing, footwear, electronic products, and other so-called sensitive commodities, which are the major manufactured exports of the East Asian developing countries/areas to the United States. The U.S.–Canadian free trade agreement of January 1989 tends to cause trade diversion and, therefore, possibly endangers exports from the East Asian countries/areas to North America, particularly because Mexico may join soon.

Japan has tended increasingly to become the most important export market for other East Asian countries/areas and the supplier of products and capital to them. From 1970 to 1982, the Japanese market proportion of the five ASEAN nations' manufactured exports rose from 1.9 percent to 10.1 percent. However, East Asian countries/areas export mainly simple processed products to Japan and suffer serious trade deficits with that economy. How can Japan be urged to open its domestic markets further, particularly markets for manufactured goods, and also speed up technology transfer? Those are the common problems facing the East Asian countries/areas.

The EC has become an important market for certain goods manufactured by the East Asian countries/areas. In 1986, of total exports from South Korea and Taiwan to the EC, machinery and electronic products accounted for 30.7 percent and 36.6 percent, respectively, while they constituted only 1.8 percent and 2.3 percent, respectively of the Community's external imports of machinery and electronic products. This indicates that the EC has the potential to absorb more machinery and electronic products from East Asian developing countries. At the same time, the EC is also an important market for textiles and light industrial goods from East Asia. However, EC member countries West Germany, France, Italy, Belgium, Luxembourg, and Portugal rank among the world's ten major exporters of textiles and clothing. The south European countries that recently joined the EC are rivals of the East Asian countries/areas in output of machinery and electronic products. The unification of the European Community's internal market will inevitably affect the manufactured exports of East Asian countries/areas to the EC. In addition, it may intensify the Community's external protection efforts, not only because the south European countries demand protection but also because the Community itself is faced with employment pressures, and the enterprises of various countries will be confronted with even fiercer competition after unification of the internal markets. Because the North American and European free trade associations have greater ability to bargain collectively with the EC, the Community's protection will likely pose greater danger to the exports from East Asian developing countries/areas.

In view of these developments, all the East Asian newly industrializing countries/areas have a common interest in cooperating and coordinating efforts to increase their strength in international trade negotiation. Given the status of the developing countries, the absence of a large trade group in East Asia, and the multilateral nature of its foreign trade, it is beneficial for the East Asian industrializing countries/areas to maintain multilateral international trade agreements. However, this effort will encounter many difficulties because of the rise of regionalism. Because of its large trade deficit, the United States will no longer act as the leader of multilateralism. In such circumstances, East Asian countries/areas should play a more active role in maintaining the broadest possible multilateral negotiations.

Efforts toward cooperation among China and East Asian developing countries/ areas in expanding manufactured exports should be part of the developing countries' efforts to establish a new international economic order. It is well known that, since the founding of the nonaligned movement in 1961 and the establishment of the Group of 77 at the United Nations' first Trade and Development Conference in 1964, the scope of economic cooperation among the developing countries has broadened considerably. It now includes cooperation in the fields of trade, finance, service, technology, and economic development. Trade cooperation began in the 1960s and 1970s with the aim of safeguarding the developing countries' common interests in the international markets for energy, raw materials, and primary products. Under present international economic conditions and development trends, cooperation among developing countries in promoting manufactured exports appears more urgent.

References

Boonekamp, Clemens. 1989. "Industrial Policies of Industrial Countries." *Finance & Development* (March).
GATT. *International Trade, 1987–88.* (Geneva).
International Business News, January 24, 1989.
Laird, Sam, and Yeats, Alexander. 1989. "Non-Tariff Barriers of Developed Countries, 1986–1988." *Finance & Development* (March).
Ministry of Foreign Economic Relations and Trade, *Almanac of China Foreign Economic Relations and Trade* (Beijing) 1988.
People's Daily, (Beijing) February 14, 1989.
UNCTAD. *Protectionism and Structural Adjustment.* Statistical and Information Annex. (Geneva) 1988.
World Bank. 1987. *World Development Report.* Chinese edition (Beijing).
World Bank. 1988. *World Development Report.* Chinese edition (Beijing).

103-34

CHAPTER 5

Manufactured Export Expansion in Hong Kong and Asian-Pacific Regional Cooperation*

Hong Kong
F14
F15
L60
O19

EDWARD K.Y. CHEN AND KUI-WAI LI

Introduction

Hong Kong's economic growth has been very rapid. During the 1961–88 period, the average annual growth rate of its real GDP was 9.3 percent, while per capita GDP grew 7 percent. Only in recent years, growth had slowed down, with GDP growing at 6.5 percent per annum during 1986–91 and GDP per capita at 5.7 percent. Rapid economic growth in Hong Kong began with its economic transformation from an entrepôt to an industrial city in the 1950s. The economic transformation was achieved without planning or even premeditation. In the 1960s and early 1970s, when Hong Kong experienced a process of rapid industrialization, the role of the government was relatively unimportant. The entire industrialization process represented a series of successful self-adjustments to changes in the internal and external economic environments. Limited by its small internal market, Hong Kong had to adopt an outward-looking policy of export-oriented industrialization from the very beginning. Due to changes in the world trade situation and internal events (such as the banking crisis in 1965 and the riots in 1967), the Hong Kong economy has experienced considerable fluctuation in its level of activity. Nevertheless, its recovery from economic setback has always been rapid and remarkable (see Table 5.1).

The process of Hong Kong's economic growth has almost invariably been

*The first three sections of this chapter are adapted and updated versions of a paper by Edward K.Y. Chen, "Foreign Trade and Economic Growth in Hong Kong," in Colin Bradford and William Branson (eds.), *Trade and Structural Change in Pacific Asia*, The University of Chicago Press, Chicago, 1987 (copyright by the National Bureau of Economic Research). The authors of this chapter are grateful to the University of Chicago Press and NBER for granting the permission to use that paper. This chapter was further updated by Dr. Shu-Chin Yang.

Table 5.1

Hong Kong: Average Annual Growth Rates of GDP and GDP Per Head
(at constant 1973 prices) (percent)

Period	GDP	GDP Per Head
1961–66	10.9	8.0
1966–71	7.6	5.4
1971–76	8.8	6.8
1976–81	12.4	9.5
1981–86[a]	5.9	4.5
1986–91[a]	6.5	5.7
1961–81	9.9	7.4
1961–88	9.3	7.0
1981–91[a]	6.2	5.1

Source: Hong Kong Census and Statistics Department, *Estimates of Gross Domestic Product* (various years).
[a]At constant 1980 prices.

accompanied by structural changes involving the intersectoral shift of resources. There have been three phases of structural changes in the territory during the past thirty years. The first phase occurred in the 1950s and 1960s, when there was a shift of resources to the manufacturing sector. The second phase began in the early 1970s, taking a direction toward the development of financial services. The third phase began in the early 1980s after China initiated its open-door policy. Since the early 1980s, Hong Kong has become a complex service center, notable for the revival of entrepôt trade, continuing expansion in financial services, and the rise of new services in telecommunication, technology transfer, and information dissemination. Many of Hong Kong's manufacturing processes have been relocated to south China and other developing countries, leaving the territory's firms to specialize in technological development, product design, and marketing.

Analysis of Hong Kong's Export Growth

Hong Kong lacks arable land and other natural resources. It depends on imports for its food supply as well as for virtually all raw materials and fuels required by domestic industrial activities. Moreover, Hong Kong's domestic market is not large enough to absorb all the manufactured products produced locally by its rapidly expanding industries. Therefore, the major manufacturing industries in Hong Kong are export-oriented.

It is frequently said that the rapid growth in Hong Kong is export-led, that the territory's rapid economic growth has been initiated and sustained by a rapid expansion in exports. In Hong Kong, industrialization can take place only if its manufactured products can find overseas markets. In this sense, export expansion makes it possible to industrialize, and industrialization gives rise to higher rates of economic growth. Export earnings enable a country to import capital goods, which have the effect of raising the level of productivity and, therefore, the rate of growth. For some other countries, the cause-and-effect relationship may not be as simple. It is equally possible for export expansion to be the result rather than the cause of economic growth: the expansion of Japan's exports is often said to be growth-led.

This chapter studies changes in the product composition of Hong Kong's exports in the past three decades. These changes will be explained on the demand side in terms of changing conditions in Hong Kong's overseas markets and on the supply side in terms of the changing comparative advantages within the domestic economy. (The first three sections of this chapter are updated and abridged versions of Chen 1987.)

It is necessary to distinguish between domestic exports and re-exports in the total figures for Hong Kong. Before the mid-1950s, the major source of income in Hong Kong was entrepôt trade, and re-exports were much larger than domestic exports. For example, in 1950 it was estimated that re-exports constituted 89 percent of total exports. There was a drastic decrease in the re-export share of total exports after the mid-1950s, but in recent years, there has been a revival of the importance of entrepôt trade as a result of the new economic policy that China adopted in 1977. In 1988, re-exports constituted over 50 percent of total exports, a dramatic increase compared with a proportion of about 20 percent in the early 1970s. In this chapter we confine ourselves to the analysis of domestic exports; unless identified otherwise, exports are domestic exports.

The economy of Hong Kong is highly industrialized and export-oriented. Manufactured products have accounted for over 95 percent of Hong Kong's total exports in the past twenty years (see Table 5.2). In fact, since the late 1960s, only 3 percent to 4 percent of Hong Kong's exports have been nonmanufactured products. At the SITC one-digit level, Hong Kong has apparently experienced a considerable change in the composition of its exports. There has been a significant decline in section 6, manufactured goods classified by materials, and a significant increase in section 8, machinery and transport equipment, (although its share has declined since late 1980s). A further analysis at the SITC two-digit level reveals that this shift at the one-digit level is due principally to the decline of the textile (spinning, weaving, dyeing, finishing) industry and the rise of the electronics industry. Changes in other divisions were relatively insignificant. Miscellaneous manufactured articles, principally labor-intensive products, accounted for two-thirds of Hong Kong's exports, reflecting the very high labor intensity of Hong Kong's manufactured exports even in recent years. An analysis at the two-digit and three-digit SITC levels shows changes in the composition of exports within the section of miscellaneous manufactured articles. Throughout the past thirty years, clothing has accounted consistently for over one-third of Hong Kong's exports. But the relative importance of footwear has declined and

Table 5.2

Hong Kong: Share of Manufactured Exports in Total Exports (percent)

Year	SITC 5	SITC 6	SITC 7	SITC 8	Total
1963	1.4	23.1	5.1	62.0	91.6
1969	1.0	15.4	11.2	68.2	95.8
1970	0.8	15.1	11.8	68.3	96.0
1975	0.8	13.5	14.6	68.1	97.0
1980	0.8	11.3	18.1	65.7	95.9
1985	1.0	9.9	22.0	62.4	95.3
1990	2.9	11.8	24.8	55.3	94.8
1991	3.2	12.1	25.8	53.5	94.6

Source: Hong Kong Census and Statistics Department, *Hong Kong Trade Statistics* (various issues).

Note: SITC 5 = chemicals; SITC 6 = manufactured goods classified chiefly by material; SITC 7 = machinery and transport equipment; SITC 8 = miscellaneous manufactured articles.

that of watches and clocks has risen rapidly. At the same time, the decrease in the relative importance of plastic flowers and household goods was offset by the rapid increase in relative importance of toys and dolls. In the mid-1980s, Hong Kong was the world's number one exporter of toys and dolls in value terms and the world's number three exporter of watches and clocks.

It is perhaps more revealing to look at the changing composition of Hong Kong's exports by types of industry. Table 5.3 shows the percentage shares of the exports of Hong Kong's major industries. These industries accounted for about three-quarters of Hong Kong's total exports. So far, clothing remains the single most important industry, accounting for more than one-third of Hong Kong's total exports, although its relative importance has shown recent signs of decline. While textiles, footwear, and plastic articles (excluding plastic toys) are declining industries, toys and dolls, electronics, and watches and clocks are enjoying rapid growth. The rise of the watch and clock industry in the past few years has been particularly noteworthy.

To examine the changes in product composition of some of these major industries, a more disaggregated analysis is necessary.

Clothing

To obtain a better idea of the product composition of Hong Kong's clothing exports, we can break down the exports by type of material, kind of wear, and method of manufacture. The import restrictions imposed on cotton products at an early stage set off a marked trend of diversification into clothing using synthetic fibers. This trend has been reversed since the mid-1970s, due partly to the exten-

Table 5.3

Hong Kong: Share of Major Industries in Domestic Exports (percent)

Year	Clothing	Textiles	Plastics and Toys	Electronics	Watches and Clocks
1959	34.8	18.1	7.0	—	—
1964	36.6	16.0	11.0	2.4	—
1970	35.1	10.3	11.3	9.5	—
1975	44.6	9.4	8.7	10.7	2.8
1980	34.1	6.7	7.9	12.0	9.6
1985	34.6	6.0	8.2	20.8	7.4
1988	30.9	7.1	5.4	25.5	8.0
1990	39.6		3.6	25.9	8.5
1991	40.2		5.8	25.3	7.2

Source: Hong Kong Census and Statistics Department, *Hong Kong Review of Overseas Trade* (various issues).

sion of trade restrictions on noncotton products by many importing countries and partly to the revived fashion appeal of cotton clothing. At present, about one-half of Hong Kong's clothing exports and two-thirds of its nonknitted outerwear exports are made of cotton. Also, cotton is more widely used in underwear than are synthetic fibers. Exports of wool clothing have declined in relative importance. Around 1969, wool accounted for about 25 percent of Hong Kong's clothing exports; in the 1980s, wool's share was less than 10 percent. This is, of course, a result of the clothing industry's attempt to diversify into higher-quality and more sophisticated products in order to overcome nontariff trade restrictions.

Hong Kong's major clothing export is outerwear. The relative importance of this item has, in fact, increased from two-thirds of total clothing exports in 1969 to more than three-quarters in recent years. The production of outerwear offers greater opportunities for product sophistication and diversification. Hong Kong has made a notable move into the area of fashion design, which has won its exporters prizes in international shows. Exports of nonknitted outerwear have increased since the mid-1970s, following the return of cotton apparel, mostly nonknitted, to fashion. On the other hand, the relative importance of knitted products in underwear and nightwear has increased over time. Today, the export value of knitted underwear and nightwear is almost as great as that of nonknitted.

In sum, the considerable changes in Hong Kong's clothing industry during the past fifteen years or so are not revealed at the two- or three-digit level of product classification.

Textiles

Hong Kong's exports of textile yarns, fabrics, and garments have declined since the beginning of the 1960s. In the earlier years the relative decline in textiles production was to a large extent the result of the increasing trade restrictions imposed on Hong Kong's textile products by the importing countries. The first severe blow to the rapid growth of textiles came in 1959, when the United Kingdom imposed restrictions on the territory's textile exports under the Lancashire Pact. In 1961 Hong Kong had to agree to the GATT Long-Term Cotton Textile Agreement (CTA), by which textile exports to the United States and the European Community were limited by a quota. At first, only textiles were restricted under this agreement. Later, clothing was included. In 1974 the CTA was replaced by the Multi-Fiber Arrangement (MFA), which also covered noncotton textiles. Both the CTA and the MFA laid down the basic principles for negotiating bilateral agreements between Hong Kong and the importing countries. In general, these agreements specified certain initial maximum quantities of textiles and clothing that might be exported from Hong Kong, allowing an annual percentage increase thereafter.

Like the clothing manufacturers, the textile industry has responded to trade restrictions with product diversification and sophistication, although perhaps somewhat less rapidly. In addition, the textile industry has turned increasingly to Hong Kong's internal market as a substitute for exports. In 1971, 45.3 percent of textiles produced in Hong Kong were exported; in 1978, the corresponding figure dropped to 23.5 percent.

The major item in cotton textiles exports is fabric. Exports of cotton yarn and thread are relatively small because most of the cotton yarn and thread are used locally for the manufacture of fabrics. Among the various types of fabrics exported, cotton fabrics have gradually regained their relative importance over noncotton, even though the local clothing industry uses an increasing proportion of the cotton fabrics produced. This confirms the fact that in recent years the worldwide emphasis has centered on the production of cotton apparel.

Electronics

There has been no clear-cut classification of Hong Kong products into electronics. The technology has been used increasingly in all kinds of industries. In the trade statistics of Hong Kong's electronics exports, two ambiguous sectors are toys and watches and clocks. With the introduction of electronic quartz watches and clocks and electronic toys such as hand-held games and toys with electronic controls, a problem of classification arises, because these products were earlier classified as electronics and later as toys and watches and clocks. Even today, there is some ambiguity about this classification. For example, a multiproduct electronics manufacturer with toys and watches and clocks as a sideline will most likely group such products under electronics rather than watches and clocks or toys. The rapid product diversification has also caused frequent reclassification of electronics products within the industry itself.

Hong Kong's electronics industry started with the manufacture of transistor radios and gradually branched into components and parts. Even today sales of radios generate a significant proportion of the export earnings of Hong Kong's electronics industry. Hong Kong began to manufacture electronics parts and components relatively early but for a long time confined itself mostly to assembly work. Only in recent years has Hong Kong begun to produce semiconductors and integrated circuits from the raw material stage. At present, a few firms design and manufacture home and commercial computers. Hong Kong is a latecomer in the production of telephones and related products, but the growth in this area has been very fast. So far, Hong Kong is not an important producer of television sets, particularly color sets. Generally speaking, the Hong Kong electronics industry has been flourishing on the basis of what has been called the "three-year cycle." This means that Hong Kong electronics firms quickly spot opportunities in the world market and produce the fashionable product for about three years. At the end of three years, the firms shift to other products because of declining demand or increasing competition from other Asian exporters. As expected, most of these products are consumer electronics, whose production does not require very sophisticated technology as shown in Table 5.4.

Toys and Dolls

For some years Hong Kong has been the world's number one exporter of toys and dolls, followed at some distance by Taiwan, Japan, and the United States, in that order. Production of toys and dolls shifted from the use of nonplastic materials to plastic. Miscellaneous toys include stuffed and rubber toys and the electronic games that have come into vogue recently. In recent years, changing comparative advantage has led many Hong Kong toy firms to invest in China and overseas (notably Thailand).

Besides plastic toys and dolls, Hong Kong also produces plastic flowers and other articles for export. Exports of plastic flowers were an important foreign exchange earner for Hong Kong in the 1960s.

Watches and Clocks

With the assistance of the electronics industry, the production of watches and clocks has grown phenomenally in the past ten years due to the application of electronic devices to these items. In the past two years, Hong Kong has been the world's number one exporter of watches in terms of quantity and the world's number three exporter in terms of value (after Switzerland and Japan). But so far, Hong Kong has confined itself largely to assembly of imported watch parts. The watches produced in Hong Kong, therefore, either have relatively low value-added content or are intended primarily for the lower price range of the market.

Table 5.4

Hong Kong: Exports of Electrical Machinery and Appliances by Industrial Origin (including electronics) (HK$ billion)

Year	Electronic Products	Electrical Parts and Components	Transistorized Radios	Electrical Appliances and Housewares	TV Receiver and Communication Equipment	Sound Reproducing and Recording Equipment and Apparatus	Electrical Industrial Machinery and Apparatus	Computing Machinery and Equipment	Electrical Apparatus and Equipment	Total
1980	3.3	—	4.3	2.0	—	1.0	—	—	0.8	12.6
1981	5.0	—	4.3	3.0	—	1.4	—	—	0.9	16.0
1982	5.3	—	4.1	2.8	—	1.7	—	—	1.1	16.6
1983	—	5.1	4.3	3.7	4.7	—	1.9	—	—	24.9
1984	—	8.4	6.2	5.2	3.8	—	2.8	—	—	33.4
1985	—	6.6	4.7	4.6	3.6	—	—	1.7	—	27.7
1986	—	2.9	5.5	4.9	6.3	—	—	6.5	—	33.8
1987	—	3.9	6.5	5.7	8.1	—	—	7.9	—	42.8
1988	—	5.3	5.2	5.5	11.4	—	—	11.7	—	53.5
1989	—	6.5	4.4	4.3	11.0	—	—	12.7	—	52.8
1990	—	8.9	4.2	3.4	11.6	—	—	13.6	—	52.4

Source: Hong Kong Census and Statistics Department, *Hong Kong External Trade* (various issues).

Value in Manufacturing Industries

Many developing countries serve as subcontracting centers for foreign firms or, at most, undertake assembly work of imported semimanufactures. In these cases, the value-added content of manufactured exports is generally low.

In the case of Hong Kong, data show that value added constituted just over 25 percent of the gross output of Hong Kong's manufactured industries as a whole. In fact, this indicates a decline in value-added content from 36.7 percent in 1973 and 34.4 percent in 1978, suggesting that the process of product sophistication was quite slow. Table 5.5 gives the percentages of value added in gross output at the three- and four-digit SITC levels of classification.

Geographic Distribution of Exports

While most of Hong Kong's exports are produced by a few industries, the direction of its sales abroad is even more narrowly confined to a few countries. Table 5.6 shows that the United States is by far Hong Kong's most important export market, accounting for over one-third of its domestic exports. The relative importance of the United Kingdom market has been declining steadily, and for some years (1975–80) West Germany was the second-largest market for Hong Kong's exports. Australia, Japan, and Canada are the other important markets for Hong Kong. The Japanese market has become more important as a result of the yen's appreciation and the restructuring of the Japanese economy. The growing significance of China as a market is notable: since 1984 it has become Hong Kong's second largest market. However, many of Hong Kong's exports to China consist of parts and semimanufactures representing intraindustry or intrafirm trade only. This is largely the result of the opening up of China, particularly its Special Economic Zones for foreign investment and participation.

The countries listed in Table 5.6 import about three-fourths of Hong Kong's domestic exports. However, the problem of market concentration may not be as serious as many observers think. As long as the territory produces the right products to satisfy the needs of overseas markets, certainly these countries can maintain or even expand their existing level of imports from Hong Kong. After all, these importers are all large countries with sizable markets. Hong Kong's existing level of exports to each of them represents a relatively small share of their markets. Table 5.7 shows Hong Kong's exports as a share of total imports of each of its major trading partners. It must, however, be noted that for some individual products such as clothing and toys, Hong Kong's exports constitute a substantial share of the total imports of some countries (such as the United States, Germany, and the United Kingdom).

The Determinants of Export Growth

Table 5.8 shows that both the unit value and the quantity of Hong Kong's exports have increased rapidly, raising the total value of its exports. Since about

Table 5.5

Hong Kong: Value Added As Percentage of Gross Output in Hong Kong's Manufacturing

Industry Group	1980	1985	1986
Food	22	26	25
Beverages	39	36	39
Tobacco	50	36	33
Wearing apparel, except knitwear and footwear	29	33	32
Leather and leather products, except footwear and wearing apparel	23	20	24
Footwear, except rubber, plastic, and wooden footwear	37	36	34
Textiles (including knitting)	23	26	27
Wood and cork products, except furniture	24	27	26
Furniture and fixtures, except primarily of metal	36	33	30
Paper and paper products	24	25	24
Printing, publishing, and allied industries	40	41	41
Chemicals and chemical products	23	30	27
Rubber products	30	32	35
Plastic products	31	30	29
Nonmetallic mineral products, except products of petroleum and coal	19	16	22
Basic metal industries	17	19	17
Fabricated metal products, except machinery and equipment	32	33	32
Machinery, except electrical	37	36	36
Consumer electrical and electronic products	20	21	19
Electrical and electronic parts, accessories and machinery	24	27	28
Professional and scientific, resourcing and controlling equipment not elsewhere classified, and photographic and optical goods	17	17	16
Transport equipment	50	52	58
Other manufacturing industries	28	29	26
All manufacturing industries	26	28	28

Source: Hong Kong Census and Statistics Department, *Survey of Industrial Production* (various issues).

Table 5.6

Hong Kong: Domestic Exports by Country Destination
(as percentage of total exports)

Year	U.S.	U.K.	W. Germany	Japan	China	Canada
1980	33.1	9.9	10.8	3.4	2.3	2.6
1981	36.3	9.5	8.7	3.6	3.6	2.9
1985	44.4	6.5	6.1	3.4	11.6	3.3
1990	29.4	6.0	8.0	5.4	21.0	2.4
1991	23.5	5.9	8.4	5.3	21.0	2.2

Source: Hong Kong Census and Statistics Department, *Hong Kong Review of Overseas Trade* (various issues).

Table 5.7

Hong Kong's Exports in Main Overseas Markets (percentage share)

Country	1980	1985	1990
United States	2.0	2.5	1.9
China	7.0	11.2	27.0
Japan	0.4	0.6	0.9
United Kingdom	1.7	1.4	1.6
Singapore	2.1	1.9	3.1
Taiwan	1.3	1.6	12.7
Canada	0.8	0.8	0.8
South Korea	—	1.6	0.9
Australia	2.2	2.1	1.8
West Germany	0.9	0.8	0.9

Source: Hong Kong Census and Statistics Department, *Hong Kong Review of Overseas Trade* (various issues).

95 percent of Hong Kong's exports are manufactured products, the high export growth rate must reflect an equally high growth rate in its manufacturing sector. Most of the major industries in Hong Kong produce for export. The figures are in fact much higher for many individual industries, such as consumer electronics, watches, clothing, and toys and dolls. The textile (spinning and weaving) industry is the notable exception, exporting less than one-quarter of its output in recent years. There is evidence that Hong Kong's growth is export-led (Chen 1980). The question here is how to explain the rapid growth of Hong Kong's manufactured exports in the past two decades.

A technique used frequently to analyze the sources of export growth is the constant-market-share method, first developed by Tyszynski (1951) and later

Table 5.8

Hong Kong: Value, Unit Value, and Quantum Indexes of Hong Kong's Domestic Exports (1981 = 100)

Year	Value Index	Unit Value Index	Quantum Index
1969	13	33	39
1971	17	38	45
1973	24	48	50
1975	28	61	47
1976	41	67	61
1977	44	69	64
1978	51	72	70
1979	70	84	83
1980	85	92	92
1981	100	100	100
1982	103	106	97
1983	130	117	111
1984	172	131	131
1985	161	131	124
1986	191	133	143
1987	243	139	174
1988	271	143	190
1989	279	147	190
1990	281	149	189
1991	287	151	190
1992 Nov.	303	153	198

Source: Hong Kong Census and Statistics Department, *Hong Kong Review of Overseas Trade* (various issues).

applied widely to many country and regional studies (for a review and extension, see Richardson 1971). Essentially, this method uses a simple conceptual framework to decompose export growth into four components:

(1) The effect of the increase in total world trade.

(2) The effect of the changes in the commodity composition of world trade. This effect will be greater with increased and more-than-proportionate growth in world trade of the commodities that Hong Kong exports in the base year.

(3) The effect of the changes in the market distribution of world trade. This effect will be greater with increased and the more-than-proportionate growth in demand in the markets to which Hong Kong exports in the base year.

(4) The effect of a country's increased competitiveness and, therefore, its ability to capture a larger share of its markets in the base year.

This decomposition method is presented by a formula published elsewhere (Chen 1987): The constant-market-share analysis is simple to operate but has a number of shortcomings (see Richardson 1971; Ooms 1967). For example, the method is arbitrary in that the share, or competitiveness, effect is nothing but an

Table 5.9

Sources of Hong Kong's Export Growth by Commodity Groups, 1976–81
(percent)

	World Trade Effect	Commodity Composition Effect	Market Distribution Effect	Competi- tiveness Effect
Textiles	119.81	6.30	3.11	−29.21
Metal	85.59	1.20	10.76	2.45
Clothing	96.51	−150.45	−48.47	202.40
Electrical machinery	72.34	−7.02	−8.89	43.58
Plastic products	6.21	−316.68	−115.13	462.59
Scientific instruments, watches, clocks	65.88	−8.08	−0.54	42.74
Footwear	104.75	177.93	−12.24	−170.37
Other	90.67	−2.15	37.24	−25.76
Total	93.27	−7.35	−10.06	24.15

Sources of data for computation: Hong Kong Census and Statistics Department, *Hong Kong Trade Statistics* (Hong Kong, 1976 and 1981); State Statistical Bureau, People's Republic of China, *Statistical Yearbook of China,* 1981; Directorate-General of Budget, Accounting, and Statistics, *Statistical Yearbook of the Republic of China* (Taipei), 1982; United Nations, *Yearbook of International Trade Statistics,* volumes 1–2 (New York, 1981).

unexplained residual; and the ordering of the terms in the actual computation affects the results. More important, this approach concentrates on the demand side. The supply factors are considered only implicitly in the competitiveness effect, which is only a residual. Also, this model treats commodity and market distribution in a static sense, with reference only to the base year. Nonetheless, such a decomposition can be useful as a partial and preliminary analysis, particularly when supplemented by other evidence, such as our analysis of Hong Kong's export growth in terms of its changing comparative advantage.

Table 5.9 gives the sources of Hong Kong's export growth from 1976 to 1981, using the constant-market-share technique. Commodity exports are divided into eight groups. Markets are divided into five regions: ASEAN and Australia; East Asia; North America; Western Europe; and others. For all exports, it is shown that 93 percent of Hong Kong's export growth in 1976–81 was due to increased world demand. The world trade effect is dominant, in fact, for all commodity groups. The commodity composition effect is unimportant except in footwear, and the market distribution effect is unimportant except in the "other" category. Overall, about one-fourth of Hong Kong's export growth can be attributed to the increased competitiveness of its products. In these sources of export growth we find considerable differences among commodity groups. Increased competitiveness was the major source of export growth in clothing and

Table 5.10

Sources of Export Growth in the NIEs (percent)

	World Trade Effect	Commodity Composition Effect	Market Distribution Effect	Competitiveness Effect
Hong Kong				
1965–70[a]	50.2	5.4	–4.4	48.9
1976–81[b]	93.3	–7.4	–10.1	24.2
South Korea				
1965–69[a]	26.2	–2.7	–1.5	78.0
1977–81[c]	92.0	–3.5	–1.8	13.3
Singapore				
1977–81[c]	65.0	7.1	2.8	25.1
Taiwan				
1965–70[a]	30.6	–6.5	3.2	72.7
1977–81[c]	70.9	–1.1	–0.1	30.3

[a]Kuo 1983.
[b]Computed by the author.
[c]Cha et al. 1983.

plastic products. These two industries have gone through a relatively rapid process of product sophistication and diversification. In electrical machinery (mainly electronics products) and scientific instruments and watches and clocks, the effect of increased competitiveness is also significant. It was, of course, no surprise to find that in such declining industries as textiles and footwear, increased competitiveness was not a source of export growth.

The constant-market-share analysis has been applied to Hong Kong for an earlier period and to other Asian NIEs as well. Table 5.10 presents the computations for Hong Kong, South Korea, Singapore, and Taiwan for two time periods (except for Singapore). Although the table is constructed from three sources, the computed results are largely comparable. All the sources used a three-digit SITC classification of commodities, but they categorized markets differently. Two observations can be made. First, there has been a trend of increasing dependence on the growth of world trade, but at the same time there has been a decrease in the relative importance of the competitiveness effect. These trends were particularly noteworthy in the cases of South Korea and Taiwan, when we compared the periods 1965 to 1970 and 1977 to 1981. The probable reasons for this are: (1) protective measures imposed by developed countries in recent years have prevented the Asian NIEs from capturing a larger share of their existing markets; and (2) many more developing countries (such as Mexico, Brazil, Malaysia, and

Thailand) have switched to an export-oriented development strategy, thus competing with the Asian NIEs in the markets of the developed countries. Thus, to a great extent in recent years, the Asian NIEs could expand their exports only at a rate corresponding to the growth in world trade.

The second observation was that, perhaps excepting Singapore, the effects of commodity composition and market distribution have not been important factors in explaining export growth. These results imply that the commodities and markets on which the Asian NIEs concentrate in the base year do not experience more than proportionate growth during the period under construction. There is, however, no indication as to whether commodity and market diversification have taken place.

It is interesting to examine the extent of product diversification undertaken by Hong Kong manufacturers in the past twenty years. One simple method is to calculate the concentration ratios of Hong Kong's commodity exports at say, the three-digit level. The computation of these ratios is based on the "H" concentration measure, which is defined as the square root of the sum of the percentage share of different commodities (or commodity groups) in total exports (Hirschman 1945; Adelman 1969; Naya 1973). When multiplied by 100, the ratio will range between 0 and 100; the more diversified the commodity pattern, the lower the ratio. The commodity concentration ratios of Hong Kong's exports indicate that there has not been much diversification in Hong Kong manufacturing at the three-digit level. There are, in fact, indications that the commodity pattern was more concentrated in the 1970s (average 42.48) than in the 1960s (average 40.46 for 1964–69); for 1980–81, the average is 41.47 (Chen 1987).

Nonetheless, it is unlikely that Hong Kong could have responded so well to the increase in world trade without diversification. At a more disaggregated level, it can be shown that within individual industries such as clothing, textiles, plastics, and electronics, very rapid processes of product diversification have taken place. Hong Kong industrialists are extremely flexible and adaptable in coping with changes in consumers' tastes within a particular subsector or product group. On the other hand, they are more reluctant to diversify into new industries, whose establishment requires much longer-term investment and greater risk. This reluctance is intensified by the lack of a definite government industrial policy.

Market diversification proved unimportant to Hong Kong's export growth in the 1960s and 1970s. During those two decades, Hong Kong continued to rely on a few markets whose growth was generally relatively slow, excepting perhaps West Germany. Some diversification into the Middle Eastern and African markets was achieved, but with limited overall significance.

Let us now consider the supply factors affecting Hong Kong's export growth. Table 5.11 shows the relationship between export performance and changes in capital intensity. Two interesting observations emerge from these data. First, the major exporting industries of Hong Kong were quite labor-intensive in 1973, and

Table 5.11

Export Performance and Capital Intensity of Principal Commodities

Commodity	Share of Total Export (%)	Average Annual Export Growth Rate (%) 1973–78 1978–86	Capital-Labor Ratio (HK$ 1,000 per worker at 1973 prices)
Clothing: outerwear			
1973	24.3		4.02
1978	25.3	23.64	4.72
1986	24.5	33.18	8.60
Clothing: underwear			
1973	8.2		2.04
1978	8.2	21.52	3.48
1986	5.8	22.06	10.20
Footwear			
1973	1.4		2.54
1978	1.0	9.82	2.83
1986	0.8	24.94	11.40
Textile yarn and thread			
1973	2.1		9.02
1978	0.8	–3.26	10.05
1986	0.6	23.15	57.60
Textile fabrics			
1973	8.9		22.83
1978	5.4	5.38	17.77
1986	5.9	39.06	96.60
Textile made-up articles			
1973	1.1		11.42
1978	0.8	11.22	7.96
1986	0.6	23.64	13.40
Toys and dolls			
1973	8.6		5.15
1978	8.3	20.42	6.80
1986	7.6	31.05	32.90
Artificial flowers			
1973	2.5		5.94
1978	1.1	–1.84	7.05
1986	0.5	7.50	2.60
Plastic articles (excluding flowers)			
1973	1.1		10.47
1978	1.1	21.72	10.66
1986	2.0	76.55	49.20

Table 5.11 *(continued)*

Commodity	Share of Total Export (%)	Average Annual Export Growth Rate (%) 1973–78 1978–86	Capital-Labor Ratio (HK$ 1,000 per worker at 1973 prices)
Iron and steel utensils,			
1973	0.5		6.60
1978	0.5	21.76	7.91
1986	0.3	21.58	20.90
Metal lanterns			
1973	0.3		6.80
1978	0.4	33.92	10.51
1986	0.2	15.40	27.50
Electric torches			
1973	0.4		5.86
1978	0.3	11.36	6.89
1986	0.2	10.63	8.10
Handbags, etc.			
1973	1.5		2.66
1978	1.5	22.44	3.30
1986	0.6	5.44	19.20
Watches and clocks			
1973	1.5		5.84
1978	6.7	166.62	7.90
1986	7.4	42.65	17.30
Cameras			
1973	0.4		6.03
1978	0.7	59.20	5.91
1986	0.6	28.53	14.10
Nonelectric machinery			
1973	1.1		8.4
1978	0.9	65.00	8.2
1986	N/A	N/A	N/A
Electric components and parts			
1973	2.4		3.85
1978	2.1	80.60	7.24
1986	3.6	69.69	69.00
Transistor radios and parts			
1973	6.3		2.65
1978	5.5	82.70	3.67
1986	2.0	4.24	12.60
Electric heating equipment and parts			
1973	0.2		4.77
1978	1.0	1,022.20	9.30
1986	1.0	35.86	29.70

Sources: Hong Kong Census and Statistics Department, *Survey of Industry Production,* various years; *Review of Hong Kong's Overseas Trade,* various years (Hong Kong).

many remained so in 1978. But capital intensity was significantly higher in most industrial sectors in 1986. Second, from 1973 to 1986, there is evidence that industries that performed better also had more significant increases in capital intensity.

If export performance is an indicator of revealed comparative advantage (Balassa 1965), our findings suggest that Hong Kong's comparative advantage is gradually changing to more capital-intensive products. This is a natural and predictable phenomenon in the process of economic development. The study of this process has been called the "stage" approach to comparative advantage (Balassa 1979; Heller 1976). It implies that a country will gradually change its trade structure in the course of economic growth and development. There are, of course, good reasons to believe that Hong Kong's comparative advantage has been changing. With the accumulation of experience and knowledge over time, levels of both labor skills and technology have increased. However, it is important to note that the change of comparative advantage to higher technology and capital intensity has been less rapid in Hong Kong than in other Asian NIEs. First, Hong Kong has traditionally been a laissez-faire economy, with the government taking very little part in building up a technological infrastructure for the promotion of the level of technology. Second, the increase in wage rates during the past twenty-five years has most likely been smaller than productivity increases. There has been a huge influx of people from China to Hong Kong, almost all of them in the working-age group. This huge supply of unskilled and semiskilled workers has had an unfavorable effect on Hong Kong's ability to keep moving up the comparative advantage ladder.

Unlike most other developing countries that seek to upgrade their industries, Hong Kong is not constrained by a shortage in its supply of capital. Acquisition of capital is not a problem because private savings rates are high and the amount of foreign direct investment has been substantial. Multinational corporations in Hong Kong have also played a positive role in technology transfer and the promotion of manufactured exports (Chen 1983).

Protectionism As an Engine of Growth

Whether in the form of tariff or nontrade barriers, protectionism is usually treated as the number one enemy of export- oriented developing countries. However, we argue here that under certain conditions, protectionism imposed by developed countries can serve as an engine of growth in export-oriented developing countries. Hong Kong is a case in point.

Trade protectionism has generated a lot of debates. Free trade advocates use the resulting economic implications as arguments. Donges (1981) and Gramm (1985), for example, argue that protectionism does as much harm to the consumers of the importing country as it does the exporting country. On the other hand, trade protection advocates have argued on the basis of a zero-sum assumption.

With free trade, cheap imports would out-compete the home supplies, and the home industries would lose profits, markets, and employment. The loss experienced by the importing country would be a direct gain for the exporting country. Industries in exporting countries would grow and employment would be generated at the expense of economic recession and loss of income in importing countries. Trade restriction in the form of quotas was thought to reverse the situation. With imports restricted, home industries would survive, while profits, markets, and employment could be maintained. On the contrary, the exporting countries would suffer from a low rate of growth as well as restricted employment, markets, and profits.

The question is whether export-oriented less developed countries (LDCs) would conform to the outcome of the zero-sum assumption. It is necessary to consider the situation from the exporting country's position. If the economy is export-oriented, with a flexible industrial structure and dynamic labor and entrepreneurial forces, its reaction to trade protectionism may not be in line with the zero-sum assumption. While some loss would be incurred in the exporting countries, it might be only temporary.

On the demand side, the quota that the developed countries impose on all exporting developing countries helps earlier exporters: the NIEs maintain their dominant market shares in the face of competition from the lower-wage latecomers such as the ASEAN countries. More advanced exporters are given a lower growth factor under the quota system, but the differences are so insignificant that while latecomers face an effective constraint, earlier exporters enjoy a guaranteed growth factor that later entrants will be unable to match. It is quite certain that Hong Kong's market share in the traditional clothing sector would have dwindled much more if not for the quota system imposed on all developing exporting countries alike. Second, domestic prices in the importing country will rise because the cost of their domestic supply is higher. In effect, the increased price, together with the restricted quantity, will generate a more inelastic demand curve for the exporters. The net result could only be a reduction in quantity, but probably not in export revenue. In reality, the quota system has provided exporters with a secure market.

On the supply side, as a form of long-term adjustment in the face of restrictive policies imposed by developed countries, exporters will undertake product diversification and sophistication, market diversification, and improved productivity either on their own or with some government support. This may involve a gradual utilization of capital-intensive production technique, better-trained workers, a higher degree of calibration of product quality, and new market promotion strategy. The result would be an improvement in competitiveness, an increase in value added, a broadened base of comparative advantage, and a new, flexible and dynamic industrial structure.

By and large, it is the textile and clothing industry that has been subject to severe protectionist restrictions. This industry began in Hong Kong in the early

Table 5.12

Annual Percentage Changes of Exports of Textiles and Clothing Under Different Protectionist Regimes

	Textile Export			Clothing Export			Total Export		
	H	L	A	H	L	A	H	L	A
1947–49 and									
1942–58	115	−22	28	—	—	—	—	—	—
Lancashire Pact									
1959–62	34	−53	−3	27	−15	4	30	−2	14
Long-Term									
Arrangements									
1962–67	18	−12	6	17	−1	13	17	10	13
1968–73									
Arrangements	52	9	21	30	12	22	28	12	20
MFA I 1974–77	44	−22	6	40	−3	18	41	−14	15
MFA II 1978–81	42	6	19	28	13	20	30	12	20
MFA III 1982–86	86	−18	15	36	−4	14	34	−5	14
MFA I–III 1974–86	86	−22	13	40	−4	17	41	−5	16

H = Highest, L = Lowest, A = Average.
Sources: Census and Statistics Department, Hong Kong, *Hong Kong Statistics 1947–67, Hong Kong Monthly Digest of Statistics,* various issues; *Hong Kong Annual Report,* various issues (Hong Kong).

1950s, when the main source of growth was the supply of cheap labor. Since the 1960s, the industry has been subjected to nontariff barriers (NTBs) imposed by developed countries. The main features of the protectionist trade policies imposed on textiles and clothing exports from Hong Kong are summarized in the appendix at the end of this chapter. These policies were mild in the beginning but gradually have become more severe and restrictive.

Has the imposition of nontariff barriers on Hong Kong exports of textiles and clothing restricted their growth in any way? In Table 5.12 we present the growth rates of textile and clothing exports under various protectionist trade regimes. The average export growth rate was 14 percent a year during the Lancashire Pact regime, 13 percent during the 1962–67 period, and 20 percent in the 1968–73 Arrangement. During the entire 1974–86 period covered by MFA the overall average annual export growth rate was 16 percent. These rates certainly exceeded the growth rates stipulated in each of the trade agreements. Textile exports tended to fluctuate more widely during the entire 1959–86 period, while clothing exports showed less volatility. Although the Lancashire Pact hit the textile industry hard, export fluctuation was more moderate between 1959 and 1962 than in the pre-Lancashire Pact period.

One could argue that protectionist trade policies could not stop the growth rate of textiles and clothing exports from rising above the restricted level. Would

Table 5.13

Quota Utilization of Hong Kong's Exports of Textiles and Clothing, 1977–88
(percent)

Year	United States	United Kingdom	Federal Republic of Germany	Average of 3 Markets (unweighted)
1977	85.2	—	—	—
1978	92.2	—	—	—
1979	79.0	—	—	—
1980	73.7	85.4	76.6	78.6
1981	76.3	85.8	71.4	78.8
1982	94.0	78.2	68.5	80.2
1983	99.7	86.7	71.4	85.9
1984	99.5	82.6	71.6	84.6
1985	95.7	78.9	59.4	78.0
1986	99.7	88.2	71.9	86.6
1987	98.5	96.2	86.7	93.8
1988	94.6	94.4	79.5	89.9
1989	96.0	86.6	75.6	86.1
1990	93.7	84.4	79.2	85.8

Source: Hong Kong Trade Department.

the exporting countries do better without foreign protectionism? We have suggested that quotas guaranteed market share to exporters. Looking at the percentage of quota utilization in Table 5.13, we find that only in 1983–84 and 1986–87 was quota utilization close to 100 percent in the U.S. market, while the percentages were lower in both the United Kingdom and German markets. Hong Kong's quota utilization rate has declined since 1987, reflecting high labor costs and the migration of its factories to mainland China. In no single year can one find quota utilization exceeding 100 percent, although it may happen with individual items. This implies that the growth allowed within quota restrictions is very close to the actual growth in the three major markets, and the performance may not change materially even when no quota restrictions are imposed.

The zero-sum assumption also seems to fail on the supply side of textile and clothing exports. As far as employment is concerned, the proportion of the labor force engaged in the Hong Kong textile and clothing industry (about 42 percent) has not changed significantly since 1961 (although it was higher from 1971 to 1977, with an average annual share of slightly more than 46 percent).

Further evidence of growth is found in capital investment in textile machinery imports. The investment in textile machinery was kept high, giving an average annual growth rate of 21 percent from 1974 to 1986. This investment has accelerated since 1984, due mainly to the shortage of labor in Hong Kong. To determine the productivity of additional capital in increasing output, one can work out the incremental capital (import of textile machinery) to output (export of textile and clothing) ratio (ICOR). Table 5.14 presents the results. The negative signs indicate either a decrease in textile machinery imports or a drop in textile and clothing exports. The average ICOR has remained positive throughout the period except during MFA III 1982–86, when there was a world economic recession, and 1982–83, when political uncertainty was aroused by the issue of Hong Kong's restoration to China in 1997. The figures were relatively high in both MFA I and MFA II periods at 0.10 and 0.05, respectively.

On the whole, there is no evidence that the Hong Kong textile and clothing industry's development has been restricted by the presence of nontariff barriers. Indeed, trade protectionism has induced firms to consolidate their positions and operations, while the quota system has helped to maintain Hong Kong's share in its export markets. (For further analysis, see Li 1991.)

Prospects

The Hong Kong economy has been growing at a very rapid rate in the past few years, after some setbacks in 1983–84. In both 1986 and 1987, its growth rate exceeded 10 percent. At the same time, the rate of inflation was relatively low, ranging from only 3 percent to 5 percent, even though the Hong Kong dollar was devalued quite significantly relative to Japanese and European currencies because Hong Kong's exchange rate system was linked to the U.S. dollar. Economic growth in the territory remained rapid even after the October 1987 stock market crash, achieving an 8 percent rate in 1988. But inflation has been increasing quite rapidly since early 1988. The domestic economy has become overheated, and a severe shortage of labor has developed.

During the past few years, the Hong Kong economy has undergone very rapid economic restructuring, shifting from the stage of industrialization oriented to the export of traditional light, labor-intensive, manufactured products to a more complex and sophisticated stage of industrialization based on the export of more capital- and technology-intensive, manufactured products. At the same time, Hong Kong has developed into an international services center. In this connection, a number of problems face the territory:

(1) The 1997 issue. Despite the Sino-British joint declaration, a lot of uncertainties overhang the future of Hong Kong where its sovereignty status changes in 1997. Those uncertainties have prevented a lot of long-term investment. At the same time, the brain drain problem has become increasingly serious. It is estimated that about 100,000 professional and skilled workers have left Hong Kong in the past few years.

(2) The government policy of nonintervention in industrial development. Because the territory's government has failed to support industry through worker development and promotion of basic and applied research, Hong Kong's industrial technological foundation is now well below that of Taiwan, South Korea,

Table 5.14

Hong Kong's Imports of Textile Machinery and Capital Productivity

	Annual Percentage Change in Imports of Textile Machinery			Incremental Capital Output Ratio (ICOR)		
	H	L	A	H	L	A
1955–58	85	–38	30	—	—	—
Lancashire Pact 1959–62	113	–34	39	1.03	–0.09	0.37
Long-Term Arrangements 1962–67	138	–29	14	0.24	–0.09	0.01
1968–73 Arrangements	96	–44	24	0.13	–0.21	0.01
MFA I 1974–77	35	–32	11	0.21	0.02	0.10
MFA II 1978–81	43	26	35	0.06	0.02	0.05
MFA III 1982–86	50	–19	18	0.06	–0.21	–0.07
MFA I–III 1974–86	50	–32	21	0.21	–0.21	0.02
1984–88	55	12	36	0.27	–0.21	0.04

H = Highest, L = Lowest, A = Average.

Sources: Census and Statistics Department, Hong Kong, *Hong Kong Statistics 1947–67; Hong Kong Monthly Digest of Statistics,* various issues; *Hong Kong Annual Report,* various issues (Hong Kong).

and even Singapore. Nevertheless, the Hong Kong government has recently taken a more positive attitude toward industrial transformation.

(3) Lack of infrastructure. The Hong Kong government has failed to take a long-term and comprehensive view to develop a physical infrastructure that can cope with Hong Kong's recent development. For example, the government has taken a long time to decide on construction of a new airport, while the ground transportation system has fallen short of meeting requirements arising from Hong Kong's rapid domestic growth and increasing economic ties with China.

(4) The China factor. China has become Hong Kong's number one trading partner. Hong Kong's investment in China accounts for about two-thirds of the total foreign direct investment in that country. Moreover, Hong Kong has relocated a significant portion of its labor-intensive production to south China. Hong Kong has also become China's intermediary in the indirect trade between China and South Korea and China and Taiwan. However, recent economic and political turmoil in China will certainly curtail that country's economic activities with the outside world. As a result, the China factor will become a less favorable influence in the future than it has been for the past few years.

(5) Increased protectionism. In the past few years, Western developed countries have become more protectionist in terms of both tariff and nontariff barriers to international trade. While the quota system can be benign, as we have argued above, the dumping complaint against Hong Kong's exports to the EC has be-

come an important concern for the territory's manufacturers. At the same time, the formation of trading blocs, particularly EC 1992, will also threaten the multilateral system established under GATT.

Despite these problems, in the context of the changing environment in the global economy and the Asia-Pacific region, we can still be optimistic about the intermediate and long-term economic outlook for Hong Kong. For example, the gap in long-term investment has been filled to some extent by capital inflow from abroad. Japanese investment in Hong Kong has increased particularly rapidly. In 1987, Japan became the number one investor in Hong Kong manufacturing. In addition, Japan has placed greater emphasis on investment in the Hong Kong service sector. The increasing cost of production in Hong Kong's traditional industries has been offset to some extent by their relocation to lower-wage countries such as China, Thailand, and Indonesia. Hong Kong has also been able to penetrate the Japanese market with considerable success during the past two years. In the China market Hong Kong has managed to increase sales of consumer products as well as capital goods and technology. The government has recognized to some extent the need for development and buildup of infrastructure; more positive steps will be taken. Because of its resilience and traditional free trade policy, Hong Kong is in a better position to fight the increased protectionism adopted by Western developed countries.

Asia-Pacific Regional Economic Relations and Prospects for Cooperation

An optimistic outlook for the Asia-Pacific region as a whole can be based on four major developments that have emerged in the past few years: (1) increasing complementarity of industrial production and economic diversification among countries in the region, (2) increased intraregional trade; (3) increased intraregional investment; (4) increased opportunity for greater regional economic cooperation. Hong Kong will have a new role in all these developments.

Subregional Division of Labor

Hong Kong has been and will be playing a very important role in increasing regional complementarity of industrial production. This development can best be described as the "flying geese pattern" of economic development. We can envisage a group of countries in this region flying together in layers, at different levels that signify their differing stages of economic development. Because of changing comparative advantages, countries at the highest level will pass their out-of-date industries down to the next level of countries. This division of labor is both horizontal, in the sense that the entire industrial product is passed on, and vertical, in the sense that subprocesses for the production of a particular product may be passed on to other countries.

The leader of the flying geese is Japan, which is followed by the Asian NIEs. Among the ASEAN countries, Malaysia and Thailand fly closer to the NIEs than do the Philippines and Indonesia. South Asia as a group falls far behind the others. China is not a goose but a huge bird flying side by side with the flock of geese. China has the potential to complement and compete with various levels of flying geese at different levels of industrial production. What emerges from this pattern of development is that countries in this region will engage in different stages of industrial development. Even countries in the same stage of development can specialize to achieve complementarity. During the past few years, a very sophisticated pattern of specialization has developed, for example, in the manufacture of semiconductors. Taiwan and South Korea have specialized in wafer fabrication, a highly capital- and technology-intensive production process. Hong Kong and Singapore have become specialized in the design and testing stage, which is highly skill- and equipment-intensive. The Philippines, Thailand, and Malaysia concentrate on the highly labor-intensive assembly stage. In terms of technological capability, Hong Kong has generally lagged behind South Korea, Taiwan, and even Singapore. But this does not imply that Hong Kong will be unable to survive. In the flying geese pattern of development, Hong Kong can still find niches in which it enjoys some unique advantages over the other economies. For example, at the technological level, while Hong Kong lags behind the other Asian NIEs in the electronic industry, it is gaining a competitive edge in specialized markets and consumer-oriented products such as the application of specific integrated circuits.

In the broader spectrum of economic diversification, some kinds of specialization have developed within the region. While South Korea and Taiwan have become largely sophisticated manufacturing bases, Hong Kong and Singapore have diversified significantly into the services sector. This does not mean that Hong Kong will give up manufacturing, but inevitably the relative importance of its services sector will increase. It is anticipated that toward the year 2000 Hong Kong will become an increasingly important regional center for the provision of trade, financial, telecommunication, and technological services. As a result, Hong Kong will have a more balanced economy that makes better use of its most precious resources—human resources.

Intraregional Trade

Another reason for optimism concerning the region's export-oriented industrialization is the increased importance of intraregional trade. This is most important because world trade has slowed and protectionism has intensified in most developed countries. For a number of reasons, intraregional trade will be increasingly important. First, the intraregional market has grown because of rapidly rising income levels in the Asian NIEs, the opening up of China, and the restructuring of the Japanese economy. Soon the aggregate GNP of the Asian NIEs, China, and ASEAN will roughly equal one-half of Japan's; the potential of their markets should not be underestimated. While the per capita income level in China is very low at only about US$300; the purchasing power of China's one billion people should not be ignored, because the nationwide average per capita income figure is misleading. Along the coast and in the economically more developed areas, per capita income is very much within the range found in middle-income countries. Although China's economy will experience a period of consolidation and slowdown, there is no question that the modernization programs and open-door policy will continue.

The Japanese market is, of course, huge. In terms of purchasing power, Japan is now the second largest economic power, although its GNP is half that of the United States. In the past the problems of the Japanese market were related to the inward-looking attitude of its consumers and the nontariff barriers imposed on imports. After the drastic appreciation of the yen, Japan switched from its conventional export-led economic growth to a domestic-demand-oriented expansion. Hong Kong's ability to penetrate the Japanese market is also impressive. In 1987, Hong Kong's exports to Japan increased by 42 percent in real terms, while exports to all markets rose only 23 percent. In the first half of 1988, Hong Kong's real exports to Japan rose 13 percent above the comparable period of 1987, while a gain of only 8 percent was recorded for all markets. In the China market, Hong Kong, of course, enjoys advantages, such as geographic proximity and cultural affinity, over other countries. It is not inappropriate to regard China as Hong Kong's semidomestic market. This market is burgeoning, and Hong Kong will benefit most from its growth.

Another cause of increased intraregional trade is the convergence toward free trade policy. While Japan has been making very serious attempts to raise its nontariff trade barriers, other developing countries in this region, such as South Korea, Taiwan, Thailand, Indonesia, and the Philippines, are gradually reducing their tariff levels.

Intraregional Investment

Traditionally, foreign direct investment in this region had come mainly from the developed countries in the West. Later on, Japanese investment became important. Most recently, the Asian NIEs have become increasingly important foreign investors in this region. Among the developing countries, Hong Kong is now one of the largest foreign investors. In 1987, Hong Kong was the number one foreign investor in China, the second largest in Indonesia, the third largest in the Philippines, Thailand, Singapore, and Taiwan, and the fifth largest in Malaysia. In making their investment abroad, Hong Kong firms have been agents of technology transfer. Moreover, in the flying geese pattern of industrial production, direct investment abroad permits relocation of industries to the next level of countries. In recent years, Hong Kong has relocated a large part of its footwear and toy industries in Thailand and the Pearl River delta in China. Foreign investment benefits Hong Kong producers as well as the host country. For example, by investing abroad, Hong Kong is actually relocating its out-of-date industries so that the process of phasing them out can be less painful and more gradual. This outward-looking investment should not be regarded as a sign of low confidence in the future of Hong Kong but, rather, as a positive measure that owners of dynamic firms take to explore their opportunities for greater profitability.

Regional Economic Cooperation

The lack of economic cooperation in this region in the past is not surprising, given the significant differences among its countries' national history, culture, economic development strategies, stage of economic development, economic system, and level of income. But in the past few years there has been a notable tendency for differing economic systems and development strategies to converge. Specifically, we observe a trend of liberalization, deregulation, and privatization in most countries of the region. At the same time, an increasing number of them have switched to outward-looking industrialization policies. As a result, the differences in the type and level of economic development have narrowed. But the most important force tending to pull Asia-Pacific developing countries together is the recent emergence of regionalism, or trading blocs, in the developed world, leading to much greater protectionism. Today, we note the trading bloc of the United States and Canada, of Australia and New Zealand, and, above all, of a Fortress Europe in 1992. Inevitably, some kind of formal organization will emerge among most of the Asia-Pacific countries, focusing on trade and development issues. The formation of a powerful economic bloc comprising Taiwan, mainland China, and Hong Kong is already under way. This group can be labeled "The Greater China." It has become a de facto economic bloc because of the rapidly increasing trade and investment interactions among its members, and their high degree of complementarity of economic resources. Mainland China has rich natural resources, a plentiful supply of trainable and cheap labor, and a huge potential capability for conducting basic research. Hong Kong has an ample supply of capital and professionals, the ability to commercialize invention, and all the infrastructure to function as a service center in finance, trade, telecommunication, and technology. Taiwan has built up a high level of technological capability to specialize in relatively sophisticated industrial manufacturing. On the demand side, the combined market of Hong Kong, Taiwan, and mainland China is huge.

In the movement toward greater economic cooperation in this region, Hong Kong can certainly play an important role. The Greater China cannot exist without Hong Kong serving as a trade and investment conduit. Hong Kong could also be instrumental in the formation of Asia-Pacific economic cooperation organizations and could logically serve as their headquarters location.

APPENDIX

**Main Features of Protectionist Policies
Applied to Exports of Textiles and
Clothing from Hong Kong**

1959–1962: The Lancashire Pact
Known as the Undertaking, the Pact was imposed by Britain and restricted Hong Kong's exports of garments and piece goods to an annual total of 164 million yards.

1961–1962: Short-Term Arrangement on Cotton Textiles (STA)
Initiated by United States. GATT participants arrived temporarily at the STA, under which importing countries could conclude bilateral agreements with exporting countries or impose restraints whenever the importing countries faced "market disruption" from imports.

1962–1967: Long-Term Arrangement on Cotton Textiles (LTA)
Consolidated the principal issues in STA. Hong Kong had concluded a number of bilateral agreements with countries such as Sweden and Norway.

1963–1965: First Extension of the Lancashire Pact
Total quota limits from Britain increased. Products were grouped into finer categories so that different quota restrictions could be exercised. An interim arrangement was extended to the first half of 1966.

1966–1972: Second Extension of Lancashire Pact
A new undertaking imposed by Britain. Greater flexibility in the form of "carry forward" and "over-use" of quota was allowed.

1968–1973: Arrangement Regarding International Trade in Cotton Textiles (CTA)
Extended the restrictions based on LTA. Restraints had gone beyond the scope of textiles.

1972–1974: Third Extension of the Lancashire Pact
A new agreement between Hong Kong and Britain was made beyond the scope of cotton textiles and covered the restriction on woven cotton and polyester/cotton fabrics, garments, and made-up articles. This undertaking lasted for fifteen months from October 1972 and was Hong Kong's last bilateral agreement with Britain, due to Britain's entry into the Common Market.

1974–1977: Multi-Fiber Arrangement I (MFA I)

Importing countries might impose restrictions unilaterally under certain conditions if consultation with exporting countries were to break down. Bilateral agreements would be concluded on "mutually acceptable terms." A Textile Surveillance Body was set up to ensure compliance with bilateral agreements. An annual growth rate of 6 percent was given to restricted items.

1978–1981: MFA II

More restrictive than MFA I as extraordinary terms were added. The "reasonable departure" clause enabled the importing countries to depart temporarily from particular elements of the agreement. Largest exporters were required to have their 1978 exports to the Common Market reduced below the 1976 level. Hong Kong faced an overall cut of 9 percent. Growth rates ranged from 0.3 percent to 4.1 percent.

1982–1986: MFA III

The "reasonable departure" clause was replaced by the "anti-surge" clause. The new clause permitted importing countries to safeguard their internal markets if exporters attempted to fulfill the underutilized quotas of sensitive products in a sudden and substantial manner. Exporters' flexibility in shifting their export composition was removed. A lower than 6 percent growth rate was placed on "highly sensitive" products.

1982–1986: Bilateral Agreement with United States

Restrained 64 percent of Hong Kong's export of cotton, wool, and synthetic fibers to United States.

1984: Country of Origin Rule

Imposed by United States, the rule prevented exports against Hong Kong's quota allowances of sweaters from panels knitted in China. Threatened 70 percent of sweater export from Hong Kong.

1985–1987: Textile and Apparel Trade Enforcement Act

Popularly known as the Jenkins Bill, it was passed by the U.S. Congress but vetoed by the president. The bill restricted all imports of fiber textiles and apparel products, called for an import licensing system, and permitted future improvements at 1 percent growth annually at the 1986 level.

1986–1991: The Hong Kong/U.S. Textile Agreement

Extended the restriction to silk and vegetable fiber textiles, which were not covered in MFA III. The annual growth rate was set at 0.5 percent in 1985–1986, rising to 2.5 percent in 1990–91, giving an average of 1.7 percent over the five-year period. Intergroup swing and carryover was 1 percent.

1987–1991: The Hong Kong/EEC Textile Agreement (MFA IV)
Covered ninety-seven categories of textile products of cotton, synthetic fiber, and wool. Annual growth rate ranged from 0.2 percent to 6 percent, depending on category. The aggregate average was 1.3 percent annual growth rate.

Sources:

Farrands, C. "Textile Diplomacy: The Making and Implication of European Textile Policy 1974–1978." *Journal of Common Market Studies*, vol. 18, no. 1, September 1979.

Lin, T.B., and Mok, V. *Trade Barriers and the Promotion of Hong Kong Exports.* Hong Kong: Chinese University Press, 1980.

The 1987–91 HK/EEC Textiles Agreement and The 1986–91 HK/US Textiles Agreement. Hong Kong: Trade Department.

Wolf, M. *Issues in the MFA Negotiations.* London: Trade Policy Research Center, 1981.

References

Adelman, M.A. 1969. "Comment on "H" Concentration Measure as a Number-Equivalent," *Review of Economics and Statistics*, February 1969: pp.99–101.

Anderson, Kym, and Baldwin, Robert E. 1965. "The Political Market for Protection and Industrial Countries: Empirical Evidence." World Bank Staff Working Papers No. 492, October.

Balassa, Bela. 1965. "Trade Liberalization and Revealed Comparative Advantage." *Manchester School of Economic and Social Studies.* May, Vol. XXXIII: 99–124.

———. 1978. *World Trade and International Economy: Trend Prospects and Policies.* Washington, D.C.:World Bank.

Balassa, Bela, 1979. "The Changing Pattern of Comparative Advantage in Manufactured Goods," in *Review of Economics and Statistics*, (Cambridge, Mass), May.

Bhagwati, Jagdish. 1988. *Protectionism.* Cambridge, Mass.: MIT Press.

Cha, D.S. et al. 1983. *A Comparative Study of the Export Competitiveness in Korea, Japan, Taiwan and Singapore.* Seoul: Korea Institute of Industrial Economics and Technology, et al. (In Korean.)

Chan, W.C. 1974. *International Trade in Manufactures: A Comparative Study of the Export Performance of Hong Kong, the Republic of China, and the Republic of Korea, 1962–71.* M.A. thesis, Chinese University of Hong Kong.

Chen, Edward K.Y. 1980. "Export, Expansion and Economic Growth in Some Asian Countries: A 'Simultaneous-Equation Model.' " In *Measurement, History and Factors of Economic Growth*, ed., R.C.O. Matthew. London: Macmillan.

———. 1983. *Multinational Corporations, Technology, and Employment.* London: Macmillan.

———. 1987."Foreign Trade and Economic Growth in Hong Kong: Experience and Prospects." In *Trade and Structural Change in Pacific Asia*, ed. Colin I. Bradford Jr. and William H. Branson. Chicago: University of Chicago Press.

Corden, Warner M. 1985. *Protection, Growth and Trade.* Oxford: Basil Blackwell.

Donges, Juergen B. 1981. *Implications on the Multi-Fibre Agreement for Developed Countries.* London: Trade Policy Research Center, December.

———. 1986. "Whitter International Trade Policies." Keil: Institut fur Weltwirtschaft an der Universitat, October.

Farrands, Chris. 1979. "Textile Diplomacy: The Making and Implementation of European Textile Policy 1974–1978." *Journal of Common Market Studies* 18, no. 1 (September): 22–39.

GATT. 1974. *Arrangement Regarding International Trade in Textiles.* Geneva,.

———. 1986. *Extending the Arrangement Regarding International Trade in Textiles — Protocol.* Geneva, July.

Gramm, B. 1985. "New Protectionism—Old Sophistry." *Asian Wall Street Journal* (October).

Greenway, David. 1983. *International Trade Policy.* New York: Macmillan.

Hamilton, Carl. 1980. "Effects of Non-tariff Barriers to Trade and Prices, Employment and Imports: The Case of the Swedish Textile and Clothing Industry." World Bank Staff Working Papers No. 429, October.

Heller, Peter S. 1976. "Factor Endowment Change and Comparative Advantage: The Case of Japan, 1956–69." *Review of Economics and Statistics* (August).

Hirschman, Albert. 1945. *National Power and the Structure of Foreign Trade.* Berkeley: University of California Press.

Hong Kong Government. 1986–91. *The HK/US Textiles Agreement.* Hong Kong: Trade Department.

———. 1987–91. *The HK/EEC Textile Agreement.* Hong Kong: Trade Department.

Hughes, Helan, and Waelbroeck, J. 1981. "Can Developing-Country Exports Keep Growing in the 1980s?" *World Economy* (June).

Jao, Y.C. 1979. "Hong Kong's Rise As a Financial Center." *Asian Survey.*

Keesing, Donald B., and Wolf, Martin. 1981. "Questions on International Trade in Textiles and Clothing." *World Economy* (March).

Koekkoek, K.A.; Kol, J.; and Mennes, L.B.M. 1981."On Protectionism in the Netherlands." World Bank Staff Working Papers No. 493, October.

Kuo, Shirley W. Y. 1983. *The Taiwan Economy in Transition.* Boulder, Colo.: Westview Press.

Laird, Samuel, and Yeats, A. 1989. "Nontariff A. Barriers of Developed Countries 1966–1986." *Finance and Development,* World Bank (March): 12–13.

Lal, Deepak. 1981. "Implication on the MFA on Developing Countries." London: Trade Policy Research Center, December.

Li, Kui-Wai. 1991. "Positive Adjustment against Protectionism: the Case of Textile and Clothing Industry in Hong Kong," in *The Developing Economics,* Vol XXIX, Vol 3. (Tokyo), September.

Lin, Tzong-biau; Lee, R. and Simons, U. eds. 1979. *Hong Kong: Economic, Social and Political Studies in Development.* Armonk, N.Y.: M.E. Sharpe.

Lin, Tzong-biau, and Mok, V. 1980. *Trade Barriers and the Promotion of Hong Kong Exports.* Hong Kong: Chinese University Press.

Lin, Tzong-biau; Mok, V.; and Ho, Y.P. 1980. *Manufactured Exports and Employment in Hong Kong.* Hong Kong: Chinese University Press.

Lundberg, Lars. 1981. "Pattern of Barriers to Trade in Sweden: A Study in the Theory of Protectionism." World Bank Staff Working Papers No. 494, October.

McMullen, Neil. 1982. *The Newly Industrializing Countries: Adjusting to Success.* London: British-North American Committee.

Naya, Seiji. 1973. "Fluctuations in Export-Earnings and Economic Patterns of Asian Countries." *Economic Development and Cultural Change* (July).

Ooms, Van Doorn. 1967. "Models of Comparative Export Performance." *Yale Economics Essays* (Spring).

Park, Ungush K. 1980. "Export Competition between and Comparative Advantages of Newly Industrializing Countries." *Korean Journal of International Business* (July).

Richardson, J. David. 1971. "Constant-Market-Shares Analysis of Export Growth." *Journal of International Economics*. 1, no. 2 (May): 227–39.

Szczepanik, Edward F. 1958. *The Economic Growth of Hong Kong*. Hong Kong: Greenwood Press.

Tyszynski, H. 1951. "World Trade in Manufactured Commodities, 1899–1950." *Manchester School of Economic and Social Studies* (September).

Wolf, Martin M. 1981. "Issues in the MFA Negotiations." London: Trade Policy Research Center, December.

Youngson, A.J., ed. 1983. *China and Hong Kong: The Economic Nexus*. Hong Kong: Oxford University Press.

135-48

CHAPTER 6

Competitiveness of Taiwan Exports in the United States Market

POCHIH CHEN*

Taiwan has enjoyed rapid export-led growth in the past two to three decades, with a huge trade surplus in recent years. As Taiwan's export growth rate typically exceeded its economic growth rate, the ratio of exports to GNP increased rapidly, from 16 percent in 1965 to 50 percent in 1985 and has more or less stabilized at that level. In the 1980s the ratio of trade surplus to GNP increased from a negligible amount to a peak exceeding 20 percent in 1986 and 1987. Since Taiwan's exports have been predominantly manufactured goods, its manufacturing sector is highly dependent on export trade. Many industries export directly or indirectly more than 80 percent of their products. As a result, factors affecting the growth or variation of exports play important roles in the development and fluctuation of Taiwan's economy. Among these factors, export competitiveness is probably most crucial. Therefore, we will analyze how Taiwan's products compete with the goods of other countries in its most important export market, the United States.

The first section reviews the importance of the U.S. market to Taiwan's exports. Section 2 introduces a model to estimate the competition among various exporting countries. Section 3 presents results of empirical estimates derived from the model. These results are used to discuss the elasticities of substitution between Taiwan products and other U.S. imports. We calculate the index of export competitiveness of Taiwan products in the U.S. market, as well as related data. Finally, we present our conclusions in the fourth section.

The Importance of the U.S. Market to Taiwan's Manufactured Exports

Since the United States has been the world's largest market and greatest importer for the past several decades, it is also, naturally, the major importer for most

* The author would like to thank Mr. Chung-Chong Chu, Ms. Yu-Long Chen, Mr. Hong-Yeh Lee, and Ms. Chun-Hua Hsu for their assistance. The first section of this chapter was updated by Dr. Shu-Chin Yang.

countries. However, Taiwan's dependence on exports to the United States has been extraordinarily high. The U.S. market took more than 20 percent of Taiwan's total exports in the early half of the 1960s. This share doubled in the early 1970s. After a mild decline during the recession following the first oil shock, the U.S. market share of Taiwan's total exports rebounded to about 48 percent in the mid-1980s. Since then however, it declined gradually to 32 percent in 1990, mainly because of United States' recession and the continuous appreciation of the Taiwan currency, under the pressure of the United States (see Table 6.1). But the ratio was still high. Such a high degree of export concentration in one country is quite unusual.

Moreover, since Taiwan's ratio of exports to GNP is also very high, this concentration implies that a significant part of the country's production relies on the U.S. market. Taiwan's export to the U.S. market as a percentage of GNP rose from 3.4 percent in 1965 to a peak of 25.6 percent in 1986 (see Table 6.1). Again, it fell appreciably since then to 13.2 percent in 1990 for the same reasons stated above. Also, the decline indicates that Taiwan has been diversifying its export markets.

Given this high dependence ratio, the fluctuations in the U.S. market would have a great influence on the Taiwan economy. In fact, the increase in sales to the U.S. market is the main source of Taiwan's export growth before 1986, and the trade surplus with the United States is almost equivalent to the overall trade surplus (see Table 6.2). In the decade before the first oil shock, which was also a period of very successful export-led growth in Taiwan, about 46 percent of the total export growth was to the U.S. market (see Table 6.1).

Taiwan's reliance on the U.S. market is based on both economic and non-economic factors. First, the United States is not only the world's largest importer, it has also been more open than other major markets during the past decades. This is particularly important for small- and intermediate-sized firms, which are more numerous in Taiwan than in most other economies. Such firms find it much easier to explore the export market in the United States than in other countries. Since the U.S. market is large enough to provide customers for small firms, they do not feel pressed to search for other outlets. Besides, they have few resources to diversify their export markets.

Second, Taiwan's products enjoyed Generalized Special Preferences (GSP) in the United States but not in the EC. As a result, compared with other exporting countries, Taiwan has sent a relatively small share of its exports to the EC and a larger share to the U.S. market. However, this does not suffice to explain why the U.S. market share of Taiwan exports was already very high in the late 1960s, before the GSP was granted.

Third, political relations between the U.S. and Taiwan have been very close, and Taiwan's educational system has been extensively influenced by the United States. A large number of Taiwanese students have studied in the American universities. Through them and their families, people in Taiwan are much more familiar with the United States than with other Western countries.

Table 6.1

The Importance of Taiwan's Exports to the United States, 1961–90

Year	Value of Exports to U.S. (NT$ billions)	Value of Exports to U.S./Total Value of Exports (%)	Value of Exports to U.S./GNP (%)	Contribution of Export Growth in the U.S. Market to Total Export Growth (%)
1961	1.71	21.9	2.5	46.2[a]
1965	3.84	21.3	3.4	46.9
1970	22.57	39.4	10.0	45.6
1975	69.19	34.3	11.8	46.5[b]
1980	243.04	34.1	16.3	43.2
1985	588.16	48.1	24.1	35.7
1986	718.97	47.7	25.6	46.2
1987	753.97	44.2	23.8	11.9
1988	688.95	38.7	19.6	−17.8
1989	651.86	36.2	16.4	10.1
1990	580.84	32.3	13.2	−2,516.5

Source: Department of Statistics, Ministry of Finance, *Monthly Statistics of Exports and Imports (Taiwan District).*

[a]1962.
[b]1976.

Fourth, Taiwan's currency (New Taiwan dollar) was virtually pegged to the U.S. dollar before 1986. The fixed exchange rate reduced uncertainty for exporters doing business with the United States.

Last but not least, the triangular economic relationship of Taiwan, Japan, and the United States was crucial. Many exportable Taiwanese goods were assembled from Japanese parts and other intermediate inputs. Thus, a significant portion of Taiwan's exports to the U.S. market actually contributed indirect exports by Japan. A great part of Taiwan's trade surplus with the United States had its counterpart in the former's trade deficit with Japan.

In order to take full advantage of the factors favoring its exports in the U.S. market, however, Taiwan has to be competitive there. In this chapter we will build a multilateral competition model and estimate the substitution effects between Taiwan's products and the exports of other countries in the U.S. market.

A Trade Demand Function for Multilateral Competition

Exports of one country often face competition from the products of the importing country as well as other exporting countries. However, empirical studies do not identify this kind of multilateral competition readily. In many empirical studies

Table 6.2

Taiwan's Total Trade Surplus and the Trade Surplus with the United States, 1971–90 (U.S. $ billions)

Year	Total Trade Surplus	Trade Surplus with U.S.	Accumulated Trade Surplus since 1976	Accumulated Trade Surplus with U.S. since 1976	Foreign Exchange Reserve since 1976
1971	0.22	0.45	—	—	—
1975	−0.64	0.17	—	—	—
1980	0.08	2.09	4.48	9.91	2.21
1985	10.62	10.03	33.17	44.03	22.56
1986	15.68	13.58	48.85	57.61	46.31
1987	18.69	16.04	67.54	73.65	76.75
1988	10.99	10.46	78.53	84.11	74.03
1989	14.04	12.03	92.57	96.14	73.95
1990	12.50	9.13	105.07	105.27	80.60

Source: Department of Statistics, Ministry of Finance, *Monthly Statistics of Exports and Imports (Taiwan District).*

of import or export demand functions, the volume of trade is assumed to be a log-linear function of the relative price and income of the importing country. For instance, we can write the export demand function of Taiwan in the U.S. market as

$$LnX = a + bLnYA + cLn(PT/PC) \qquad (1)$$

where X denotes the real value of Taiwan's exports to the U.S. market; YA, the real income of the U.S.; PT, the export price of Taiwan; and PC, the price of the products competing with Taiwan products. While functions of this kind have the advantage of giving us both price and income elasticity, the meaning of price elasticity in this function is not clear. In some empirical studies, PC is assumed to be the price index of the importing country. Then the coefficient c may capture the substitution between Taiwan exports for the products of the importing country but not exports from competing exporting countries. Other empirical studies use some kind of composite price index of other exporting countries as PC. In this case, the coefficient would represent the substitutability between the products of various exporting countries. The actual meaning of c depends on the method used to calculate the composite price index PC. However, since products from various exporting countries and the products of the importing country may compete with each other in the real world, we must incorporate prices of all countries, or at least prices of the

Figure 6.1. **A Hypothetical Structure of Competition in the Import Demand**

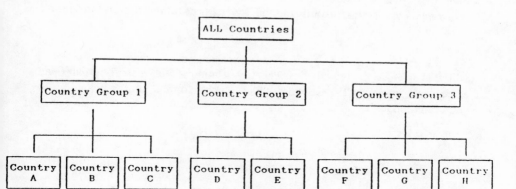

real world, we must incorporate prices of all countries, or at least prices of the major competitors, in the export demand function. But when the substitutabilities between different pairs of products are unknown, we cannot design a composite price index PC to represent the prices of all competitors. It is too complicated to incorporate all prices directly in the demand function without any *a priori* restriction.

The Armington model (1969a, 1969b; Deardorff and Stern 1986) seems an acceptable way to simplify the complicated phenomenon of multilateral competition. Armington used the concept of the utility tree and arranged different products from different countries in a two-level CES utility function. With this simplification, the estimation of the otherwise complicated phenomenon becomes possible although still not easy. If we imitate this idea and use a multi-level CES function, we may be able to estimate the diverse substitution effects between products of different countries.

This idea will be illustrated by using a hypothetical three-level CES function in the following paragraphs. Suppose first that total imports are separable in the utility function of the importing country, and that we can classify all competing countries in several different groups. Assuming further that countries belonging to different groups will not compete with each other directly, we can have the structure of competition shown in Figure 6.1. Countries belonging to the same group compete with each other first.

Then their products form a composite product and compete with the composite products of other groups at a higher level of competition. Under this assumption, the export price of a country belonging to group 2 or 3 will not affect the exports of country A directly. However, by affecting the implicit prices of groups 2 and 3, the export price from country D to H can still influence the

Let us further assume that at each level of competition the choice of the importing country follows some kind of CES utility function. Then we may construct a hypothetical quantity of total imports Q as follows:

$$Q = (A_1 Q_1^e + A_2 Q_2^e + A_3 Q_3^e)^{(1/e)} \qquad (2)$$

where Q_i is again the hypothetical quantity of imports from country group i and can be written as a CES function of the imports from countries belonging to country group i:

$$Q_1 = (AaQa^f + AbQb^f + AcQc^f)^{(1/f)} \qquad (3)$$
$$Q_2 = (AdQd^g + AeQe^g)^{(1/g)} \qquad (4)$$
$$Q_3 = (AfQf^k + AgQg^k + AhQh^k)^{(1/k)} \qquad (5)$$

When the total value of imports is given, the import choice of the importing countries can be viewed as if it is maximizing Q, subject to the budget constraint of the total value of imports. With our CES assumption, it is much easier to determine the competition between the products from different countries. For countries belonging to the same group, the competition is determined mainly by the elasticity of substitution within this group and the share of each country in the group. Their shares of total imports and the elasticity of substitution between their products at the higher level of competition are less important but not necessarily negligible. However, for countries belonging to different groups, competition is determined solely by their shares of total imports and the elasticity of substitution between their products. In general, these substitution effects differ for different countries. Moreover, if there are more levels in the CES function, the substitution effects become more diversified. Thus the multilevel CES utility function is flexible enough to encompass the complicated phenomenon of competition in international trade. We simply have to determine market shares and elasticities of substitution within each group.

Nevertheless, we may not have enough prior information to determine the levels of competition and classify countries in different groups. It is also difficult to estimate a CES function with many levels of competition and many countries. Sato (1967) introduced a two-level CES function and suggested a step-by-step method of estimation. Brown and Heien (1972) treated the two-level CES function as a utility tree or nested utility function and used the maximum likelihood method for its estimation. When the number of levels in the CES function increases, it becomes more difficult to classify countries into different groups and estimate the multilevel CES function. Therefore, in this chapter we try to find a more tractable method for estimating the multilevel CES function.

The work of W. J. Keller (1976) is a good starting point. He derived, among other things, a simple demand function for an individual commodity in a multilevel CES utility function. His demand function can be written in a log-linear form as:

$$LnQa = A + E_1 LnPa/P(1) + E_2 LnP(1)/P(2)$$
$$+ E_3 LnP(2)/P(3) + \ldots E_k LnP\ (k-1)/P(k) \qquad (6)$$

where Qa is the quantity demanded for a specific commodity, and Pa is its price. A in (6) represents other factors in the demand function, including constant term and the income effect. $P(i)$ is the shadow price of the commodity group that contains our specific commodity Qa and competes with other commodity groups at the level of competition. Finally, the coefficient Ei is the elasticity of substitution within the commodity group that contains commodity Qa at the ith level of competition.

The functional form is quite simple and familiar. Indeed, it looks like a straightforward extension of equation (1). The economic interpretation of equation (6) is also conceivable. We can accept that Qa competes first with the commodity group represented by $P(1)$ with an elasticity of substitution E_1; then Qa and other commodities represented by $P(1)$ as a group compete at the higher level with the commodity groups represented by $P(2)$ with an elasticity of substitution E_2, and so on. We can also imagine that a decision maker uses $P(k)$ and $P(k-1)$ to determine the fraction of his total expenditures that will be spent first on the commodity group represented by $P(k-1)$, then he will use $P(k-1)$ and $P(k-2)$ to determine the fraction spent on the commodity group represented by $P(k-2)$; and so on.

Unfortunately, the estimation of equation (6) is not as easy as it looks because all the $P(i)$s are actually unobservable shadow prices. Nevertheless, when the market share of each commodity or commodity group is already known, $P(i)$ of each commodity group can be approximated by a Divisia price index (Chen 1976; Gollop and Jorgenson 1980:23). The rate of increase of this index equals the weighted average rate of increase of each commodity in this group, weighted by the market shares of each commodity in this group. If we use these approximate price indices in place of actual $P(i)$s, it will become much easier to estimate equation (6). In fact, it can be estimated simply by using the ordinary linear least square method.

Though equation (6) can be estimated easily by our method, it still has the same shortcoming as other kinds of demand functions in empirical studies of international trade. Almost all export demand functions in empirical studies, including equation (6), imply that to increase a country's exports, it is necessary that its products become cheaper than the products of its competitors or the income or total imports of the importing country increase. But when we review the export growth history of the East Asian countries, it is hard to believe that their export expansion was caused by a sharp decline in their terms of trade or the income growth of their trading partners. One may surmise that export growth in the East Asian countries results from the augmentation of their supply capacity. However, we should remember that when the demand curve is fixed, changes in the supply function can affect the quantity demanded only by changing the variables incorporated in the demand function. Therefore, introducing supply into the model in the normal way cannot eliminate this shortcoming of equation (6).

There are at least two traditional ways to avoid this shortcoming. The first is to assume that the income elasticity of the import demand function is very high. This assumption may be supported by the fact that some empirical studies using equation (1) have indeed resulted in a high income elasticity estimate. However, instead of representing actual behavior of the importing country, the high income elasticities might reflect the inability of changes in relative prices to explain the trend of increasing exports.

The second traditional way to avoid the shortcoming of the demand function is to use the small-country assumption and discard the demand function altogether. When a country is small enough, it will take international prices as given. Then the quantity of exports is determined by the supply function rather than the demand function. This assumption is often used in theoretical studies. However, it is not useful for our study because it assumes away the possibility of imperfect substitution between the products from different countries.

In this chapter we design a third method that allows changes in supply to affect the demand function explicitly. Following the Dixit-Stiglitz (1977) model in the theory of industrial organization, we can assume that a country's exports actually include many kinds of products, and the quantity of exports of any country in equations (3) to (5) is merely a hypothetical quantity of the composite products. For instance, Qa in equation (3) can be written as

$$Qa = (B_1C_1b + B_2C_2b + \ldots B_nC_nb)^{(1/b)} \tag{7}$$

where C_i is the quantity of ith product exported by country A and n is a very large number. Let us further assume that only a small subset of these n kinds of products is actually exported. Without loss of generality, we can assume that the exports are products 1 through m, and C_i is equal to zero when i is greater than m. Exports can be expanded by an increase in either C_i or m. Under these assumptions, there will be an economy of scope in the utility function. That is, when the volume of total exports, or the sum of C_is, is kept constant, an increase in m can raise the total utility. If we define the units of these products properly, so that the unit price of each product (Pi) is equal to P, the economy of scope can be seen indirectly in the shadow price of Qa. Since Qa is a linear homogeneous function of C_is, it can be proved that the shadow price of Qa is merely the average cost of Qa (Chen 1989):

$$\begin{aligned} Pa &= (P_1C_1 + P_2C_2 + \ldots + PnCn)/Qa \\ &= P\{(1/C_1)^{1/b-1} + (1+C_2)^{1/b-1} + \ldots \\ &\quad + (1/C_m)^{1/b-1}\}^{b-1/b} \end{aligned} \tag{8}$$

Because b is generally assumed to be between zero and one in the analysis of product differentiation, it is clear from equation (8) that an increase in m will reduce the shadow price of Qa if P is kept constant. Therefore, equation (8) is an indication of the economy of scope. In other words, when the exports of one country are diversified, the importing country will react as if they have become cheaper.

An equally important implication of equation (8) is its difference from the price index. When m is increasing, equation (8) implies that the price index compiled by conventional methods will normally overestimate the shadow price of Qa. Since the difference between Pa and P is determined by the number of products exported, we can assume that the discrepancy between a price index compiled by conventional methods (Px) and the theoretical Pa can be represented by an increasing function of the degree of product diversification (D):

$$Px = Paf(D) \tag{9}$$

As a result, we cannot deflate the value of exports by Px to obtain an unbiased index of the quantity. What we obtain is actually

$$Xa = (P_1C_1 + P_2C_2 + \ldots + PmCm)/Px = Qa/f(D) \tag{10}$$

Unfortunately, since Pa is unobservable, we have to use Xa as the quantity index of exports in empirical studies. Theoretically, the $P(i)$'s in equation (6) should all be calculated from Pa. Therefore, equation (6) cannot be used to estimate directly the export demand function. Further assumptions are needed. Assume that the value of total imports is given; the decision to take imports from different countries follows a multilevel CES utility function, and our exports actually contain differentiated products; thus the export demand function for Xa can be obtained by inserting equations (9) and (10) into equation (6).

$$LnXa = B + Ln[M/P(k)] - (E_1+1)Lnf(D) + E_1Ln[Px/P(1)]$$
$$+ E_2Ln[P(1)/P(2)] + \ldots + EkLn[P(k-1)/P(k)] \tag{11}$$

where B is the constant term, M is the value of total imports, and $P(k)$ is the shadow price of imports from all countries. Although $P(i)$s in equation (11) are unobservable, their differences from the $P(i)$s calculated from the observed export prices are affected only by the degree of differentiation among products of the exporting countries. If we can integrate some variables into the demand function to represent the effects of product differentiation, we can pretend that there is no product differentiation and still use the observed export prices when we calculate $P(i)$s. Therefore, we will assume that the effects of changes in the degree of product differentiation can be determined by noting changes in the potential GDP of the exporting country and changes in real imports of the importing country. Then equation (11) can be rewritten as

$$LnXa = B + EmLn[M/P(K)] + EyLnYp + E_1Ln[Px/P(1)]$$
$$+ E_2Ln[P(1)/P(2)] + \ldots + EkLn[P(k-1)/P(k)] \qquad (12)$$

where Em and Ey are unknown coefficients and Yp is the potential GNP of the exporting country. This equation also looks like a natural extension of equation (6). Even if the assumptions of multilevel CES function and product differentiation in this section are deemed unacceptable, equation (12) can still be used as a heuristic functional form for decisions about exports where foreign demand, domestic supply capacity, and the relative prices of competitors all play important roles. In the next section we will use equation (12) to estimate the import demand function of the United States for Taiwan products.

The Elasticities of Substitution in the U.S. Market

Using quarterly data from the first quarter of 1976 to the fourth quarter of 1986, we estimated equation (12) as the export demand faced by Taiwan's exports in the U.S. market. Many different combinations and differing levels of competition were tried, and most of the results gave us a very high explanatory power. Therefore, we could not select the best model simply by comparing the R^2's of different equations. To determine which equation is better, we set up the following rules:

• All explanatory variables in the regression except the constant term and seasonal dummies must be statistically significant.

• All signs of the estimated coefficients must be the same as we expect from the theory.

• The elasticity of substitution at the higher level of competition must be smaller than the elasticity of substitution at the lower level of competition.

In accord with these rules, we selected the following equation as the best model for the U.S. demand function for Taiwan's exports:

$$Ln(Xa)_t = -8.73 + 0.4386\ Ln(Xa)_{t-1} + 0.7222\ Ln(M/Pm)_t$$
$$\qquad\qquad (2.9866) \qquad\qquad\quad (3.6733)$$

$$- 0.4917\ LnYp - 2.5427\ Ln[Pa/P(2)]_t$$
$$\quad (2.1751) \qquad\quad (-2.0611)$$

$$- 0.8418\ Ln[P(2)/P(6)]_{t-1}$$
$$\qquad\quad (-2.0557)$$

$$- 0.7652\ Ln[P(6)/Pm]_{t-1} + 0.0752D_1$$
$$\ (-2.6919) \qquad\qquad\qquad (2.3757)$$

$$+ 0.0851D_2 + 0.1615D_3$$
$$\quad (2.4270) \quad (5.3247)$$

$$R^2 = 0.9855 \qquad \bar{R}^2 = 0.9815 \qquad\qquad\qquad (13)$$

where Xa is the value of Taiwan exports to the U.S. market deflated by the export unit value index of Taiwan; M and Pm are, respectively, the value of total imports and the unit price index of U.S. imports; Pa is the export unit price index of Taiwan; Yp is the index of Taiwan's potential GDP adopted from Chen and Chu (1989); $P(2)$ is the composite export unit price index of Taiwan and Korea; $P(6)$ is the composite export unit price index of Taiwan, Korea, Japan, Hong Kong, and Singapore; and Di's are seasonal dummies. All the prices were calculated in terms of U.S. dollars, and the number under each coefficient is the t value for that coefficient.

We can see from this regression result that South Korea is indeed the major competitor for Taiwan in the U.S. market, as many businessmen in Taiwan believe. The short-run and long-run elasticities of substitution between their products are as high as 2.5476 and 4.538, respectively. Therefore, when the price of a product rises in one country, many of its exports would be replaced by the exports of another country. Taking the products of Taiwan and Korea as a group, their elasticities of substitution with the products of Hong Kong, Singapore, and Japan are 0.8418 for the short run and 1.4995 for the long run. The elasticities of substitution of these five areas with products of other exporters in the U.S. market are 0.7652 for the short run and 1.363 for the long run. All these results imply that price competition is certainly important for these countries in the U.S. market. The result that the potential GDP of Taiwan is a significant explanatory variable also supports the hypothesis that increasing product differentiation or increasing supply capacity is an important reason for expansion of Taiwan's exports to the U.S. market.

The assertion that South Korea is Taiwan's major competitor in the United States can also be supported by the similarity of their export product composition. We took 151 SITC items of manufacturing products and calculated the correlation coefficients of their market shares of U.S. imports. We found that the correlation between the market shares of Taiwan and Korea is higher than those of other areas; however, the correlation between Taiwan and Hong Kong is only slightly smaller than that between Taiwan and Korea (see Table 6.3).

Also noteworthy in Table 6.3 is the time pattern of the correlation coefficients. The correlation coefficients between Taiwan and South Korea, Hong Kong, and Singapore are declining. Suggesting that these NIEs are now developing their own export routes. On the other hand, the correlation coefficients between Taiwan and Thailand and mainland China are increasing, indicating that they present increasing competition to Taiwan.

From our regression results, we can also calculate the price elasticity and cross price elasticities in the U.S. import demand for Taiwan's products. Table 6.4 presents some of these long-run elasticities, calculated on the basis of 1986 market shares.

The price competitiveness of Taiwan in the U.S. market is another important indicator we can calculate from the empirical results. The relative price terms in

Table 6.3

Correlation Coefficients between Taiwan and Other Countries/Areas for Their Shares of Manufactured Exports in the U.S. Market

Year	Korea	Hong Kong	Singa-pore	Thailand	India	Mainland China	Japan	West Germany
1981	0.61	0.50	0.20	0.02	0.00	0.13	−0.04	−0.33
1982	0.55	0.49	0.17	0.01	0.02	0.13	−0.08	−0.30
1983	0.49	0.44	0.10	0.05	0.06	0.15	−0.11	−0.33
1984	0.47	0.44	0.10	0.06	0.09	0.16	−0.10	−0.32
1985	0.46	0.41	0.08	0.08	0.07	0.19	−0.09	−0.31
1986	0.49	0.37	0.07	0.17	0.06	—	−0.09	—

Note: Calculated from the OECD tapes of Foreign Trade Statistics.

Table 6.4

Price Elasticity and Selected Cross Price Elasticities for Taiwan's Exports in the U.S. Market

Asia	Elasticity	Other Regions	Elasticity
Taiwan	−2.6336	Canada	0.2387
Korea	1.3138	Australia	0.0101
Japan	0.3651	New Zealand	0.0035
Hong Kong	0.0426	France	0.0360
Singapore	0.0268	West Germany	0.0909
Thailand	0.0074	United Kingdom	0.0582
Malaysia	0.0098		
Indonesia	0.0114		
Philippines	0.0076		

Note: Calculated from equation (13).

our regression result represent the effects of price changes on Taiwan's exports to the U.S. market. Therefore, this part can be combined as an index of price competitiveness. To facilitate the comparison with other price indicators, the index in Table 6.5 is calculated on the scale that a 1 percent rise in this index is equivalent to a 1 percent decline in Taiwan's export prices. As Table 6.5 indicates, the variations in price competitiveness were rather modest despite the high elasticities of substitution between the products of the competing countries. However, Taiwan's competitiveness dropped sharply when the N.T. dollar appreciated against the U.S. dollar in two recent years.

Concluding Remarks

We have designed a model to estimate the export demand function faced by Taiwan in the U.S. market. According to our findings, South Korea is Taiwan's

Table 6.5

Index of Taiwan's Export Price Competitiveness in the U.S. Market, 1976–87 by Quarter (1980 = 100)

Quarter	U.S.	Quarter	U.S.
1976:2	98.7752	1983:1	103.9750
3	98.1683	2	105.1880
4	99.2094	3	103.4630
		4	103.0550
1977:1	98.2948	1984:1	102.2070
2	97.8587	2	102.3060
3	98.8202	3	101.6040
4	99.7312	4	102.5620
1978:1	99.8438	1985:1	102.5570
2	100.5320	2	103.1970
3	98.3433	3	103.1120
4	97.8318	4	104.1860
1979:1	95.5372	1986:1	103.6350
2	97.6109	2	102.0900
3	96.6046	3	99.2399
4	98.4308	4	97.7277
1980:1	99.4877	1987:1	96.4507
2	100.4710	2	94.1389
3	100.2580	3	94.5377
4	99.9829	4	94.6419
1981:1	100.7430		
2	101.2240		
3	102.1440		
4	100.8710		
1982:1	102.1400		
2	104.5340		
3	103.6390		
4	103.4890		

Note: calculated from equation (13).

major competitor. The increase in supply capacity or product differentiation may be an important factor in expanding Taiwan's exports. Moreover, the short-run elasticity of substitution between the products of the four Asian NIEs and Japan on one hand and the products of other exporting countries on the other is only 0.76. Thus U.S. imports from these countries cannot be reduced by forcing their currencies to appreciate against the U.S. dollar.

There are also some gaps in our analysis. We have been unable to find more adequate indicators of product differentiation in the competing countries. If we could have found them, our estimates would be more consistent with our theoretical assumptions. Another important gap is the fact that we did not include mainland China in any subgroup of competing countries because we lacked export price data for that country. We hope these gaps can be reduced in further studies.

References

Armington, Paul S. 1969a. "A Theory of Demand for Products Distinguished by Place of Production." Washington, D.C., International Monetary Fund, Staff Papers, pp. 150–178.
———. 1969b. "The Geographic Pattern of Trade and the Effects of Price Changes." Washington, D.C.: International Monetary Fund, Staff Papers, pp. 179–201.
Brown, Murry and Heien, Dale M. 1972. "The S-branch Utility Tree: A Generalization of the Linear Expenditure System." *Econometrica*, Vol. 40(4), July: 737–77.
Chen, Pochih. 1976. *A Statistical Analysis on the Export Competitiveness of Taiwan*. Taipei: Executive Yuan.
———. 1989. "A Multi-Level Export Demand Function with Product Differentiation." Paper presented at the Conference on Taiwan's Trade Issues, Academia Sinica, Taipei.
Chen, Pochih, and Chu, Chung Chong. 1989. *Export Competitiveness by Importing Area*. Taipei: Taiwan Institute of Economic Research.
Deardorff, Alan V., and Stern, Robert M. 1986. *The Michigan Model of World Production and Trade*. Cambridge, Mass.: MIT Press.
Dixit, Avinash K., and Stiglitz, Joseph E. 1977. "Monopolistic Competition and Optimum Product Diversity." *American Economic Review*, June: 297–308.
Gollop, Frank M., and Jorgenson, Dale W. 1980. "U.S. Productivity Growth by Industry." In *New Development in Productivity Measurement and Analysis*, J.W. Kendrick and B.N. Vaccara eds., 17–124. Chicago: University of Chicago Press.
Keller, Wonter J. 1976. "A Nested CES-Type Utility Function and Its Demand and Price-Index Functions." *European Economic Review*. February, Vol. 7(2), 175–86.
Sato, Kazuo, 1967. "A Two-level Constant Elasticity of Substitution Production Function." *Review of Economic Studies*, April, Vol.XXXIV(2) 201–18.

CHAPTER 7

South Korea's Manufactured Exports and Industrial Targeting Policy

JUNG-HO YOO

S. Korea
F14
L60   L52
F13

Introduction

Led by extremely fast export growth, South Korea's economic growth has been very rapid in the past quarter-century. Government intervention has been extensive and, until very recently, took place under authoritarian regimes that suppressed human rights and the labor movement. The general perception has been that the country's unusually rapid export expansion was possible primarily because the government, through a series of five-year economic plans, nurtured certain sectors to become export industries by providing such incentives as subsidies, tax incentives, tariff and nontariff import barriers, etc. Government intervention is usually justified by the argument for nurturing infant industry, as well as the existence of linkage effects among industries, economies of scale, and the absence of efficient capital markets.

In the South Korean economy, a good example of government intervention was seen in the 1970s when the authorities pursued an industrial targeting policy with utmost vigor. This chapter investigates the effects of the 1970s industrial policy on resource allocation among manufacturing industries to see whether the government can really improve the economy by imposing its will on the market process. The effects of government intervention on industrial organization and income distribution are also very important, but they are not considered here; neither are the effects on performance of other sectors.

Section 2 describes briefly the industrial policy of the 1970s and the major tools the government employed. Section 3 traces the growth of value-added components and trends in factor employment in South Korea's manufacturing industries since the 1970s. Section 4 presents estimates of capital efficiencies in manufacturing industries, to assess the effect of government industrial policy on resource allocation. Section 5 examines South Korea's changing share of world exports, which reflects the effects of industrial policy on the international competitiveness of the country's products. Section 6 describes the changes in South

149

Korean economic policies since the late 1970s. The chapter concludes with an assessment of the government's role in South Korean economic growth.

Industrial Policy in the 1970s

On January 12, 1973, the late President Park Chung-hee declared in a press conference, "The government hereby announces a heavy and chemical industry policy that places heavy emphases on the measures to promote the development of heavy and chemical industries" (Office of the Secretary to the President 1976).[1] This marked the official launching of the heavy and chemical industry policy (HCI). There were several reasons underlying the policy. One of the most important reasons, apparently, was concern for national security. In 1971 the United States reduced by one-third the number of its troops stationed in South Korea. This was seen as the beginning of full withdrawal of American troops in the near future. The government felt the need to build up certain industries for defense purposes. Among economic reasons for the HCI policy were the perceived threats to South Korea's export-led growth. On one hand, the rapid export expansion and economic growth of China and other second-tier NICs (newly industrializing countries) raised the prospect that South Korea would soon lose markets for labor-intensive products to these countries with still lower wage rates. On the other hand, protectionism was rising in the industrial countries, particularly against labor-intensive products. These developments led the government to conclude that South Korea needed an industrial structure resembling those found in the advanced industrial countries.

Throughout the 1970s until the spring of 1979, when it announced the Comprehensive Stabilization Program, the South Korean government carried out the HCI policy to promote development of certain "important" or "key" industries. The industries included iron and steel, nonferrous metals, shipbuilding, general machinery, chemicals, electronics, and others designated by the president. Policies for taxes, trade, credit, and interest were all mobilized to promote development of the heavy and chemical industries.

The tax system provided various incentives for qualifying firms in these industries. The major incentives were tax holidays, special depreciation of fixed capital, and a temporary investment tax credit. Legal bases for preferential treatment were provided by laws promoting the development of important industries as well as the Tax Exemption and Reduction Control Law. The latter law underwent a major revision in line with the HCI policy in late 1974, while the laws promoting individual industries were already in place at the beginning of the 1970s.

Kwack (1985) constructed the effective tax rates on marginal return on capital for firms in various industries, assuming that the firms would take full advantage of the major incentives provided by the tax system. His estimates took into account statutory tax rates, various tax incentives, inflation rates, and so on. They covered nine manufacturing industries, some of which were favored by the

Table 7.1

South Korea: Effective Corporate Tax Rate on HCI and Non-HCI Industries (percent)

Year	HCI[a]	Non-HCI[b]
1970	39.2	39.4
1971	34.9	34.7
1972	27.7	29.8
1973	33.5	38.6
1974	29.9	37.7
1975	15.9	52.1
1976	18.0	51.0
1977	17.5	49.5
1978	16.9	48.4
1979	18.3	48.5
1980	18.3	48.8
1981	20.6	51.1
1982	47.1	48.2
1983	40.4	42.2

Source: Kwack 1985, Table 3–5.
[a]Simple average of corporate tax rate for heavy and chemical industries (HCI).
[b]Simple average of corporate tax rate for non-heavy and chemical industries (non-HCI).

HCI policy. For a summary of simple averages of estimated effective corporate tax rates for the HCI and the non-HCI industries, see Table 7.1.

As shown in this Table, there was a great difference in the way the corporate tax system treated the favored and non-favored industries. From the mid-1970s until the early 1980s, firms in the favored industries could take advantage of tax incentives to bring the effective tax rate on their marginal return on capital below 20 percent. During the same period, the effective tax rate for the firms in other industries remained close to 50 percent. These estimates, of course, were not the actual tax rates, but they show clearly the large discriminatory tax incentives given to the favored industries. The preferential treatment almost disappeared in 1982, because the tax system was revamped during the preceding year with the specific objective of eliminating this advantage.

During the 1970s, trade policy severely limited imports of foreign goods that competed with products of the favored industries, reversing the liberalizing trend that began in the mid-1960s. In 1967 the import regime shifted from a "positive list system" to a "negative list system," whereby the Public Notice regarding Exports and Imports, issued periodically by the Ministry of Commerce and Industry (now the Ministry of Trade and Industry), listed the import items that could not be imported without prior government approval.

Liberalization of the import regime in the latter half of the 1960s is reflected in Table 7.2, which shows import liberalization ratios by manufacturing indus-

Table 7.2

South Korea: Import Liberalization Ratio by Manufacturing Industries
(percent)

Industry	1966	1970	1975	1980	1983	1985
All manufacturing industries	8.1	41.7	40.1	56.6	64.1	77.1
Industries favored by the HCI policy:						
chemical	18.9	38.5	35.0	25.7	46.6	66.6
oil refinery	12.5	6.3	12.5	12.5	51.2	53.5
iron & steel	4.9	64.6	67.1	84.2	93.3	95.6
nonferrous metals	16.5	75.9	73.4	88.1	86.4	88.6
nonelectrical machinery	14.1	56.3	33.8	47.6	64.4	76.5
electrical machinery	0.0	23.5	17.6	31.0	46.9	64.5
transport equipment	0.0	65.0	57.5	63.6	49.6	67.2

Source: This table is based on Kim 1988: Appendix Table 1.

Note: Import liberalization ratio is here defined as a ratio of the number of import items that need no prior approval from the government over the number of import items in the industry, excluding import items that can be restricted for noneconomic reasons, such as health or safety standards.

tries for a few selected years.[2] In 1966, the ratio for the manufacturing sector as a whole was at an extremely low level of less than 8 percent. By 1970 it rose to 41.7 percent.

Reversing this trend, the import liberalization ratio declined slightly in the 1970s. For the manufacturing sector as a whole, the ratio decreased from 41.7 percent in 1970 to 40.1 percent in 1975. For purposes of this chapter, the important point is that the decline was due mostly to large drops in the liberalization ratios for the industries promoted by the HCI policy. The policy increased protection for the favored industries by returning some products to the negative list which required prior government approval for imports. This is more noticeable from 1975 to 1980 for nonelectrical machinery and transportation equipment, as well as chemicals. It was made virtually impossible for anyone except exporters to import foreign products if domestic firms produced similar or substitute goods in the designated key industries. Exporters continued to have access to foreign goods at international prices through the tariff rebate system.

Allocation of investment funds was the most powerful tool the government used to implement the industrial policy. The government was directly involved in allocating these funds not only to different manufacturing industries but to individual investment projects as well. To finance numerous large-scale investment projects in the chemical and heavy industries, the National Investment Fund was established in 1974. The commercial banks, which were practically owned by the government at that time, were also directed to make loans to these investment projects. Loans to heavy and chemical industries and other ear-

Table 7.3

South Korea: Share of Policy Loans in Domestic Credit (percent)

Year	Unearmarked	Foreign Trade	Earmarked	All
1970	29.7	5.6	12.2	47.4
1971	30.2	6.1	11.9	48.3
1972	26.7	6.7	20.3	53.8
1973	25.5	10.5	19.4	55.4
1974	23.9	11.3	17.5	52.7
1975	27.2	9.0	16.6	52.7
1976	26.3	10.0	16.2	52.4
1977	29.2	10.4	16.2	55.8
1978	32.3	10.8	17.5	60.7
1979	33.4	10.6	15.0	59.0
1980	34.5	11.5	14.2	59.8
1981	31.3	12.7	14.6	58.7
1982	29.6	12.3	12.5	54.4
1983	28.0	12.7	14.0	54.7
1984	26.5	12.7	14.8	54.0
1985	25.1	12.8	14.8	52.8

Sources: Economic Planning Board, *Korean Economic Indicators*, 1986, and Bank of Korea, *Economic Statistics Yearbook*, various issues (Seoul).
Notes:

"Domestic credit" includes all loans and discounts to the private sector by the Bank of Korea, deposit money banks (commercial banks and special banks), and two development institutions, the Korea Development Bank and the Korea Export Import Bank.

"Unearmarked" includes the loans funded by the National Investment Fund and government fund, loans in foreign currency, and all loans by the Korea Development Bank.

"Foreign trade" includes the loans for foreign trade by deposit money banks and all loans by the Korea EXIM Bank.

"Earmarked" includes the loans for agricultural industries, small and medium-sized firms, home building, etc.

marked ventures were called "policy loans" and were offered at preferentially low interest rates. While the industrial policy was implemented, the policy loans were expanded, representing an increasingly large share of available domestic credit. Table 7.3 shows the shares of various types of policy loans available in domestic credit to the private sector and the changes in the 1970–85 period. The share of all policy loans is shown in column 4, and it may be broken down into three categories. The share of policy loans for foreign trade is shown in column 2; these were used mainly to finance exports in general and were not related directly to industrial targeting. Column 3, titled "earmarked," shows the share of loans designated for the agricultural sector, small- and medium-sized firms, home building, and so on; these loans were not directly related to the industrial policy. The share of unearmarked loans is shown in column 1; these were the most likely source of investment funds directed by the government to favored projects in the heavy and chemical industries.

In the early 1970s, the industrial policy loans already constituted nearly one-half of domestic credit to the private sector. By the late 1970s and early 1980s the policy loans had increased further, accounting for 60 percent of all domestic credit to the private sector. By 1985 the policy share dropped again to slightly above the 50 percent level. This rise and fall in the policy loan share is due almost entirely to the change in the share of unearmarked loans. From the mid-1970s to the end of the decade, the share of these loans rose by approximately 6 percentage points from 27 percent to around 33 percent. Then it declined to around 25 percent by the mid-1980s. Thus, at one point, the government had 60 percent of all domestic credit under its control, and more than one-half of these loans went to projects favored by the industrial policy.

The significance of the credit policy can be better understood by looking at the interest rates on the industrial policy loans. Table 7.4 compares interest rates on ordinary loans, two kinds of policy loan, and the inflation rate. The loans for foreign trade always enjoyed the lowest interest rate, as shown in column 2. The loans for fixed investment favored by the HCI policy carried the next lowest interest rates. For example, the interest rate on the Korea Development Bank loans to finance investments in capital equipment in key industries is shown in column 3. Compared with the discount rate charged by the commercial banks on commercial bills in column 1, it was 5 to 12 percentage points lower in the first half of the 1970s and about 3 percentage points lower in the second half of the decade. Except for one year, it was always lower than the inflation rate in the 1970s. This anomaly of a negative real interest rate did not disappear until prices stabilized in the 1980s.

In early 1979 the government estimated that 74 percent of all fixed investment in the manufacturing sector in 1976 and 82 percent in 1979 went to the heavy and chemical industries (Economic Planning Board 1979). This was primarily the result of the government's intervention in the allocation of investment funds, but strong incentives were also in place for the private sector to invest in the favored industries because the preferential loans carried negative real interest rates. In addition, trade policy must have played an important and indispensable role in complementing other policy measures, which furthered misallocation of resources by strengthening the bias of the incentive structure. By guaranteeing the market for domestic firms and thereby reducing their risks and artificially increasing their profitability, the government's trade approach made the private sector a willing partner of the HCI policy.

Evolution of South Korean Manufacturing Industries since 1970s

The South Korean manufacturing sector grew very rapidly and underwent many changes during the 1970s. Growth experience of individual industries in the

Table 7.4

South Korea: The Interest Rate and Rates of Inflation (percent)

Year	Discount on Bills	Loans for Foreign Trade	Loans for Equipment to Key Industries (by Korea Development Bank)	Consumer Price Index (Percentage Change)
1970	24.30	6.00	12.00	16.01
1971	23.00	6.00	12.00	13.51
1972	17.79	6.00	11.17	11.51
1973	15.50	6.67	10.00	3.20
1974	15.50	8.83	10.00	24.48
1975	15.29	7.67	12.00	25.20
1976	16.33	7.42	12.42	15.27
1977	17.25	8.00	13.00	10.17
1978	18.02	8.58	14.17	14.46
1979	18.75	9.00	15.00	18.26
1980	23.33	12.00	20.50	28.70
1981	19.50	12.00	18.00	21.30
1982	12.38	10.75	12.75	7.25
1983	10.00	10.00	10.00	3.38
1984	10.27	10.00	10.31	2.30
1985	10.75	10.00	9.56	2.47

Source: Bank of Korea, *Economic Statistics Yearbook*, (Seoul, various issues).

Note: The interest rates (columns 1 to 3) are weighted averages, weights being the number of months they were in use in a given year. When the rate is given as a range, the midpoint is taken.

sector varied widely. This section describes the salient features of changes in the manufacturing industries, particularly those related to the HCI policy.[3]

Growth of Value-Added

The outstanding feature in the evolution of the manufacturing sector in the 1970s is its rapid growth. In terms of constant-price value-added, the growth rate of the manufacturing sector as a whole at times exceeded 20 percent per year (see Table 7.5). However, the pace of growth was not uniform throughout the period covered in this chapter. It slowed down considerably in the last few years of the 1970s and in 1980, when the South Korean economy experienced negative growth. In the 1980s the manufacturing sector regained some of its earlier growth pace.

Growth rates in various industries were not uniform either. Industries in the HCI group generally grew faster than the rest (see Table 7.5). From 1970 until 1978, the HCI growth rate was roughly 50 percent higher than the non-HCI pace.

Table 7.5

South Korea: Growth of Value-Added of the Manufacturing Sector

A. Value-Added, Industry Groups (in billions of 1980 won)

	1970	1973	1975	1978	1980	1983	1985
All manufacturing	2,613	4,534	5,896	10,259	11,214	1,409	616,805
HCI	658	1,290	1,805	3,796	4,132	5,536	7,096
HCI(-chem)	278	687	1,062	2,484	2,605	3,985	5,302
Non-HCI	1,956	3,244	4,091	6,463	7,082	8,560	9,709

B. Average Annual Percentage Changes, Industry Groups

	1970– 73	1973– 75	1975– 78	1978– 80	1980– 83	1883– 85	1970– 78	1978– 85
All manufacturing	20.2	14.0	20.3	4.6	7.9	9.2	18.6	7.3
HCI	25.2	18.3	28.1	4.3	10.2	13.2	24.5	9.3
HCI(-chem)	35.1	24.3	32.7	2.4	15.2	15.4	31.5	11.4
Non-HCI	18.4	12.3	16.5	4.7	6.5	6.5	16.1	6.0

Sources: See Appendix, page 171.

The HCI(-chem) excludes the chemical industries; it grew at an extremely rapid average annual rate, exceeding 30 percent from 1970 to 1978. This group, comprising basic metals and all types of machinery, including transportation equipment, doubled its real value-added every three years or less. Its growth rate was roughly twice that of the non-HCI group.

From 1978 to 1985, the growth rates of all three groups dropped precipitously. But except for the last few years of the 1970s, the HCI and HCI(-chem) groups grew more rapidly than the non-HCI group. As a result, the relative sizes of these groups changed considerably. In real terms, the value-added of the HCI group was about one-third the amount of the non-HCI group in the early 1970s and rose to seven-tenths as large in 1985. The HCI(-chem) value-added became even larger during the same period. It was less than 15 percent of the non-HCI value-added at the beginning of the same period and rose to more than 50 percent of the amount in 1985.

Employment Growth

The growth of employment in the manufacturing sector was similar to the value-added growth (see Table 7.6). Employment grew at an average annual rate of nearly 11 percent in the 1970–78 period but less than 2 percent from 1978 to 1985, a much sharper decline than in value-added growth. The HCI and non-HCI groups show similar contrast between the two time periods. However, the employment growth was much faster in the former group in both periods. After a

Table 7.6

South Korea: Employment Growth in the Manufacturing Sector

A. Employment, Industry Groups (1,000 persons)

	1970	1973	1975	1978	1980	1983	1985
All manufacturing	1,188	1,561	2,114	2,681	2,648	2,858	2,993
HCI	176	278	397	592	616	751	846
HCI(-chem)	154	248	362	549	573	710	803

B. Average Annual Percentage Changes, Industry Groups

	1970–73	1973–75	1975–78	1978–80	1980–83	1983–85	1970–78	1978–85
All manufacturing	9.5	16.4	8.2	−0.6	2.6	2.3	10.7	1.6
HCI	16.5	19.4	14.3	2.0	6.8	6.1	16.4	5.2
HCI(-chem)	17.0	20.9	14.9	2.1	7.4	6.3	17.2	5.6
Non-HCI	8.2	15.7	6.7	−1.4	1.2	1.0	9.5	0.4

Sources: See appendix, page 171.

surge in 1974 and 1975, non-HCI employment nearly stopped growing from 1978 to 1985, while growth resumed in the HCI group, albeit at a relatively low rate.

Capital Accumulation

Capital accumulation in the manufacturing sector was also very rapid during the 1970–85 period, at an average annual rate of 14.5 percent. Like the trend in value-added, the rate of capital accumulation slowed down considerably in the 1978–85 period but not as sharply as employment. The HCI rate of capital accumulation was much higher than that of the non-HCI. The rate for the HCI(-chem) was particularly high, two or more times faster than the non-HCI between 1973 and 1978. However, in the last few years of the 1970s, capital accumulation proceeded more rapidly in the non-HCI than in the HCI; in the 1978–85 period, it slowed down much less than the pace for the non-HCI (see Table 7.7).

Changes in Capital Intensity

Because employment growth was slower than capital accumulation, the entire manufacturing sector's capital intensity (the capital-to-labor ratio) more than tripled from 1970 to 1985. The rise was more rapid in the 1978–85 period, chiefly because employment growth almost stopped, particularly in the non-HCI group (see Table 7.8).

For the 1970–85 period as a whole, capital intensity did not rise as rapidly in the HCI as in the non-HCI. In 1970 the HCI capital-labor ratio was 2.3 times that

Table 7.7

South Korea: Capital Accumulation in the Manufacturing Sector

A. Capital Stock, Industry Groups (in billions of 1980 won)

	1970	1973	1975	1978	1980	1983	1985
All manufacturing	5,050	9,355	13,063	19,879	26,381	33,488	39,245
HCI	1,433	2,877	4,674	7,893	10,013	13,281	16,100
HCI(-chem)	680	1,568	3,009	5,872	7,584	10,161	12,482
Non-HCI	3,617	6,478	8,389	11,986	16,368	20,207	23,146

B. Average Annual Percentage Changes, Industry Groups

	1970–73	1973–75	1975–78	1978–80	1980–83	1983–85	1970–78	1978–85
All manufacturing	22.8	18.2	15.0	15.2	8.3	8.3	18.7	10.2
HCI	26.2	27.5	19.1	12.6	9.9	10.1	23.8	10.7
HCI(-chem)	32.1	38.5	25.0	13.6	10.0	10.8	30.9	11.4
Non-HCI	21.4	13.8	12.6	16.9	7.3	7.0	16.2	9.9

Sources: See appendix, pages 171–172.

of the non-HCI; in 1985 it declined by 1.8 times, due mainly to the slower rise in the chemical industry's capital intensity.

One of the most noteworthy phenomena was the decline in the non-HCI capital-labor ratio in the middle of the 1970s and its considerable rise subsequently. From 1973 to 1975 the ratio declined from 5.05 million 1980 won per laborer to 4.89 million won. This took place while the capital intensity was rising 7 percent a year on average in the HCI group as a whole and accelerating to nearly 15 percent a year in the HCI(-chem). It should be noted that before this drop, capital intensity was increasing almost as rapidly in the non-HCI group as in the HCI.

Capital intensity decreased mainly because employment increased more rapidly than capital accumulation, even though real wages were rising. In the first half of the 1970s per capita income increased more than 9 percent and the manufacturing wage rose nearly 6 percent per year, both in real terms. Along with this rising "factor price," employment in the non-HCI surged in 1974 and 1975. This caused the drop in the non-HCI capital-labor ratio, because there was no accumulation of capital. In fact, capital stock in the non-HCI increased at a respectable rate of about 14 percent per year in the 1973–75 period. Consequently, the non-HCI capital-labor ratio was only 14 percent greater in 1978 than in 1973, compared with a 69 percent increase of the ratio for the HCI(-chem) during the same period.

However, this relative position was abruptly reversed in 1979 and 1980, when the capital-labor ratio for the non-HCI rose at an average annual rate of 18.5

Table 7.8

South Korea: Capital-Labor Ratio in the Manufacturing Sector

A. Capital-Labor Ratio (in millions of 1980 won per laborer)

	1970	1973	1975	1978	1980	1983	1985
All manufacturing	4.25	5.99	6.18	7.41	9.96	11.72	13.11
HCI	8.14	10.34	11.78	13.32	16.25	17.67	19.04
HCI(-chem)	4.40	6.33	8.32	10.69	13.24	14.31	15.55
Non-HCI	3.57	5.05	4.89	5.74	8.05	9.59	10.78

B. Average Annual Percentage Changes, Industry Groups

	1970–73	1973–75	1975–78	1978–80	1980–83	1983–85	1970–78	1978–85
All manufacturing	12.1	1.5	6.3	15.9	5.6	5.8	7.2	8.5
HCI	8.3	6.8	4.2	10.4	2.8	3.8	6.3	5.2
HCI(-chem)	12.9	14.6	8.7	11.3	2.6	4.3	11.7	5.5
Non-HCI	12.2	−1.6	5.5	18.5	6.0	6.0	6.1	9.4

Sources: See appendix, page 171 and Tables 7.5, 7.6, and 7.7.

percent versus 11.3 percent for the HCI(-chem) and 10.4 percent for the HCI as a whole. This trend continued in the 1980s, mainly because of the relatively low rate of employment growth in the non-HCI group.

Factor Market Distortion

One can safely infer from the contrasting capital-labor ratio changes within the HCI and non-HCI that the two groups faced widely differing wage-rental ratios. During the 1970–78 period, the wage-rental ratio must have been rising for the HCI group but falling or rising very slowly for the non-HCI. For the 1978–85 period, almost the opposite was the case: although the wage-rental ratio was rising for both groups, it must have been rising more rapidly for the non-HCI.

As the two groups faced the same wage rate, the wage-rental ratio for the HCI and non-HCI could diverge only if the two groups experienced different rental rates. The key to the explanation must lie in the HCI policy, which strongly favored investment in industries in that group during the 1970s. Various incentives and direct government involvement in credit allocation lowered the cost of capital for the HCI but raised it for the non-HCI. The high cost of capital for non-HCI entrepreneurs could have resulted simply from unavailability of investment funds from the banks at the government-controlled interest rates or from excessively high interest rates charged outside. Thus, in the 1970–78 period the wage-rental ratio for the non-HCI remained relatively low despite the rising real wage rate, but it rose for the HCI along with the increase in the real wage rate.

The rise in manufacturing real wages accelerated from an average annual rate of 6 percent in the first half of the 1970s to 12.6 percent in the second half of the decade. Obviously, this tended to raise the wage-rental ratio for all manufacturing industries, but it must have pushed the ratio higher for the non-HCI group because the HCI policy had made its capital cost higher than the cost for the HCI.

Moreover, changes in the real interest rate tended to raise the wage-rental ratio faster for the non-HCI group. As inflation was brought under control in the 1980s, the nominal interest rate did not decline as rapidly, thereby raising the real interest rate (see Table 7.4). In this process, the interest rate on the preferential policy loans declined more slowly than rates on other loans, as part of the government's effort to curtail discriminatory practices. Consequently, the real interest rate rose more rapidly for the HCI than for the non-HCI. This also had the effect of raising the wage-rental ratio more rapidly for the non-HCI group than for the HCI.

A rise in the wage-rental ratio has greater impact when capital intensity is lower (or labor intensity is higher). Indeed, another way of describing the contrasting capital intensity experiences of the HCI and non-HCI is to state that until 1978 the HCI group had achieved a greater reduction of its labor intensity than the non-HCI did. Therefore, the rising wage-rental ratio meant a greater increase in production cost for the non-HCI group. This had occurred in the second half of the 1970s. In response, in the late 1970s and 1980s many industries in the non-HCI group laid off workers or raised their capital intensity by accumulating capital faster than they increased employment.

The Effect on Resource Allocation: Capital Efficiency

A good yardstick to measure the success or failure of an industrial policy is the degree of efficiency in an economy's use of its domestic resources. The greater the improvement in efficiency that an industrial policy permits, one may say, the more successful the policy is. This immediately raises a question: How shall we measure efficiency itself? The critical answer depends on the society's objective function. For purposes of this chapter we assume that the sole argument in the objective function is enhancement of the gross national product. Since we focus only on the manufacturing sector, we want to find out how the HCI policy affected the efficiencies of various manufacturing industries in their use of the society's resources to create the value-added.

Obviously, it would be advisable to compare the value-added that an industry creates with some kind of combined input of resources into the industry. When there is more than one factor of production, we need to know the prices that reflect accurately the worth of those factors to the society. One should use these prices when combining the inputs of different production factors to determine how much of the society's resources the industry uses. But these prices, which are the opportunity costs or shadow prices of the factor services, are not readily available.

Instead, we estimate the efficiency in use of one factor, capital, and look for evidence of the HCI policy effects on this efficiency. The efficiency of capital in a given industry may be measured by the amount of value-added created by a unit of capital employed in the industry. First, we estimated the value-added created by labor in the industry. The labor contribution was subtracted from the industry's value-added and the remainder was considered the portion created by capital. We took the ratio of the remainder of the value-added to the capital stock employed in the industry as the measure of capital efficiency.

The value-added created by labor was estimated by using the Input-Output (I-O) Tables of the Bank of Korea. The Employment Table, a part of the I-O Tables, reports the number of paid employees and unpaid workers (self-employed people and family members), the sum of which is the total employment in a given industry. The Transactions Table, another part of the I-O Tables, reports the value added by the I-O industries and the compensation to paid employees. The reported compensation certainly understates the value-added created by the labor employed in the industry sector, since some value-added must have been created by unpaid workers. To estimate the total value-added created by all labor in an industry, the reported compensation was divided by the number of paid employees and the quotient was multiplied by the total number of employed persons. The result is the compensation that would have been paid to all laborers if the unpaid workers had received the same average wage as the paid employees. This imputed compensation is assumed to equal the value-added created by labor in the industry. These results for individual I-O industries were aggregated to obtain the desired estimates at the three-digit Korean Standard Industrial Classification (KSIC) level or at even higher aggregate levels.

The estimates of capital efficiencies for the HCI and non-HCI groups are presented in Table 7.9. For the manufacturing sector as a whole, the estimated efficiency was relatively stable around 30 percent in the 1970s and dropped to around 25 percent in the 1980s. When manufacturing industries were grouped into those favored or not favored by HCI policy, the estimated capital efficiency of the favored group (HCI) was generally lower than that of the nonfavored group (non-HCI) during the 1970s but became higher in the 1980s. The capital efficiency of the HCI group showed a greater sensitivity to business fluctuations, dropping substantially in 1975 and 1980, when the domestic economy and the world economy slumped after the oil crises of those years.

Examination of individual industries constituting an industry group reveals that capital efficiency estimates vary widely. For this reason we divide the aggregate HCI industry into two subgroups: "chem," which includes the chemical industries, and the rest of the HCI, which is termed "HCI(-chem)." The latter comprises basic metal industries and all kinds of machinery industries. The disparity in estimated capital efficiency was greater between the two subgroups than between the HCI and the non-HCI (see Table 7.9). Capital efficiency ranged

Table 7.9

South Korea: Capital Efficiency of the Manufacturing Sector (percent)

	1970	1973	1975	1978	1980	1983	1985
All manufacturing	31.8	31.8	30.2	31.9	24.8	24.8	25.1
HCI	31.0	31.3	27.3	32.3	25.9	26.7	27.9
Chemicals	42.4	39.0	37.5	52.4	51.8	43.2	42.6
HCI(-chem)	22.7	27.5	22.2	26.3	18.4	22.2	24.3
Non-HCI	32.3	32.0	31.8	32.0	24.3	23.7	23.4
Adjusted HCI	18.1	24.9	21.6	27.0	20.2	23.3	24.9
Adjusted Non-HCI	27.9	28.3	28.1	28.4	21.2	20.6	20.7

Sources: See appendix, page 171 and Tables 7.5, and 7.7.

between 40 and 50 percent for chem but only between 20 to 30 percent for HCI(-chem).

The main reason for the chem group's high efficiency was the unusually high capital efficiency of the petroleum refinery industry. One of the non-HCI industries also had an unusually high capital efficiency: the tobacco industry. In both instances, monopoly power was apparently the reason for high capital efficiency. The petroleum refinery industry was and still is dominated by a few firms, while tobacco manufacturing was a government monopoly.

The estimates of capital efficiency, excluding these two industries, are presented in Table 7.9 as "adjusted HCI" and "adjusted non-HCI." During the 1970s capital efficiency for the adjusted HCI was substantially lower than for the adjusted non-HCI. The simple average of the four years reported during the 1970s was slightly less than 23 percent for the adjusted HCI and somewhat higher than 28 percent for the adjusted non-HCI. The difference of 5 percentage points (a difference of roughly 20 percent) is significant. Also significant is the degree to which the marginal product of capital (assuming the productions are linearly homogeneous) was lower in the industries favored by HCI policy than in other industries during the 1970s. In a static world, an optimum allocation of a scarce resource requires equality of its marginal product among differing uses. The marginal products of capital in the favored and nonfavored industries could have been brought more closely in line with each other if capital accumulation had been slower in the favored industry group and faster in the non-favored groups, if the law of diminishing returns had operated in manufacturing industries. But this was not the case; in fact, there was too much investment in the favored industries during the 1970s (see "Capital Accumulation" on page 158 and Table 7.7).

Obviously, the HCI policy was at least partly responsible for the misallocation of capital. The HCI industries were protected from foreign competition, and strong tax and financial incentives were provided to attract investment to this group. Moreover, the government was directly involved in allocating the investment funds to favored industries. As a result, the capital-labor ratio rose more rapidly in the favored industries than in the rest of manufacturing when the HCI policy was vigorously pursued. For most of the 1970s, the rate of increase in the capital-labor ratio was particularly rapid in the HCI(-chem) group compared with the non-HCI group.

However, the relative magnitudes of capital efficiency in the favored and nonfavored industry groups were reversed in the 1980s: the capital-labor ratio rose more rapidly in the nonfavored industries than in the favored groups. Thus, as capital intensity rose faster in the non-HCIs than in the favored industries, its capital efficiency dropped below that of the favored group. Capital efficiency is expected to decline if the law of diminishing returns holds true. When the petroleum and tobacco industries are excluded, the average difference in favor of the adjusted non-HCI was 5 percentage points in the 1970s; in the 1980s the average difference was 2 percentage points in favor of the adjusted HCI, or a difference of 3.5 percentage points when the year 1980 is excluded.

Export Competitiveness

We may take South Korea's market share of world exports as an indicator of the competitiveness of its industries. We will first compare the share of South Korea's total exports on the world market with that of the competing countries. Then we will compare market shares of the favored and nonfavored industries of South Korea.

South Korea's market share of world exports rose rapidly after 1974 and peaked in 1978, fell during the next two years, and rose again. This pattern holds when OPEC exports are excluded from the world total to eliminate the direct effects of oil price rises (see Table 7.10).

In contrast, the combined world market share of the six competing countries whose export product composition most closely resembled South Korea's in the late 1970s continued to rise after 1978.[4] This rise actually accelerated in the latter half of the 1970s. Thus, there was apparently no shift of world demand from South Korea to cause the decline in its share of world exports. The decline must have been due to a deterioration of the country's competitiveness, caused by conditions inside South Korea.

Table 7.11 presents the world market shares of the HCI and non-HCI groups of South Korea's major export products. Each group includes the major (but not all) export goods of its component industries. These products accounted for 80 percent or more of all the country's manufactured exports. The world market shares of these two groups of export products show distinctly divergent trends.

The HCI group's share of the world market rose throughout the 1970s and up to 1983, excepting only the worldwide recession year of 1975. However, the world market share of the non-HCI group expanded relatively smoothly and

Table 7.10

South Korea's Market Share in World Exports (percent)

Year	Korea's Share in Total World	Korea's Share in World Excluding OPEC	Competitor's Share
1970	0.296	0.315	3.682
1973	0.615	0.669	4.327
1976	0.854	1.007	4.493
1979	0.988	1.153	4.898
1980	0.937	1.121	5.183
1981	1.157	1.367	5.474
1982	1.271	1.461	5.540
1983	1.462	1.637	5.776
1984	1.654	1.826	6.442
1985	1.697	1.854	6.625
1986	1.749	1.856	6.611

Sources: International Monetary Fund, *International Financial Statistics,* Washington, D.C. (various issues). United Nations, *Yearbook of International Trade Statistics,* New York, (various issues).

Note: Competitors include Hong Kong, Israel, Portugal, Spain, Taiwan, and Yugoslavia.

rapidly in the first half of the 1970s, then fluctuated considerably in a basically upward trend. The periods of decline and slow growth could be effects of the HCI policy, which slowed down capital accumulation in the non-favored industries that produced traditional major export goods. There is evidence to support this suspicion. According to Yoo's estimates (1984), an increase of 1 percent in production capacity reduced export prices of the heavy and chemical industries by 0.37 percent and export prices of light industries (very similar to the non-HCI group in this chapter) by a full percentage point. Yoo's estimate was based on quarterly data from the first quarter of 1972 to the third quarter of 1982. The result suggests that the export products of light industries could have been more competitive if there had been more fixed investment in this sector.

Of course, one should also consider the effects of the won overvaluation in the latter half of the 1970s. The exchange rate was kept constant at 484 won to the U.S. dollar from 1974 to 1979, while the rate of inflation was higher in South Korea than in the United States. The won overvaluation probably reinforced the adverse effects of the HCI policy on the competitiveness of the light industries' export products and, ultimately, of the country's total exports in the late 1970s.

Table 7.11

South Korea's Selected HCI and Non-HCI Products in the World Market
(percent)

Year	Main HCI Products	Main Non-HCI Products	% of South Korea's Total Manufactured Exports
1968	0.03	1.35	83.18
1969	0.07	1.50	81.66
1970	0.07	1.83	87.24
1971	0.09	2.13	88.05
1972	0.20	2.45	87.83
1973	0.33	3.52	84.69
1974	0.42	3.44	84.46
1975	0.33	4.13	84.23
1976	0.48	5.51	84.38
1977	0.54	5.56	80.32
1978	0.70	5.92	83.93
1979	0.71	5.52	82.72
1980	0.80	5.27	82.62
1981	1.04	6.40	82.19
1982	1.25	6.10	83.36
1983	1.60	6.23	85.00

Sources: Same as Tables 7.3 and 7.10.
Notes:
Included in HCI products (with SITC codes in parentheses) are chemical elements and compounds (51), petroleum products (332), iron and steel (67), nonferrous metals (68), nonelectrical machinery (71), electrical machinery (72), transport equipment (73)
Included in non-HCI products are rubber products (62), plywood (631), textiles (65), travel goods (83), clothing (84), footwear (85), miscellaneous manufactures (89).
The last column shows the percentage of South Korea's manufactured exports of the exports of the products included in columns 1 and 2.

The 1979 Stabilization Program and the 1980s Policies

Table 7.12 shows how the South Korean economy performed in the 1970s. Inflation, which was subsiding after the first oil crisis in the mid-1970s, reaccelerated toward the end of the decade. Nominal wages, which had risen at an annual rate of approximately 30 percent since the mid-1970s, began to decelerate marginally in 1979 as the real GNP growth was slowing down. In foreign trade, export growth in real terms started to decelerate sharply in 1977, while absolute export volume declined in 1979. Economic growth slackened suddenly, causing the growth rate to drop by 4.8 percent in 1980.

South Korea's negative growth is often attributed to unfavorable external developments. Chief among these was the second oil crisis in 1979, which adversely affected the world economy and international trade. The political uncer-

Table 7.12

Performance of South Korea's Economy, 1971–86

Year	GNP	WPI	CPI	Wage	Real Export	Trade Balance (US$ millions)
			Percentage Changes			
1971	9.1	8.6	13.5	16.2	29.45	−1,046
1972	5.3	13.8	11.7	13.9	50.22	−574
1973	14.0	6.9	3.1	18.0	57.20	−566
1974	8.5	42.1	24.3	35.3	9.26	−1,937
1975	6.8	26.5	25.3	27.0	22.76	−1,671
1976	13.4	12.2	15.3	34.7	35.79	−590
1977	10.7	9.0	10.1	33.8	19.06	−477
1978	11.0	11.6	14.1	34.3	14.36	−1,781
1979	7.0	18.8	18.3	28.6	−0.96	−4,395
1980	−4.8	38.9	28.7	22.7	11.39	−4,384
1981	5.9	20.4	21.3	20.1	17.65	−3,628
1982	7.2	4.7	7.2	14.7	6.43	−2,594
1983	12.6	0.2	3.4	12.2	16.29	−1,763
1984	9.3	0.7	2.3	8.1	15.66	−1,036
1985	7.0	0.9	2.5	9.9	7.56	−19
1986	12.9	−1.5	2.8	9.2	12.98	4,206

Source: Economic Planning Board, *Major Statistics of Korean Economy,* 1987 (Seoul).

tainty following the assassination of President Park in late 1979 was also an important factor. Moreover, unusually cool weather during the summer of 1980 severely reduced agricultural output. However, these developments could not have been responsible for the worsening economic performance in 1978 and 1979 or for the rapid slowdown of real export growth that began as early as 1977.

In the late 1970s, it seemed that the accumulated ill effects of the industrial policy were finally halting the long-sustained growth momentum. Fortunately, the government recognized the seriousness of the situation and began to introduce substantial changes during the spring of 1979. In April 1979, the South Korean government announced the Comprehensive Stabilization Program, which attempted to redress the excesses of the HCI policy of the 1970s. The program was based on recognition that the industrial policies had caused havoc in all aspects of the country's economic life: management of macroeconomic policies; management of small and large firms, whether in the favored or neglected industries; daily lives of average- and low-income families; competition in the international markets; and Korea's credit standing in the international financial market. The macroeconomic policies, which should have bounded and contained the industrial policies, had become hostage to the industrial policies.

The new program cited the following problems as directly related to excessive investment in the favored heavy and chemical industries: increased investment that outstripped the industry's increased supply of skilled labor and capacity to absorb the related technology; development of bottlenecks in the supply of light industry products; and low rates of capacity utilization. The seriousness of the capacity utilization problem was clearly indicated in the Comprehensive Stabilization Program announcement of April 1979. The major contents of the program included:

- restrictive budget management, with expenditure cuts and deferral of public investment projects;
- restrictive monetary policy, with particular attention to improved operation of preferential policy loans and interest rates;
- plans to adjust investment in the heavy and chemical industries;
- measures to facilitate the supply and stabilize the price of daily necessities;
- measures to prevent real estate speculation;
- measures to support low-income people.

Implementation of the monetary and fiscal policies envisaged in the program was under way when, later in the year, the government switched to a reflationary policy package in response to the second oil crisis and the ensuing global recession. Nevertheless, the Comprehensive Stabilization Program may be viewed as the turning point in economic policy: it set a new direction toward pursuit of a "private-sector-led economy" instead of a "government-led economy." The basic tenets, which became more firmly established in subsequent years, were to attain price stability, establish an unbiased incentive structure, and promote competition within the domestic market and from abroad. Emphasis shifted from the promotion of particular industries to improvement of overall economic efficiency, and from intervention at the industry and firm level to greater reliance on the market.

By 1983, conservative management of fiscal and monetary policies had succeeded in reducing the double-digit inflation rate to less than 3 to 4 percent a year, as measured by the wholesale price index (WPI) and consumer price index (CPI) in Table 7.12. The effort to bring inflation under control was helped by the decline in world prices of crude oil and other raw materials, imports of which South Korea depended heavily on. As the inflation rate declined, the government reduced the subsidy elements in the preferential policy loans by lowering interest rates on nonpreferential policy loans faster than rates on favored policy loans. As Table 7.4 indicates, the interest rate differential between the two kinds of loans had largely disappeared by 1983. Government-owned stocks of commercial banks were sold to the public to increase bank independence of government influence.

To counterbalance the increased concentration of economic power in a small number of business conglomerates, a side effect of the HCI policy, the Anti-Monopoly and Fair Trade Act was enacted toward the end of 1980 and a Fair

Trade Commission was created. The Act reduced the number of items whose prices had been government-controlled on grounds that they were produced by monopolies or oligopolies. Establishment of small- and medium-sized firms was encouraged, and various support measures were devised to compensate for their inability to compete on an equal footing with the giant conglomerates. Over the years, dissatisfaction with the plethora of special laws designed to promote particular industries had been increasing. These laws were either abolished altogether or replaced in 1986 by the Industrial Development Law, which was based on the principle that policy supports to specific industries should be abandoned in favor of functional supports.

Import liberalization had been discussed and implemented to some extent as the balance of payments improved in the middle of the 1970s. This approach gathered support as an essential remedy for inflation and the distorted incentive structure. The government removed an increasing number of importable items from the list of products that had required prior government approval for importation, despite broad-based public opposition. Thus, the import liberalization ratio was raised even during the late 1970s and early 1980s, when the balance of payments was deteriorating sharply.

Conclusion: An Assessment of the Government's Role

The government's intervention in the economy had been extensive and, at times, pervasive until it began to decline after the announcement of the Comprehensive Stabilization Program in 1979. The extent of government intervention did not differ much during the two preceding decades, but the content of economic policies differed significantly. In the 1960s, export expansion was the primary goal of nearly all economic policies. In the 1970s, changes in the international economic and noneconomic scenes led the government to attempt to build a more "advanced industrial structure," similar to those in the advanced industrial countries. To pursue this goal, the government had become directly and extensively involved in resource allocation at the sectoral, industry, and even firm levels. But in the 1980s, government intervention declined substantially.

Insofar as export promotion is concerned, economic policies of the 1960s worked much better than those of the 1970s. There was substantial protection of domestic industries, but the main policy emphasis of the 1960s was to encourage private sector exports with a variety of incentives. Policy was results-oriented and did not discriminate among industries and firms. In contrast, the 1970s policy was process-oriented, attempting to achieve the goal by promoting selected industries. The government was deeply involved in choosing the "right" industries for promotion, supplying them with the "right" amount of investment and complementary factors at the "right" time and place, and so on.

Moreover, the government's 1960s export promotion policies were intended largely to offset the bias against exports that had been engendered by protection of domestic industries for import substitution in the 1950s. The incentives to firms to export or sell their products in the domestic market were almost equal in the late 1960s (Westphal and Kim 1982).[5] While the 1960s policy created a largely neutral incentive system, the 1970s policy created a strong bias toward domestic sales. South Korean exports expanded faster and the economy performed better in the 1960s, when the private sector faced a neutral incentive system, than in the 1970s, when the government attempted to substitute intervention for the private-sector market forces and created a bias toward domestic sales.

One may disagree with this assessment of the effects of government intervention and call attention to the rapid export expansion and economic growth of the 1980s to argue that the 1970s industrial policy made possible the more recent strong economic performance. This argument sounds plausible because the most visible gains in South Korean exports during the 1980s were posted by such products as consumer electronics, semiconductors, other computer-related products, telecommunication equipment, and passenger cars. These were mainly the products of "heavy" industries that had been greatly favored under the 1970s industrial policy. Therefore, some people think that the 1970s industrial policy should receive some credit for Korea's economic performance in the 1980s. However, this conclusion is questionable and needs further investigation.

First, the rapid 1980s increase in South Korean exports was due mostly to the increased volume of sales to the United States. From 1980 to 1987, total exports increased by $30 billion, with 46 percent of this going to the United States. The large increase in South Korean exports to the United States was part of an overall surge in U.S. imports, which was due primarily to: (1) the Reagan administration's fiscal policy, which raised government expenditures without raising tax revenues; (2) the depreciation of the real effective exchange rate, due to an 8 percent depreciation of the won in 1985 against the U.S. dollar; and (3) the steep appreciation of the Japanese yen and German mark since 1985, which reduced competitiveness of their exports vis-a-vis South Korean products.

Second, U.S. restrictions on imports from Japan diverted some demand to South Korean products. These developments were particularly favorable to exports by the industries that had been targeted by the 1970s industrial policy. These external developments contributing to the rapid increase in South Korean exports to the United States and the rest of the world occurred in the 1980s. There is no reason to believe that the South Korean government foresaw them and took them into account in formulating its industrial policies of the 1970s.

Nevertheless, the government should be given credit for having recognized in time the problems created by the industrial targeting policy. By adopting the Comprehensive Stabilization Program in 1979, it laid the foundation for Korea's subsequent economic revival.

One may also ask what would have happened if the government had not promoted the heavy and chemical industries during the 1970s. A direct answer to this question is very difficult, but for an indirect response one may look at the performance of an economy in similar circumstances during the mid-1970s that did not adopt the same kind of industrial policy. Taiwan comes fairly close to being such an example. Taiwan's exports did not suffer because it lacked an industrial policy, indeed they expanded faster than South Korea's. Thus it seems highly likely that even without the industrial policies of the 1970s, South Korea could have taken advantage of expanding export opportunities that developed in the United States and other parts of the world. However, the composition of its export products might have been different.

In short, the effect of the South Korean government's interventionist role in the country's economic development was very different from the popular perception that it engineered the phenomenal increase in the country's exports and economic growth. When the economy performed well under the extensive government intervention of the 1960s, the net effect of intervention was a neutral incentive system. When the government attempted to put in place the "advanced industrial structure" it deemed desirable, the industrial targeting policy was not successful. The case for the government's role in economic development seems stronger when its policies are not actively interventionist, when it seeks instead to control inflation through conservative management of fiscal and monetary policies; maintain a trade regime that gives exporters access to foreign intermediate goods at international prices; liberalize imports or undertake the necessary depreciation of the currency (despite broad-based opposition).[6]

Probably the government's greatest contribution was its willingness to reconsider policies once they were found to be unworkable. The ultimate criterion for policy decisions was economic performance, and policy adapted flexibly to changing domestic or international conditions. Ironically, the flexibility in economic policy was demonstrated by authoritarian governments. Having come into power with questionable legitimacy, the two previous governments had relied heavily on strong economic performance to build and maintain their legitimacy. The power elite left economic decision making largely in the hands of the technocrats. In general, South Korean technocrats and bureaucrats have not had strong vested interests in the welfare of specific social classes or sectors or industries of the economy. Their choice of policies was guided by considerations of overall economic performance.

This characterization seems to describe accurately the behavior of decision makers when their policy choices involved issues that could have had a decisive impact on the economy as a whole, such as major decisions on exchange rate policy, money supply, fiscal management, and trade policy. This is not to say that the South Korean political system and bureaucracy were immune to the influence of special-interest groups or were corruption-free. More likely, pressures from special-interest groups affected only decisions on details within the overall policy framework, particularly those that did not materially affect overall economic performance.

Appendix: Description of the Data

Value Added

Manufacturing industries' value-added is a component of the national income estimates prepared by the Bank of South Korea. The estimate was available in 1980 won at the three-digit KSIC level.

Labor and Labor Share

The number of laborers employed in the manufacturing industries was obtained from Employment Tables, which are part of the Input-Output Tables estimated by the Bank of South Korea. The Employment Table reports two groups of laborers: paid employees and unpaid workers, who include the self-employed and family members. The number of laborers used in this study is the simple sum of the two groups.

Capital Stock

Pyo's estimates (1988) of capital stock are used. Included in Pyo's estimates of capital stock are buildings and structures, machinery and equipment, and transportation equipment. Employing the polynomial-benchmark method, Pyo used investment data from two national wealth surveys for the years 1968 and 1977 as well as census and annual surveys of the mining and manufacturing sectors. He has made two series of capital stock estimates: gross and net. The estimates were available at the three-digit KSIC level.

In this study I used Pyo's estimates of gross capital stock in 1980 constant prices, with some adjustment of the estimate. In a few instances Pyo estimated the combined capital stock of two 3-digit KSIC industries.[7] In these instances the estimated capital stock was split into two parts, one for each of the component industries. First, Pyo's capital stock for 1973 was split into two by referring to the component industries' book value of capital stock as reported in the mining and manufacturing census for the same year. The split was done in accord with the component industry's share of the sum of the book value of the capital stock. In the second step, annual increments in Pyo's capital stock were again split into two. This time, an increment was split according to the component industry's share in the sum of the acquisition of new capital stock. In the final step, to obtain a new time series of capital stock for a component industry, the split increment of capital stock was added to the split capital stock for the years after 1973 or was subtracted from it for the earlier years.

Notes

1. Source is in Korean; English translation of the quoted text is the author's.
2. The import liberalization ratio in an industry is usually defined as a ratio of import

items that need no prior approval from the government for importation under the Foreign Trade Act over the total number of import items in the industry. The definition of the ratio used in Table 7.2 differs from this usual definition in that it excludes from the numerator items whose importation can be restricted by other laws or regulations, such as those intended to enforce health or safety standards.

3. A few preliminary notes should be made at this point on the presentation that follows. This chapter covers the 1970–85 period. Data are shown only on those years for which the Bank of Korea estimated the Input-Output Tables. The availability of the tables restricts the number of observations. In all, twenty-three-digit Korea Standard Industrial Classification (KSIC) industries are considered. In order to facilitate explanation, these industries are aggregated into a few groups. One is a group of seven three-digit industries that were favored by the HCI policy and is labeled "HCI." (The favored industries are identified in the tables presented in this paper.) Another group is labeled "non-HCI," and it includes all the rest of manufacturing industries. The group labeled "HCI(-chem)" excludes chemical industries from HCI. Data used are described in the appendix.

4. The countries were Hong Kong, Israel, Portugal, Spain, Taiwan, and Yugoslavia. After excluding natural-resource–based products, the product compositions of forty-seven bigger trading countries' manufacturing exports of the late 1970s were compared with South Korea's at the two-digit SITC level. Austria, Italy, and India had compositions more similar to South Korea's than some countries recognized here as competitors, namely, Yugoslavia, Portugal, and Spain. However, they were not included as competitors on the grounds that their per capita income was very different from Korea's.

5. For a more general discussion of export promotion policy and import substitution policy, see Krueger, Anne O., 1980.

6. Until and through the last depreciation of won in 1985, public sentiment was against the depreciation, even though it was necessary to prevent overvaluation of the currency. Since the last depreciation, public sentiment has turned against the appreciation, as it is seen as a submission to foreign pressure. The vagary of public sentiment on this matter would be an interesting subject of investigation into human behavior.

7. The pairs of industries whose combined capital stock was estimated were apparel (KSIC 322) and footwear (KSIC 324), industrial chemicals (351) and other chemical products (352), petroleum refinery (353) and petroleum and coal products (354), and, last, iron and steel (371) and nonferrous metal (372). Either these industries were individually interesting, or, as in the case of petroleum refinery and industrial chemicals, the industry favored by the HCI policy was lumped together with one that was not favored.

References

Bank of Korea. *Economic Statistics Yearbook.* Various issues.
Economic Planning Board. 1979. *Comprehensive Stabilization Program.* April 17.
———. *Major Statistics of Korean Economy.* Various issues.
———. 1986. *Korean Economic Indicators.*
International Monetary Fund. *International Financial Statistics.* Various issues.
Kim, K. S. 1988. *The Economic Effects of Import Liberalization and Industrial Adjustment Policy.* Korea Development Institute. In Korean.
Krueger, Anne O. 1980. "Trade Policy As an Input to Development." *American Economic Review* 70, no.2 (May).
Kwack, Taewon. 1985. *Depreciation and Taxation of Income from Capital.* Seoul: Korea Development Institute. In Korean.

Nam, Sang-woo. 1985. "Integrated Economic Stabilization Programs in South Korea." Presented at the International Seminar on the Process of South Korea's Industrialization, Seoul, South Korea, March 8–21.

Office of the Secretary to the President. 1976. *Collection of President Park Chung-hee's Speeches*, vol. 5. Seoul: Daehan Gongron-sa. In Korean.

Pyo, Hak-Kil. 1988. *Estimates of Capital Stock and Capital/Output Coefficients by Industries for the Republic of Korea (1953–1986)*. KDI working paper 8812.

United Nations. *Yearbook of International Trade Statistics*. Various issues.

Westphal, Larry E., and Kim, Kwang-Suk. 1982. "South Korea." In *Development Strategies in Semi-Industrial Countries*, ed. Bela Balassa et al. Baltimore: Johns Hopkins University Press.

Yoo, Jung-ho. 1984. "Estimation of Some Desegregated Export and Import Functions." *The Korea Development Review* (Fall 1984). Seoul: Korea Development Institute. In Korean.

CHAPTER 8

Changing Strategies of Manufactured Export Expansion in Singapore

VICTOR FOOK AI NG AND SHU-CHIN YANG

Introduction

The Singapore experience in economic growth and export expansion is an interesting case of strategy changing promptly because of political circumstances and economic environment. Singapore's economic development strategy up to 1965, while the country was part of Malaysia, was based almost exclusively on Malaysia's policies. Thus, from 1963 to 1965, the economic strategy was based on import substitution and the idea that there would be this domestic market. In August 1965 Singapore was separated from Malaysia, however, and soon after that the strategy refocused entirely on export development. The slogan was: The world is our market. Along with rapid economic growth, manufactured export expansion, and increased competition from other developing countries, manufacturing industries in Singapore have to move upward. In an island economy like Singapore, they have to be associated with multinational corporations (MNCs) in capital, technology, and production. Hence, the slogan was soon broadened to: The world is our market, and the world is our factory. With remarkable success in constantly upgrading its manufacturing industry and exports, Singapore has recently been facing greater competition from other newly industrializing economies and increasing protectionism from developed countries. Thus, toward the end of the 1980s it gradually shifts to a strategy of developing into an international total business center for manufacturing and services, particularly in financial and information services.

Early Export Development Strategy and Performance

With a domestic market of only 3 million people in mid-1990, Singapore's economic development strategy has been dictated by international geopolitical factors. Since it had no natural resources, it had to import virtually all components and other inputs for the manufacturing sector. It is, therefore, not

175

surprising that Singapore had to subscribe to and practice free trade. Duty-free and hassle-free imports mean cheaper inputs for the export manufacturing sector.

The export incentives to Singapore's development fall under two broad categories as included in the Economic Expansion Incentives (Relief from Income Tax) Act of 1967. Basically, the first category of incentives was designed to attract foreign manufacturing investment in Singapore, while the second was designed to promote export of manufactured goods.

To attract new investment in the industrial sector, the government modified old fiscal incentives and introduced new ones. Any firm in an industry that is designated a pioneer status was, and still is, exempted from tax on company profits for a period of five to ten years, depending on such factors as the level of investment, its capital and skill intensity, research and development expenditures, and so on. For projects involved in advanced technology and long gestation periods the tax exemption period can exceed ten years. In addition, to attract foreign investment generally no limits were placed on foreign participation. Foreign firms were allowed to repatriate profits and to import workers with skills not available locally (Lim and Fong 1986: 19; Chng 1987: 383).

The main incentives for encouraging exports, introduced in 1967 and liberalized then, allow taxing approved export profits at 4 percent rather than at the usual rate of 40 percent. The incentive period is normally five years, but it can be extended to fifteen years for projects with fixed capital assets of over S$150 million, provided Singapore permanent residents own at least 50 percent of the paid-up capital. Besides, firms that do not qualify for pioneer status or export incentives, are provided with an investment allowance, a tax credit of up to 50 percent of new fixed investment for an approved manufacturing and technical servicing project (Lim and Fong 1986: 19).

Initially, the foreign investment strategy was simply to attract export-oriented foreign investment. Thus, in the 1960s and early 1970s, Singapore was very popular among MNCs from the United States, the EC, and Japan. The bulk of such investments was relatively labor-intensive, what one could call "screwdriver operations." The export incentives benefited the local and relatively small Singapore manufacturing companies.

The chief salesman of Singapore, it was often said, was the first prime minister, Mr. Lee Kuan Yew who pioneered the strategy of attracting foreign direct investment (FDI) and promoting exports. The entire national psyche is geared toward sales, exports, and going international. During his administration several investment and export promotion agencies were set up.

The Singapore Economic Development Board (EDB) established in 1960 has been and still is the agency to administer the development of pioneer industries. The Singapore Trade Development Board (TDB) is the official body responsible for trade promotion. This statutory body has the flexibility of a private-sector organization and the credibility of a government agency. In addition, several

Table 8.1

Singapore: GDP by Industry, 1960–90 (at 1985 market prices) (percent)

	1960	1970	1980	1990
Agriculture, fishing, and quarrying	3.8	2.4	1.4	0.5
Manufacturing	16.6	24.8	29.5	29.0
Utilities	1.7	1.9	2.0	2.1
Construction	5.3	9.5	7.1	5.3
Trade	24.6	22.0	18.9	17.6
Transport and communication	8.8	7.3	12.0	14.2
Financial and business services	14.0	16.9	20.5	27.7
Other services	19.6	14.9	11.6	10.1
Adjustment items	5.6	0.3	–3.0	–6.0
Total GDP	100.0	100.0	100.0	100.0
GDP growth rate per annum (%)		9.2	9.1	7.1
		(1960–70)	(1970–80)	(1980–90)

Source: Department of Statistics, Singapore *Yearbook of Statistics, 1991* (Singapore).

other government agencies provide supporting services to the TDB and export-ers. These agencies include the Singapore Institute of Standards and Industrial Research (SISIR), the National Computer Board (NCB), and the National Pro-ductivity Board (NPB).

The only government-registered trading company set up specifically to pro-mote the export of Singapore-manufactured products is Intraco Ltd. It is a con-glomerate whose activities range from export and import trading to investment in resource-based activities, manufacturing, and distribution of Russian-made auto-mobiles. Intraco is a commercial success but a policy failure. It is a failure as a trading company set up to promote Singapore's manufactured products. To be fair, Intraco has been very successful in certain pioneering activities such as strategic investment in China as well as critical links with the Eastern European bloc countries.

Voluntary trade associations play an important role in the promotion of Singapore's manufactured products. The primary organization for this purpose is the Singapore Manufacturers' Association. Various Chambers of Commerce tend to engage in trade and commercial activities, as their name implies. These organiza-tions are now under pressure to upgrade and provide specialized services.

With industrial and export promotion largely across-the-board and unselec-tive, the initial period of Singapore's open industrialization exploited fully its given comparative advantage then—the abundant unskilled labor. Thus, the labor-intensive industries, particularly the textiles and clothes, grew very rapidly. Rapid growth also occurred in new labor-intensive, export-oriented electric and non-electric manufacturing. In 1970, the share of the manufacturing sector in

Table 8.2

Singapore: Principal Statistics of Manufacturing, 1960–91

	Unit	1960	1970	1980	1990	1991
Establishments[a]	Number	572	1,774	3,369	3,707	3,867
Employment	Number	32,900	125,121	287,227	351,843	357,626
Output	S$ Million	1,661	4,613	32,710	71,458	74,870
Value Added	S$ Million	185	1,129	8,573	21,615	23,139
Direct Exports	S$ Million	1,043	2,044	19,875	47,100	49,180
Direct Exports as % of output	%	31.7	44.3	60.8	65.9	65.7

Source: Ministry of Trade and Industry, Singapore. *Economic Survey of Singapore,* 1991. p.124.
[a]Refers to establishments engaging 10 or more persons and includes rubber processing.

GDP increased to 24.8 percent from 16.6 percent in 1960. It surpassed the trade sector and became the largest sector of the economy (see Table 8.1). Manufactured exports (SITC 5–8, excluding entrepôt trade) more than quadrupled (see Table 8.3). Total direct exports' share in total output increased from 31.7 percent in 1960 to 44.3 percent in 1970. In 1972, the value of domestic manufactured exports for the first time exceeded manufactured re-exports. Employment increased sharply from 32,900 to 125,121 (see Table 8.2).

Soon, Singapore's industrialization entered into a new stage. In 1972, the Tripartite National Wage Council (NWC) was established to oversee orderly wage adjustments in line with equity, price stability, and the maintenance of Singapore's competitiveness in the world market. Meanwhile, the government perused a more selective and vigorous industrial promotion strategy. In 1975, the Capital Assistance Scheme was introduced, and the Joint Venture Bureau was established. In 1976, the Small Industries Finance Scheme (SIFS) was launched and then extended (ESIFS). The Pioneer Industries now (1975) focused on metal engineering, ship machinery and equipment, optical products, chemicals, petroleum chemicals and pharmaceuticals, and electronic and electrical equipment—all capital, skill and technology-intensive industries.

During the 1970s, in spite of the oil crises and world recessions, the manufacturing sector still grew fairly rapidly, more than the GDP growth rate of 9.1 percent. Its share in GDP increased from 24.8 percent in 1970 to 29.5 percent in 1980 (Table 8.1). Direct manufactured exports accounted for 60.8 percent of manufactured output in 1980 as compared with 44.3 percent in 1970 (Table 8.2). Direct manufactured exports in 1980 was almost ten times that in 1970. All this indicates a strong export-lead industrialization.

Table 8.3

Singapore: Domestic Exports by Major Commodity, 1960–91
(at current prices in U.S.$ million)

SITC	Commodity	1960	1970	1980	1990	1991
0	Food	48	105	601	958	1,125
1	Beverages and Tobacco	21	12	103	386	398
2	Crude Materials	9	30	152	460	449
3	Mineral Fuels (including oil bunkers)	—	792	14,180[a]	17,137	17,202
	Oil bunkers	—	280	2,568	2,785	3,012
4	Animal & Vegetable Oils	20	49	394	587	556
5	Chemicals	27	43	573	3,619	4,208
	Medicinal Products	2	8	258	251	253
	Plastic Materials	—	3	100	958	1,447
6	Manufactured Goods	51	170	1,323	2,127	2,247
	Veneer & Plywood	1	41	334	94	79
	Textile Yarn & Fabrics	8	23	262	193	239
	Iron & Steel	2	12	116	153	194
7	Machinery & Equipment[b]	17	198	6,567	32,352	34,477
	Office Machines	—	34	264	14,519	15,194
	Industrial Machines	—	34	264	512	477
	Electric Motors & Resistors	—	6	346	1,004	1,119
	Radio & Television Receivers & Parts	—	20	1,872	4,846	4,726
	Electronic Components & Parts	—	N/A	2,203	5,148	5,984
	Ships, Boats, & Oil Rigs	—	10	588	303	274
8	Miscellaneous Manufactures	25	144	1,886	4,866	5,096
	Clothing	5	65	757	1,793	1,779
	Optical & Photographic Equipment	—	0	154	146	173
	Watches & Clocks	—	3	143	184	221
	Musical Instruments	—	2	90	274	260
9	Miscellaneous	—	289	27[a]	262	273
	TOTAL	217	1,832	25,805	62,754	66,031

Source: Ministry of Trade and Industry, Singapore. *Economic Survey of Singapore, 1991*. p.146.
[a]Oil bunkers were transferred from miscellaneous to mineral fuels.
[b]Prior to 1984, automatic data processing machines were excluded.

Strategy and Performance in the 1980s

Two decades of rapid growth and industrialization had turned Singapore from a labor-surplus economy to a full employment economy toward the end of the 1970s. With rising real wages, Singapore began to feel the pressure of increasing competition in exports. This was particularly so, as most Southeast Asian developing countries had also gradually changed from import institution industrial development strategy to export promotion strategy. As their wage levels were (and still are) lower than Singapore's, the comparative advantage of labor-intensive manufactured exports was being shifted away from Singapore to other countries in the region. Meanwhile, as low growth and unemployment in developed countries persisted, protectionism mounted. In view of these developments, Singapore had to reshape its industrialization strategy to defend further growth.

In 1979, the government launched a long-term indicative plan—the Ten Year Plan (Goh 1981), in which a new strategy of industrial restructuring—dubbed the "Second Industrial Revolution"—was announced to aim at promoting higher value-added skill and technology intensive industries.

The key macroeconomic target in the plan for the 1980s was to achieve real GDP growth of 8–10 percent per annum. If that could be achieved by 1990, Singaporeans would enjoy the same standard of living as the Japanese did in 1977–78: a per capita income of S$16,300. The decade of the 1970s had seen a rapid rise in Singaporean living standards, with per capita income growth averaging 8 percent annually in real terms. The goal, therefore, was to repeat that performance for the 1980s.

The underlying assumption of the ten-year plan was that the high-growth scenario of the 1970s would prevail in the 1980s. This meant continued demand for Singapore's goods and services, which, in turn, implied that Singapore would remain internationally competitive. From the supply side, the plan envisaged one major change: Whereas growth in the 1970s was based on labor force increases, growth in the 1980s would have to come from productivity increases. The plan, therefore, set a crucial target for the 1980s: productivity growth of 6 percent to 8 percent. This target could be achieved only through a drastic restructuring of the Singapore economy.

There were two interlocking options for restructuring the economy. First, Singapore could upgrade current economic activities by enhancing the value-added per worker: higher labor productivity and more extensive automation and mechanization. Second, Singapore could promote new economic activities: new investment in higher-skilled, high-knowledge, and high-technology manufacturing, as well as service activities.

The ten-year plan mapped out several strategies to hasten the pace of economic restructuring. The key strategies were:

- three-year wage correction policy to bring wages, then up 20 percent across the board, in line with market levels and to induce more efficient use of labor;

- tax incentives to encourage substitution of capital for labor through greater automation, mechanization, and computerization;
- investment promotion strategies aimed at attracting higher value-added and skill-intensive activities; and
- increased emphasis on skills development in the training and educational institutions, leading to a more skilled work force.

For the manufacturing sector, the plan's targets were:

- real value-added growth of 11 percent to 13 percent per year;
- share of GDP to increase to 31 percent (in constant prices) in 1990;
- productivity growth of 8 percent to 10 percent per year; and
- employment growth of 2.6 percent per year.

In 1981, the selection of pioneer industries for promotion was refocused toward more technology-oriented and high-value added industries, such as heavy engineering, machine tools and precision instruments, petrochemicals, pharmaceuticals, plastics, electronics and electrical industries, and research and development.

However, in the mid-course of the plan period, the performance of the manufacturing sector was mixed. With the impact of higher labor cost (partly as a result of government policy) the pace of manufacturing growth decelerated. While growth of real value-added in manufacturing showed a strong upward trend until 1981, the average annual growth rate was only 5 percent during the 1980–84 period, well below the 9 percent average rate of the 1975–79 period and the plan target rate of 11–13 percent. The sector's share of GDP in current factor costs was 27 percent in 1980 but declined to 23 percent in 1984. In 1984–85, world recession finally extended to Singapore; GDP declined by 1.8 percent for 1985, the most severe setback in twenty years.

But with greater availability of trained manpower and under the pressure of higher labor cost, the pace of automation in industry accelerated. Gross fixed assets increased more rapidly, resulted in doubling gross fixed assets per worker during 1979–83. Thus, labor productivity increased sharply in 1979–84 at a rate of 5.9 percent per annum, compared with 0.4 percent per annum in 1973–79 (Chng, Low, and Toh 1989: 18), almost reaching the lower end of the plan target.

However, moving to a more mature phase of development implied that further growth in manufacturing would be harder to achieve. Growth would have to be achieved by doing the right things right and restructuring instead of merely expanding. Singapore would have to watch its cost competitiveness more closely, particularly because the world economy was going through a period of slow growth with continued high unemployment and protectionism. In view of all this, the Economic Committee, established in April 1985 and chaired by the

Minister for Trade and Industry, reshaped the strategy in its 1986 report, (Ministry of Trade and Industry 1986) as follows:

- Move beyond being a mere production base. Encourage establishment of operational headquarters here; do research and development; provide financial, administrative, technical, and management services to subsidiaries in the region.
- Exploit other growth niches such as:
  — high-value, low-volume, performance-sensitive products;
  — parts and components, which are less sensitive to protectionism and incur lower freight costs to major markets;
  — activities in which speed and efficiency command a premium;
  — highly profitable activities in which tax incentives have maximum impact, investment in new growth areas;
  — improving the range and quality of supporting industries;

- Increase the number and quality of trained technical personnel;
- Reduce costs; improve business efficiency.

Regarding investment incentive, the Committee recommended improving the existing package by adding:
  — a post-pioneer (after expiration of the period designated as a pioneer industry) incentive that grants a reduced tax rate of 10 percent on post-pioneer profits;
  — a R&D incentive in the form of a reserve equal to 20 percent of pre-tax profits, which can be set aside for R&D expenditure;
  — for venture capital investors, a front-end tax deduction against other income, equal to 50 percent of the equity investment; establishment of venture capital funds to attract high-technology companies;
  — tax changes to encourage the use of leased plants and equipment;
  — wider use of loan schemes such as the Capital Assistance Scheme (CAS) to promote desirable projects;
  — use of the CAS to provide equity capital to companies, with buy-back options on reasonable terms, particularly for important and strategic projects; and
  — incentives for companies undertaking R&D activities to hire more engineers and technicians.

In relation to cost reduction and improvement of business efficiency, the Committee recommended the following specific objectives:
  — reduce costs of production by lowering employer's contributions to the Central Provident Fund (the government's forced savings scheme) to 10 percent, and maintaining wages at existing levels for two years;

— encourage three-shift operations, which would have a great impact on total cost reduction;

— improve product design and development capability through more liberal financial support;

— improve the educational system, particularly the universities, by emphasizing creativity and innovation;

— extend the 90 percent tax exemption on royalty income to other forms of creative work;

— build up a strong infrastructure to support R&D work;

— bring management up to date by exposing managers to modern organizational methods and systems and continuously upgrading the skills of workers, technicians, and engineers;

— encourage spending and investment to counteract recession with a reduction of corporate and personal income taxes to 30 percent; and

— encourage plant up-dating with a 30 percent investment allowance for expenditures in new plant and machinery.

As a result of the efforts in cost reduction and efficiency improvement, Singapore has been able to maintain its international competitiveness. With this strength and world and local economic recovery since late 1986, Singapore experienced strong export and GDP growth (again over 9 percent a year) for the rest of the decade. Meanwhile, new policies for achieving the long-term strategy were introduced. "The wage bargaining process was revised to allow for greater flexibility and productivity related awards. Further reductions in personal and corporate taxation were accompanied by the introduction of value added tax. Efforts to diversify the economy were renewed, with tax changes introduced in the 1988 budget aimed at promoting the services industries, overseas investment, and the development of Singapore as a financial centre." (EIU 1992–93: 11).

For the decade of the 1980s, Singapore's GDP growth slowed down to 7.1 percent per year from over 9 percent for the previous two decades. The manufacturing sector grew slightly at a slower rate than GDP, thus its share in the GDP fell from 29.5 percent in 1980 to 29 percent in 1990. Financial and business services, and transportation and communications, both mostly in connection with international business, showed the fastest growth, and their share in the GDP increased to 27.7 and 14.2 percent respectively (see Table 8.1). Evidently, the economic structure of Singapore has been changing to more international service-oriented than manufactured exports-oriented, although the latter is still very important and closely service related.

Direct Manufactured Exports

Within the manufacturing sector, electronic production has increased rapidly and has become the largest industry. In 1991, its value-added accounts for one third

Table 8.4

Singapore: Top Ten Industries in Manufacturing, 1991
(value added in percent)

Electronic Products	33.8
Petroleum Products	8.6
Transport Equipment	7.4
Paints, Pharmaceutical & Other Chemical Products	6.3
Machinery Except Electrical & Electronic	6.1
Fabricated Metal Products	6.0
Industrial Chemicals & Gases	4.7
Printing & Publishing	4.4
Electrical Machinery, Apparatus & Appliances	4.2
Food	2.7
Total Manufacturing[a]	100.0

Source: Ministry of Industry and Trade, Singapore, *Economic Survey of Singapore*, 1991, p.51.
   Note: [a]Excluding rubber processing.

of the total manufactured value-added. Far behind that, are petroleum products and transport equipment, and then paints, pharmaceutical and other chemical products, non-electrical machinery and fabricated metal products (all between 6 to 8.6 percent of total manufactured value-added in 1991) (see Table 8.4). All these sub-sectors are capital, skill, and technology-intensive. The labor-intensive industries such as textiles, clothing, footwear, wood products, etc. are no more in the top ten list, all below 2.7 percent of total manufacturing value-added (see Table 8.4). Clearly, Singapore's industrial restructuring strategy has achieved to a large extent the upgrading of the manufacturing sector.

Direct manufactured exports' share in total manufacturing output increased further in the 1980s, albeit at a slower rate than the previous two decades. The share increased from 61 percent in 1980 to about 66 percent in 1990 and 1991, apparently reaching a plateau (see Table 8.2). However, the newly promoted high skill, capital, and technology-intensive manufactured exports have grown much faster than the average. Among the large items of these manufactured exports have been chemicals, particularly plastic materials, and machinery and equipment, particularly microcomputers and other office equipment, radio and television receivers and parts, and electronic components and parts.

Challenges and Strategies for the 1990s

Entering into the 1990s, the development of the small island open economy of Singapore is facing challenges from both demand and supply side. On the supply side, it has to deal with high and rising wages in competition of manufactured

exports with a growing number of Asian countries, some are low-wage economies such as China and Indonesia, and some are newly industrializing economies
with skilled labor, capital, and technology comparable to or catching up with
Singapore. On the demand side, it is confronting with rising protectionism in its
major trade partners in the West.

Regarding protectionism, for instance, in the 1980s, as the declining dollar
failed to narrow its trade deficit, the United States introduced a number of trade
bills and conducted a number of bilateral negotiations to constrain imports. In
1986, Singapore faced petitions launched by U.S. companies to graduate three
export items from the U.S. Generalized System of Preferences (GSP). The three
products were non-folding wooden chairs, wooden furniture other than chairs,
and certain steel structures. With effect from January 1989, Singapore would no
longer be eligible for benefits under the U.S. Generalized System of Preferences.

Antidumping and countervailing duty (CVD) actions have been two common
problems faced by Singapore. In 1986, antidumping actions were filed in the
United States for the first time against Singapore's exports of steel tubes and
color television picture tubes. In 1988, two new investigations on ball bearings
and industrial belts were initiated. In 1991, a new antidumping case was filed
against Singapore's exports of portable electric typewriters.

The United States is also considering the application of countervailing duty
(CVD) to some Singapore exports. Investigations include carbon wire rods, ball
bearings, and industrial belts. The immediate effect of antidumping and CVD
investigations was a slowdown of exports of these products while the investigations were underway. In 1991, Singapore and the United States signed a land-
mark Trade and Investment Framework Agreement. The Agreement established
the mechanism for consultation on bilateral trade and investment issues and for
identifying trade opportunities.

Singapore's exports also attracted antidumping charges in Australia. First was
monoethylene glycols (MEG). The case was terminated in October 1990 upon
Singapore's termination of the export. In 1988, Singapore exports of power
cables and lavamisole hydrochloride, a drug used for the manufacture of a wide
range of veterinary products, faced Australia's antidumping charges. In 1991, a
total of 6 antidumping cases were filed against Singapore companies. New Zealand also conducted its first investigation on Singapore's exports of lead-acid
batteries in 1991.

Problems arising from protectionism in the EC were less serious. However,
high tariffs, subsidy programs, quota restrictions and anti-import campaigns continued to be targeted at agricultural products sourced from the region through
Singapore. Singapore's exports of color television sets and umbrellas also continued to be subjected to import restrictions by the importing countries (Singapore Ministry of Trade and Industry, *Survey* 1986: 32; 1988: 36; 1991: 92).

The international trade environment is now clearly different from the 1970s,
and the new protectionism in the developed countries and intensifying competi-

tion with the other industrializing countries have already slowed and will continue to slow down Singapore's manufactured exports.

The Singapore government has been very dynamic in dealing with changing situations. It has been very prompt in adapting its development strategy to meet any new challenge. The 1986 Report of the Economic Committee had already recognized that economic planning for the 1990s and beyond would require new strategies and policy initiatives to sustain long-term competitiveness. The focus of the new strategy is for Singapore "to become an international total business center for manufacturing and services" and a major exporter of services focused on information technology. (Sullivan in LePoer, 1989: 137). The extension from the concept of "the world is our factory and market" to "being a world total business center" by adding the development of the service and information sectors is again based on the country's basic and new comparative advantage: good geographical international business location, political stability, good and efficient government, efficient transportation and communication facilities and other infrastructure, high level education and skill, free market, free enterprise, and flexibility.

To implement this strategy, several schemes have already been initiated (see particularly Ministry of Trade and Industry, 1990: 60–61; 1991: 60–61, 81 and IEU, 1992–1993: 21) as follows:

- Promotion of automation. This is a key strategy to alleviate labor shortage and enhance productivity. Three programs in particular were implemented to promote automation:
  — Automation feasibility studies: The Applied Automation Centre provides consultancy to help companies identify areas within their operations which could be automated to save labor. As at end–1990, automation feasibility studies have been completed for 161 manufacturing companies.
  — Automation leasing and purchasing program: by end–1990, 114 projects were financed under the program to purchase automation equipment.
  — Industry-Wide Automation Development Program: at end–1990, ten projects have been identified in eight different industries, including insertion of odd-sized components for the printed circuit board assembly industry, sewing line transporter system for the garment industry and automated system for electroplating for the surface-finishing industry.

- The development of the "Growth Triangle."
  To overcome the land limitation and extend the comparative advantage, Singapore initiated the idea of the "Growth Triangle" to promote Singapore, Malaysia's Johor state, and a number of Indonesian island groups as a single economic unit, thus combining Singaporean manufacturing skills and developed infrastructure facilities with the lower land and labor costs of its neighbors. Two agreements (cover-

ing investment promotion and protection and other matters) were signed with the Indonesian government in 1990, and Singaporean firms are already establishing themselves in the Batam Industrial Park and other locations. As of April 1992, a total of S$5.3 billion from Singapore and other countries had been invested in Batam.

- Promotion of local enterprises
The high tech strategy has least impact on the domestic manufacturers and efforts are now being formulated to improve finance, regulation, and support to change this. The government is now encouraging small- and medium-sized enterprises to expand abroad, in order to stay competitive. It is also masterminding an intensive effort to diversify export markets, concentrating on Japan and western Europe. Local enterprises account for 70 percent of total employment and 59 percent of total value-added in the manufacturing, commerce, and service sectors.

- Foreign Investment and MNCs
Foreign investment generated more than 70 percent of manufacturing output and more than 80 percent of manufactured exports. The MNCs not only contribute to the know-how, the management and entrepreneurship, but also bring world market to the doorstep and subcontracts to local enterprises. They also keep close contact with the changes in world demand and taste and can adapt promptly with the changes. Much of their recent investment has been in emerging sectors such as electronics and pharmaceuticals. MNCs will generate more growth in earnings in financial services. In addition to the incentives already granted to foreign investment, the government is also trying to moderate wage and labor benefits increases to keep costs low. It also gives incentives for MNCs to train local workers to upgrade their skills.

- Research and Development
National expenditure on research and development (R&D) increased from 0.2 percent of GDP in 1978 to 0.9 percent in 1990. The private sector provided more than half currently. The National Technology Plan aims to achieve a total national expenditure on R&D to 2 percent of GDP in 1995. A Research and Development Assistance Scheme has established to funding (S$2 billion over five years beginning in 1991) private company-sponsored research. Other programs include financing manpower development and technology infrastructure. The National Science and Technology Board was established in early 1991.

- Trade Promotion
The Government continued to promote Singapore's goods and services abroad and develop Singapore as a premier international trading hub. De-

sign has been recognized as an important strategic competitive tool for marketing Singapore products overseas. The Design Council was established to mount strategies to develop national design resources. To promote Singapore-made goods, and project the image of Singapore as a producer of world-class products, showcase outlets of Singapore products were opened. The drive to diversify markets for Singapore's products and services continued. Special attention was paid to newly liberalizing economies in Asia, the former Soviet Union and Eastern Europe as well as to post-Gulf war business opportunities in the Middle East.

Conclusion

Singapore's manufactured export expansion and economic growth have been remarkable. The good performance is a result of combined efforts of the government, business, and workers. The government's choice of development strategy has been very dynamic. It has recognized promptly the changes in international and domestic economic conditions and tried to meet the challenges ahead of the game. Having fully exploited its dynamic comparative advantage, Singapore has progressed rapidly from import-promotion to export promotion of manufacturing, from labor-intensive manufacturing and export to skill, capital, and technology-intensive manufacturing and export. It is now engaging in activities in developing into an international manufacturing and services center, with rapid development of financial, communications, and information services. In a way, it has led and still is leading other Asian developing countries in the process of industrialization and development.

References

Chung Ming Wong, "Trends and Patterns of Singapore's Trade in Manufactures," in Colin I. Bradford, Jr. and William Branson, ed., *Trade and Structural Change in Pacific Asia*, National Bureau of Economic Research, The University of Chicago Press (Chicago), 1987.

Chng Ming Kng, Linda Low and Toh Mun Heng. 1989. *Industrial Restructuring in Singapore*, Chopman Publishers, (Singapore).

Goh Chok Tong. 1981. "Highlights of Singapore's Economic Development Plan for the Eighties," Appendix I of *Towards Higher Achievement, Budget Speech, 1981*, March (Singapore).

The Economist Intelligent Unit (EIU), 1992–93. *Singapore: Country Profile, Annual Survey of Political and Economic Background*; Published by *Economist*, (London).

Lim, Linda and Pary Eng Fong. 1986. *Trade, Employment and Industrialization in Singapore*, International Labor Office (Geneva).

Ministry of Trade and Industry, Economic Committee. 1986. *The Singapore Economy: New Direction*, February 1986. (Singapore).

Ministry of Trade and Industry, Singapore, 1986, 1988, 1991. *Economic Survey of Singapore, 1986, 1988 and 1991*. (Singapore).

Sullivan, Margaret. 1989. "The Economy," Chapter 3 in Barbara Leitch LePoer (ed), *Singapore, A Country Steady*, December 1989, Library of Congress (Washington, D.C.).

189-206

CHAPTER 9

Manufactured Exports from Thailand: Performance and Prospects*

SOMSAK TAMBUNLERTCHAI

Thailand
F14
L60
O29

Introduction

The international community has focused much attention on Thailand recently, in the expectation that the country will soon join the club of newly industrializing economies (NIEs). Thailand's high economic growth rate in recent years, combined with the rapid expansion of its manufactured exports, has obviously contributed to this expectation.

It is true that over the years Thailand has been able to achieve respectable economic growth with reasonable stability. Its manufacturing sector has become increasingly important, with manufactured exports expanding substantially. But considering the per capita income level of its people (US$1570 in 1991, see Chapter 1, Table 1.1) and the state of industrial development, Thailand still has a long way to go before it can match the economic status enjoyed by the NIEs at present. Further expansion of Thailand's manufactured exports will face quite a number of problems. The international environment surrounding Thailand in the years to come will be quite different from what the NIEs encountered when they first embarked on export promotion.

This chapter presents a profile of Thailand's manufactured export sector, investigates various factors contributing to its past performance, and assesses the prospects for further growth of such sales. The first section provides an overview of the manufacturing sector's role in the Thai economy. We review structural changes in the Thai economy over the past three decades, as well as changes in industrialization policy emphasis. In the next section, we investigate the performance and prospects of the manufactured export sector in some detail and identify several factors contributing to its past growth. In the final section, we assess prospects for further growth of manufactured exports from Thailand in light of the changing international trading environment. We

---

* This chapter was updated and slightly expanded by Dr. Shu-Chin Yang.

identify positive as well as negative factors affecting future growth of the country's manufactured exports.

The Manufacturing Sector in the Thai Economy

Growth and Structural Change

Since Thailand embarked on the path to economic development by introducing its First National Economic Development Plan in 1961, the country has undergone significant growth and structural change.

During the 1960s, the Thai economy was able to grow rapidly, paced by strong public sector investment in infrastructure expansion and agricultural commodity production. Private-sector investment in the manufacturing sector, particularly in import-substituting industries was also actively encouraged. Since the early 1970s, Thailand belatedly shifted to export-led development strategy. This set out a subsequent rapid industrialization and growth. Despite two oil crises in the 1970s and two world economic recessions in the 1980s, Thailand's GDP grew at a respectable annual average rate of 7.3 percent in 1965–80 and 7.9 percent in 1980–91 (see chapter 1, Table 1.1). GDP increased further in 1992 by 7.5 percent (Bank of Thailand, 1993).

Among the structural changes the most significant of the past three decades has been the shift out of agriculture toward manufacturing and other nonagricultural sectors. Agriculture as a share of gross domestic product has declined steadily from 40 percent in 1960 to 27 percent in 1970, 20.6 percent in 1980, and 14.5 percent in 1990 and 13.5 percent in 1991. In contrast, the role of manufacturing has increased substantially from 11.7 percent of total GDP in 1960 to 16 percent in 1970, 21.7 percent in 1980, and 24.7 percent in 1990, and 24.9 percent in 1991. According to the latest series of GDP estimates, since 1979 manufacturing has overtaken the agricultural sector as the largest generator of income. Other sectors have also become more important in the Thai economy, among them public utilities (electricity and water supply); transportation and communication; banking, insurance, and real estate; and services (see Table 9.1).

Agriculture's share of the labor force and exports has also declined over the years. The former's share fell from more than 80 percent in 1960 to about 60 percent in 1987, while the latter's share decreased from 82.7 percent in 1961 to 27.9 percent in 1987 and further to 15.1 percent in 1991. Manufacturing sector products made up only 2.4 percent in 1961 and rose sharply to 76.2 percent of the country's export earnings in 1991. (see Tables 9.2 and 9.3)

The structural changes in Thailand's economy extended beyond the sectoral level and were widespread at the product level as well. There has been significant diversification of products within each broad economic sector. For example, within the agricultural sector, rice accounted for as much as 37.7 percent of the value and 30 percent of total exports in 1960, but its share fell

Table 9.1

Thailand: Distribution of Gross Domestic Product by Economic Sector, 1970–91 (at 1972 constant prices)

Sector	1970	1980	1990	1991
Agriculture	27.0	20.6	14.5	13.5
Mining and quarrying	2.9	2.6	2.9	2.9
Manufacturing	16.0	21.7	24.7	24.9
Construction	5.3	4.5	5.3	5.2
Electricity and water supply	1.0	2.0	3.0	3.1
Transportation and sommunication	6.5	6.7	7.2	7.1
Wholesale and retail trade	17.4	16.9	17.6	17.6
Banking, insurance and real estate	2.5	2.8	5.3	5.2
Ownership of dwellings	5.6	4.8	3.7	3.7
Public administration and defense	4.4	5.2	3.9	3.8
Services	11.5	12.2	12.3	12.9
Gross Domestic Product	100.0	100.0	100.0	100.0

Source: National Economic and Social Development Board (NESDB), *National Income Statistics of Thailand,* New Series, various issues, 1970–92 (Bangkok).

to 20.3 percent of the value and 16.2 percent of agricultural sector's exports in 1987. Other agricultural products that have become more important since the 1960s include maize, sorghum, cassava, rubber, and mung beans. More recently, high-value-added crops such as fruits and vegetables have become more significant in terms of output and exports. The fisheries sector has also become a major generator of income and exports in the economy. For example, frozen shrimp and cuttlefish are now major Thai export products.

In the manufacturing sector, too, there has been significant structural change with diversification of products (see Table 9.3). Food, beverages, and tobacco were important industries in 1960; combined, they constituted 60 percent of the manufacturing value-added in 1960. While they are still important industries, their share of total manufacturing value-added has declined steadily over time. The latest GDP series shows that the combined share of these three industrial groups declined from 36.7 percent in 1970 to 28.3 percent in 1987. Because many new food products have emerged, there has been no clear declining trend for this industry since 1970. The beverage, tobacco, wood and wood product, petroleum product, and transport equipment industries have declined in importance. In contrast, textiles, wearing apparel, printing and publishing, chemicals and chemical products, electrical machinery and supplies, and "other manufacturing" have shown clearly increasing shares of manufacturing value-added over time (NESDB various issues).

Table 9.2

Thailand: Exports by Economic Sector, 1961–92

Sector	1961	1971	1981	1990	1991	1992
Agriculture	82.7	62.2	47.7	24.8	15.1	15.0
Fishing	0.4	2.0	4.3	5.5	6.6	5.9
Forestry	3.3	1.5	0.1	0.1	0.1	—
Mining	6.6	13.7	7.7	1.2	1.0	—
Manufacturing	2.4	10.0	35.8	75.3	76.2	77.6
Others	4.7	3.3	4.3	1.4	2.0	1.5
Total	100.0	100.0	100.0	100.0	100.0	100.0

Source: Bank of Thailand, *Monthly Bulletin,* various issues (Bangkok).

Changes in Policy Emphasis on Industrialization

Industrialization was a common aspiration of most developing economies in the postwar period. Thailand was no exception. In the decade following World War II, the government was eager to promote the process of industrialization. In those days the strategy was to set up a number of state enterprises producing a variety of industrial products, including cement, paper, sugar, tobacco, and an array of consumer products. The government's initiatives turned out to be failures, because the operations of most public enterprises were inefficient due to poor management and widespread corruption (Ingram, 1971, chapter 12).

Furthermore, the government's direct involvement in industries through the establishment of state-owned enterprises made private entrepreneurs reluctant to invest in manufacturing activities that could compete with these enterprises. Private manufacturing industries were thus confined to mostly small-scale operations in industries such as rice milling, sawmill operation, and household handicrafts.

In the late 1950s, the government sharply reversed its industrialization policy. It began to reduce its direct involvement in the manufacturing sector and switched instead to playing a supporting role to private enterprises through the granting of investment incentives and the provision of public infrastructure, at the same time limiting public control of the private sector.

In the 1960s, the government invested heavily in public infrastructure projects to support the private sector. The major investments included irrigation systems, electric power plants, and highway projects.

To promote private-sector investment, the government enacted an investment promotion law and established a Board of Investment (BOI) in 1959 to administer the provision of tax and other incentives to individual investors. The tariff structure was also revised several times to protect domestic industries.

Table 9.3

Thailand: Principal Export Commodities, 1958–91 (percent)

Product	1958	1968	1978	1988	1990	1991
Rice	46.0	27.6	12.6	8.6	4.7	4.2
Rubber	20.6	13.3	9.7	6.7	4.0	3.4
Maize	2.8	12.0	5.2	1.0	0.7	0.5
Tin	4.0	11.0	8.7	0.6	0.3	1.2
Tapioca	3.0	5.6	13.1	5.4	3.9	3.4
Teak	3.7	1.2	0.3	—	—	—
Wood products	—	0.1	1.2	1.0	0.7	0.7
Sugar	—	—	4.8	2.4	3.0	2.0
Shrimp	—	2.0	1.8	2.4	3.4	3.7
Mung beans	0.4	1.0	1.4	0.3	0.2	0.1
Jute & Kenaf	1.1	4.9	0.5	0.3	0.2	0.2
Tungsten	0.1	0.3	1.2	—	0.7	0.7
Fluorite	—	0.8	0.2	—	2.3	2.1
Textile products	—	—	8.3	14.5	14.3	15.1
Jewelry	—	—	2.5	5.9	2.2	1.7
Tobacco leaves	1.3	1.5	1.4	0.3	0.3	0.4
Integrated circuits	—	—	2.6	2.2	3.7	3.5
Canned pineapple	—	—	1.4	1.2	0.9	1.0
Cement	0.2	0.1	—	—	—	—
Other exports	16.8	18.6	23.1	47.2	54.5	56.5
Total exports	100.0	100.0	100.0	100.0	100.0	100.0

Source: Bank of Thailand, *Monthly Bulletin,* various issues (Bangkok).

The industrialization policy of the 1960s was based mainly on the promotion of import-substituting industries. The BOI encouraged consumer goods industries, including assembly-type activities that utilized imported parts and components. Furthermore, the tariff structure gave additional protection to finished goods and some intermediate products. Labor-intensive and resource-based industries such as textiles and agricultural processing were also included in the BOI promotion list. However, they were classified in Group C, which received fewer import duty protection and tax incentives than other industries. The BOI's promotion placed greatest emphasis on industries that were capital-intensive and produced on a relatively larger scale, such as metal smelting, vehicle tires, and chemicals. Next on the BOI's priority list were a number of assembly-type industries, including motor vehicles and electrical appliances.

Compared with the NIEs, Thailand was rather late in instituting an outward-looking industrialization strategy. Not until the early 1970s did manufactured exports receive promotional support from the authorities. This was probably due to the fact that the country had always been able to rely on the export of primary products based on its abundant natural resources to earn the needed foreign exchange. It was therefore less urgent to promote manufactured exports. In addition, the import substitution policy coupled with rapidly increased domestic demand for industrial products during the 1960s made it difficult to promote industrial exports.

The policy of promoting manufactured exports was first set out in Thailand's Third National Economic and Social Development Plan (1972–76). During this period, the investment promotion law was revised to give more incentives to the producers of industrial exports. Its chief measures included rebates of duties paid for imported inputs used in the production of manufactured exports and provision of short-term loans at preferential interest rates for manufactures exported through the central bank's rediscount facility. In addition, export industries promoted by the BOI could be granted an income tax holiday for a period of five to eight years, together with exemption from duty and taxes for imported machinery and equipment.

The gradual shift from an import-substitution policy toward an export-promotion policy was brought about through a realization that the scope of further import substitution is limited, as growth of many such industries slowed down due to a saturated domestic market. Furthermore, it was realized that the high protection afforded industries under the import-substitution policy was creating economic inefficiency, a heavy reliance on imported inputs, and the concentration of industrial activities around Bangkok.

On the other hand, policy makers saw the NIEs succeed in achieving high economic growth by adopting outward-looking strategies.

The shift toward export promotion continued into the 1980s. Various cumbersome export procedures were eased, while investment promotion tilted strongly toward export industries. Currency devaluation in 1984, coupled with a new exchange rate policy to promote exports, also gave strong impetus to industries that produced them.

With continuous expansion of manufactured exports and comfortable balance of payments position, Thailand in recent years has been increasingly liberalizing its foreign trade, with more controls being removed and further reductions in tariffs. For instance, in late 1990, import duty on all machinery has been reduced from 20 percent to 5 percent, irrespective of whether an industry is rewarded promotional privileges. The move was a part of a longer-term strategy to restructure import duty rates for a wide range of goods, thereby reducing and rationalizing protection. Also, the Ministry of Industry proposed in 1992 to ease the burden of local assemblers by dropping the local contents regulation which requires local assemblers to use at least 54 percent of local parts in their assembly (EIU, 1991–92 issues).

The lowering of the level of protection will enhance further export-led industrial growth. However, in view of the emerging shortage of skilled labor and rising real wage, Thailand's development strategy now focuses more on industrial deepening, greater output sophistication and higher productivity. The new approach would require efforts to overcome the present skill bottlenecks. Thus, the country's education and training system is being adapted to produce more engineers and more science and management personnel with a vocational setting. This would also mean shifting output away from labor-intensive products to more capital- and technology-intensive industries, with higher quality of human capital and productivity. In manufacturing, particular emphasis is being placed on the role of small and medium enterprises, which have the potential of export-competitiveness in supplying parts or components on the one hand; and on the other hand, bring about larger employment, more equitable distribution of income and wider geographical diversification. All these have been embodied in the 1992–96 Seventh National Development plan. The plan also addresses among other issues, the need for strengthening the over-burdened infrastructure, including roads, parks, sewage, and telecommunications (World Bank 1992).

Performance and Prospects for Manufactured Exports

Structure of Foreign Trade and Trade Balance

As external trade has expanded more rapidly than domestic production, the Thai economy became more open over the years, and the export/import share of GDP has increased. In 1960, merchandise exports and imports accounted for around 30 percent of the country's GDP. This share increased to 71 percent in 1990. If the services trade were also included, the degree of openness would reach over 80 percent in 1990 (IMF 1993).

Over the past two decades, exports from Thailand have expanded rapidly, and the country has to gradually gained share of world trade. But Thailand is still a small trading country: in 1990 the value of its exports accounted for only 0.7 percent of the world's total export value (IMF 1993).

The structure of Thailand's foreign trade has changed markedly over the past three decades. In the 1960s, agricultural products accounted for the bulk of the country's exports, and the value of manufactured exports was very low. Over the past two decades, manufactured products have rapidly increased their share of the country's total merchandise exports. The value of manufactured exports constituted only 2.4 percent of Thailand's total merchandise exports in 1961, rose dramatically to 10 percent in 1971, 35.8 percent in 1981, and 76.2 percent in 1991, and further to 77.6 percent in 1992. Since 1985, the value of manufactures has surpassed that of agricultural products in the Thai export market. The share of fishery products has also increased over the years, while the importance of mineral and forestry products, has declined significantly (see Table 9.2).

The structure of Thailand's merchandise imports has also changed considerably over the past three decades. Following the policy of import substitution in

Table 9.4

Thailand: Imports by Economic Classification, 1961–91 (percent)

Sector	1961	1971	1981	1987	1991
Consumer goods					
nondurable	32.2	10.8	6.3	4.9	3.8
durable	7.3	7.1	4.4	5.0	5.3
total consumer goods	39.5	17.9	10.7	9.9	9.1
Intermediate products & raw materials					
chiefly for consumer goods	10.9	18.8	15.6	24.8	23.7
chiefly for capital goods	7.0	10.4	9.1	10.3	10.2
total intermediate products raw materials	17.9	29.2	24.7	35.1	33.9
Capital goods					
machinery	13.4	21.7	17.0	23.1	31.6
others	12.0	10.7	9.4	7.9	8.6
total capital goods	25.5	32.4	26.4	31.0	40.2
Other Imports					
vehicle & parts	7.9	8.2	4.4	4.5	4.9
fuel and lubricants	10.1	10.2	30.1	12.9	9.1
others	−0.7	2.1	3.7	6.6	2.6
total of others	17.3	20.5	38.2	24.0	16.8
Grand Total	100.0	100.0	100.0	100.0	100.0

Source: Bank of Thailand, *Monthly Bulletin,* various issues (Bangkok).

the manufacturing sector, consumer goods as a share of total imports decreased steadily from 39.5 percent in 1961 to 17.9 percent in 1971 and to 9.1 percent in 1991. On the other hand, the intermediate goods and capital goods share of total imports increased considerably over time. The increased price of oil since 1973 has contributed significantly to the rapid rise in total value of oil imports as well as to structural change in imports. Thailand's import bill for oil accounted for around 10 percent of the country's total imports before the first oil crisis. This share exceeded 20 percent in the mid-1970s and jumped to around 30 percent during the 1980–82 period. After that, the decline in world crude oil prices, along with the discovery of natural gas in Thailand, reduced both the value and the share of oil imports. The oil share total imports dropped to around 9 percent in 1991 (see Table 9.4).

Although export expansion has been rapid over the past two decades, imports have also increased significantly, bringing Thailand larger trade deficits. In fact, the country has suffered a trade deficit every year since 1957. But the oil price increase substantially aggravated the trade deficit. The deficit was particularly large after the oil crisis of 1979–80, averaged at 8.6 percent of GDP in 1979–1981, and widened to a peak of 9.8 percent in 1983.

Thailand's worsening trade balance since the mid-1970s has to a significant extent resulted from the deterioration of terms of trade. The oil crisis of 1973–74 occurred almost simultaneously with the world commodity boom. Thus, rising prices of Thailand's major export items during 1972–74, including rice, rubber, tin, and maize, helped to prevent deterioration of Thailand's terms of trade. But export commodity prices moderated after 1975 while imported oil prices remained high. Therefore, Thailand's external terms of trade deteriorated substantially. During the early 1980s the marked decline in its export commodity prices contributed significantly to the country's adverse trade balance. Around the mid-1980s Thailand's terms of trade improved greatly due to the marked decline in oil prices as well as higher world prices for some of Thailand's major export commodities, such as rice, rubber, and maize. The trade deficit declined significantly in 1986. But as the economy recovered, with demand for investment and consumer goods increasingly rapidly, the country's trade deficit widened significantly again since 1988. In 1990 the trade deficit was around 12.7 percent of GDP (IMF 1993).

Performance of Manufactured Exports

Clearly, Thailand's manufactured exports have grown much more rapidly than exports generated by other sectors of its economy. Their rapid growth began in the early 1970s and has continued since then. Starting from a small base, manufactured exports grew at an average annual rate exceeding 30 percent from 1970 to 1987 (in terms of baht). This growth rate is quite respectable although not as high as the corresponding pace among the Asian NIEs.

As a result of this expansion, the manufacturing sector has become more export-oriented. A calculation of the export-to-output ratio based on the Input-Output Tables in 1975 and 1980 shows that the ratio was 13.8 percent in 1975 and 20.0 percent in 1980, the latest available estimate. Since 1980, manufactured exports have grown much more rapidly than manufacturing sector production. Judging from this explanation, the export-output ratio for the manufacturing sector should be substantially higher now than it was in 1980.

Manufactured exports are now among Thailand's major export items. In fact, textile products including garments have been the most important earners in the export market since 1985. Since 1986, garments alone have been the country's top export item, replacing rice, which had been Thailand's most significant export earner since the country entered foreign trade. In 1958 only eight items qualified as principal exports with value exceeding 1 percent of total exports, and all of them were primary products (see Table 9.3). Rice and rubber already accounted for three-fourths of total export value. In the late 1960s, many more commodities qualified as principal exports, although primary products such as

Table 9.5

Thailand: Distribution of Manufacturing Exports by Industry (percent)

Industry	1970	1981	1985	1987
Processed food	26.0	29.0	21.3	16.6
Textiles	20.3	14.2	12.5	9.4
Garments	0.9	12.8	15.4	19.3
Footwear	0.1	1.2	2.5	3.2
Wood products	0.3	2.7	2.0	2.1
Furnitures & fixtures	0.1	1.3	1.4	1.8
Paper & paper products	0.8	0.3	0.6	0.7
Leather products	1.5	1.4	1.4	2.1
Rubber products	0.8	1.1	1.2	1.4
Plastic products	1.1	1.3	1.3	1.2
Chemical products	7.5	1.0	1.4	1.3
Nonmetallic mineral products & glass products	9.9	1.1	1.3	1.2
Metal products	8.3	3.4	3.6	2.8
Nonelectrical machinery	0.5	0.6	2.6	2.7
Electrical machinery & supplies	0.4	12.4	10.0	10.1
Transport equipment	0.1	0.3	0.4	0.4
Scientific equipment	2.0	1.1	1.3	0.8
Jewelry	17.1	9.4	9.1	11.1
Miscellaneous	2.5	4.8	10.7	12.1
Total	100.00	100.00	100.00	100.00

Source: Bank of Thailand, *Monthly Bulletin,* various issues (Bangkok).

rice, rubber, maize, tin, and tapioca were still the dominant export items. By the late 1970s, textile products (including garments), gems and jewelry, integrated circuits, and canned pineapple were among the principal export items. It is noteworthy that despite the increased number of items qualifying as principal exports, the share of "other exports" in Table 9.3 also rose considerably over time; by 1991, the combined share of "other exports" reached 56.5 percent. This implies that the country's export commodities have greatly diversified, due in large part to the expansion of manufactured products.

To see the structure of manufactured exports more clearly, we classify data for exports of manufactures, obtained from the Bank of Thailand, in the nineteen groups presented in Tables 9.5 and 9.6. In Table 9.5, we see that processed food, textiles, garments, electronic machinery and supplies (mainly integrated circuits), and jewelry (including precious stones) constituted a significant proportion of manufactured exports. These five industrial groups have accounted for over two-thirds of the country's manufactured exports in the late 1980s. The processed food share was the largest until it was exceeded by the garments group in 1987. Textiles (including garments) have shown a slight decline and jewelry a greater decline in relative share in recent years.

Table 9.6

Thailand: Growth Rates of Manufactured Exports by Industry (based on export value in baht)

Industry	Average Annual Growth Rate of Exports (percent)						
	1970 −74	1974 −78	1978 −81	1981 −84	1985	1986	1987
Processed food	115.7	9.3	31.5	2.3	19.8	26.8	21.0
Textiles	83.1	29.4	11.7	9.1	19.3	20.2	23.0
Garments	215.7	34.0	39.8	20.4	20.0	38.9	77.4
Footwear	159.0	78.8	118.2	29.0	15.4	34.5	85.7
Wood products	259.3	20.3	12.4	7.1	14.1	19.3	66.4
Furnitures & fixtures	290.7	30.0	52.3	7.9	29.4	41.7	81.5
Paper & paper products	115.9	−9.5	22.6	9.2	120.4	72.1	47.8
Leather products	12.8	53.7	6.6	22.1	−6.3	31.3	126.6
Rubber products	14.8	31.8	52.6	12.7	31.9	35.8	64.4
Plastic products	75.6	20.9	50.3	23.5	−2.7	12.1	56.6
Chemical products	70.3	−18.9	31.7	0.9	145.4	15.2	50.5
Nonmetallic mineral products, glass products	68.5	−13.5	14.8	3.1	20.8	28.7	47.4
Metal products	64.6	10.3	−38.0	11.7	34.4	37.8	9.5
Non-electrical machinery	70.8	64.8	7.2	123.9	265.8	−5.9	110.9
Electrical machinery & supplies	194.9	77.2	44.9	9.4	7.0	45.7	36.3
Transport equipment	134.0	33.1	27.3	8.9	37.8	19.4	65.2
Scientific equipment	18.1	42.4	62.1	19.4	58.7	8.9	10.9
Jewelry	54.6	25.5	34.8	13.5	16.0	57.7	51.3
Miscellaneous	156.4	−2.7	45.9	9.0	74.2	39.8	58.8
Total	95.0	18.4	30.4	10.2	25.7	33.5	47.3

Source: Bank of Thailand, *Monthly Bulletin,* various issues (Bangkok).

In terms of export growth rates, we see from Table 9.6 that most product groups registered high growth, although growth rates fluctuated during various time periods. Among the product groups that showed high growth rates during the 1970s were processed food, textiles, garments, footwear, wood products and furnitures, electronic goods, transport equipment, and miscellaneous manufactured goods. These product groups continued to expand in the 1980s but mostly at reduced growth rates. In the 1980s, leather products, rubber products, nonelectrical machinery, transport equipment, jewelry, and miscellaneous manufactures have been among the product groups that registered high growth rates.

Most of Thailand's exports have been directed to developed countries. The European Community, the United States, and Japan are its most important markets. The U.S. market has grown particularly rapidly over the past decade. Since 1984, the United States has replaced Japan as the largest importer of Thai products. But the EC countries as a group are the most important market for

Table 9.7

Shares of Thailand Exports by Major Country, 1970, 1980, and 1990 (percent)

Country	1970	1980	1990
United States	13.4	12.6	22.6
Japan	25.5	15.1	17.2
Asian NIEs			
Singapore[a]	6.9	7.7	7.3
Hong Kong	7.5	5.1	4.5
Taiwan	4.9	1.3	1.6
South Korea	0.3	0.7	1.7
ASEAN[a]			
Malaysia	5.6	4.5	2.5
Indonesia	2.3	3.6	0.6
Philippines	0.1	0.3	0.7
Brunei	—	0.1	0.1
China	—	1.9	1.5
Australia	0.5	1.1	1.6
European Community			
Netherlands	8.6	13.2	4.8
West Germany	3.6	4.1	5.1
United Kingdom	2.1	1.8	4.0
Italy	1.9	1.9	1.8
France	1.0	1.6	2.4
Belgium	0.7	2.5	1.5
Saudi Arabia	2.2	1.7	1.4
Iran	0.2	1.6	0.5

Source: Bank of Thailand, *Monthly Bulletin,* various issues (Bangkok).
[a]Singapore is a member of ASEAN.

Thailand's goods. The Netherlands, West Germany, the United Kingdom, and France are among its more important markets in the EC. The Middle East has also become a significant market for Thai exports. Among the ASEAN countries, Singapore is Thailand's most important trading partner. Among the Asian NIEs, Hong Kong is the most important importer of Thai products. Thai exports to China have also increased over the years (see Table 9.7).

Japan has absorbed relatively small amounts of manufactured exports from Thailand compared with the EC and the United States. However, Thailand's sales of manufactured goods to Japan have expanded rapidly in recent years. Japan had imported mainly natural resources and processed primary products from Thailand, but in recent years some manufactured products, notably jewelry and garments, have gained substantial ground in the Japanese market. However, the Japanese market for Thai garments is still very small compared with the United States and the EC. At present, processed food, jewelry, textiles, and garments are the most important Thai exports to the U.S. market. To the EC market, Thailand's major manufactured export items are textiles, garments, and precious stones. Smaller items such as leather products, ceramic and plastic products, and processed food items have also posted substantial growth in the EC market in recent years.

Factors Contributing to Past Export Growth

Five major factors have contributed to the rapid growth of manufactured exports from Thailand over the past two decades (Akrasanee and Tambunlertchai 1990).

First, Thailand's manufactured exports comprised mostly resource-based and labor-intensive products that are consistent with its perceived comparative advantage. Processed food, textiles and garments, gems and jewelry, and integrated circuits in the assembly stage are examples of manufactured goods that are either resource-based or labor-intensive. Thailand began to promote manufactured exports in the 1970s, when the tide of protectionism was high in the world market. But as marginal exporters for most products, Thai producers did not seem to be seriously affected by trade-restricting measures in major importing countries until recent years. In fact, it has been argued that the expansion of textile and garment exports in the early 1970s benefited in part from the developed countries' quota restrictions on textiles from major exporting economies such as Taiwan and Hong Kong. Thailand was able to obtain some of the spillover demand for these products. But if Thailand had lacked comparative advantage in textile products, its textile exports would not have expanded rapidly even if demand for these products had increased.

Second, the government's policy shift in the early 1970s encouraged manufacturers to reorient emphasis from domestic sales to exports. Government incentives to exporters have been modest, and industries competing with imports have been favored by the tariff structure. But the declared emphasis on exports, coupled with government promotional measures, has helped to create a favorable environment for export-oriented industrial development.

Third, the change of international currencies has had, on balance, a positive impact on Thailand's exports. The pegging of the Thai baht to the U.S. dollar, together with the 1970s realignment of major currencies, resulted in the depreciation of the baht relative to most other units. The depreciation of the U.S. dollar and its tie to the baht might have helped to improve the competitiveness of Thai manufactured exports and accelerate their expansion since the early 1970s. When the U.S. dollar appreciated in the first half of the 1980s, the Thai government carried out two major devaluations, in 1981 and 1984. The 1981 devaluation was quickly offset by the further appreciation of the U.S. dollar in subsequent years. The 1984 devaluation, however, was followed by the sharp depreciation of the U.S. dollar after the Plaza Accord of September 1985 (Tambunlertchai, 1989; Akrasanee and Tambunlertchai 1990). The international currency realignment from 1986 until the present time, along with more flexible management of the exchange rate in Thailand, has helped to maintain the price competitiveness of Thai products in the world market.

Fourth, foreign direct investment in export-oriented industries has helped Thailand develop new commodities for overseas sale. Integrated circuits and canned pineapple are frequently cited examples of export products created by transnational company investment. In the late 1980s there have been accelerated inflows of foreign direct investment in export-oriented industries, as producers have relocated from economies such as Japan and Taiwan that face currency appreciation. The favorable investment climate in Thailand has also encouraged this inflow of funds. With foreign investment, Thai companies have produced export goods such as plastic toys, rubber gloves, ball bearings, automotive parts and components, and a number of food items. Recent political uncertainties have caused some slow-down in the application of foreign investment. However, given the restoration of political stability and the stable financial conditions, foreign investment is coming back gradually.

Finally, we have to recognize the Thai manufacturers' and exporters' efforts to promote manufactured product sales. Manufacturers and traders have responded enthusiastically to the government's export promotion policy despite the modest incentives offered to them. Recognizing the limited growth potential in the domestic market and the need for export sales to expand their industries, entrepreneurs in the private sector have made strenuous efforts to improve their productivity and product quality as well as to find additional sales channels. These private-sector efforts have turned Thailand's export promotion policy into reality.

Problems and Prospects for Further Export Growth

World Trading Environment and Protectionism

As its economy has become more open, Thailand has been affected increasingly by the changing world trading environment. Major factors that led to a change in the international trading environment during the early 1980s included the following: the decline in growth of developed market economies that have traditionally absorbed a large proportion of exports from developing countries; increasing numbers of nontariff trade barriers in the developed economies; high interest rates and fluctuating exchange rates; and the marked decline in world commodity prices. Thailand was affected by all these factors. The decline in prices of its major export commodities, along with reduced world demand for manufactured products, had serious effects on the Thai economy from 1980 to 1985. Economic growth decelerated while the country's trade deficit rose substantially. Foreign debt accumulated, and the debt service ratio jumped to 21.9 percent in 1985. The government was unable to finance economic expansion because the large budget deficit, and public debt accumulation limited its resources. In fact, the government was forced to adopt austerity monetary and fiscal policy measures that further depressed the domestic economy.

Since 1986, there has been a significant turnaround in Thailand's economic growth and export expansion. Facilitating its economic upturn were the decline in oil prices, recovery in commodity prices, currency realignments, reduction of international interest rates, and recovery of the overall world economy. But Thailand has been confronted increasingly by trade protectionism, and the growth of its manufactured exports tends to be impeded by trade-restricting measures in the major importing countries.

Thai commodities such as tapioca, rubber, tin, and sugar have long been subject to restrictions imposed either by importing countries or by international commodity agreements. Among its manufactured exports, textile products have been subject to restriction under the Multifiber Arrangements (MFA). The impact of this restriction has been felt increasingly as the rates of utilization of textile quotas gradually approach their limits.

More important, rising protectionistic sentiment in the United States, Thailand's major export market, has heightened tensions in Thai-U.S. relations. Since 1984, there have been several cases involving the imposition of either an antidumping duty (AD) or a countervailing duty (CVD) by the United States on imports from Thailand. Products affected include textile fabric and garments, steel pipes and tubes, and ball bearings. Although the duties are generally not high, these restrictive measures aroused uncertainties and confusion among Thai exporters.

Recently the United States has pressed Thailand on issues involving the protection of intellectual property rights. Thailand actually has protected intellectual property rights through its laws on patents, trademarks, and copyright, but the U.S. government has claimed that Thailand lacks adequate protection for such items as pharmaceutical patents and copyrights on computer software, which have been excluded from coverage by Thai laws. Finally, in January 1989 the U.S. government decided to exclude eight items from the list of GSP benefits to Thailand, including wooden furniture, ceramic tiles, metallic ornaments, and artificial flowers. Thailand's main concern now is the U.S. administration's threat to impose further restrictions on Thai products under section 301 of the new Omnibus Trade Act. While the latest round of GATT multilateral negotiations has proceeded, the United States has resorted increasingly to bilateralism and, at times, actions that violate GATT principles. As long as the United States cannot correct its huge trade deficit, many countries, including Thailand, expect continued restrictive trade measures from this country.

With respect to Europe, there was a danger that unification of EC members into a single market in 1992 would cause an inward orientation of this largest trading bloc in the world and raise the level of trade protection against nonmember countries. Although the integration is temporarily delayed, EC has been pressing Thailand for stronger wording of an agreement on tape piracy, threatening that EC may retaliate on the European Generalized System of Preference (GSP) for Thailand.

Thailand has a large trade deficit with Japan. The appreciation of the yen has helped Thai exporters penetrate the Japanese market, but Thailand also has to import Japanese products at higher domestic prices. More important, the investment boom of the past two years has prompted increased imports of capital goods as well as intermediate goods from Japan. But despite the opening of the Japanese market in recent years, it is still difficult to sell various Thai products in Japan. A complicated distribution system, stringent quality and sanitary requirements, and other administrative barriers are well known deterrents to penetration of the Japanese market. At present, most Thai exports to Japan are primary products and raw materials. Thai exporters will have to work hard to sell more manufactured products in Japan. It remains to be seen whether increased Japanese investment in Thailand's export-oriented industries will improve prospects for overseas sales of their products.

Along with protectionism and trade barriers in major importing countries, Thailand's exporters of manufactured products will face more severe competition from other developing economies. Thailand currently enjoys considerable comparative advantage in certain labor-intensive products. But developing economies such as China, Sri Lanka, Indonesia, and Burma have abundant labor and much lower wage costs than Thailand. Thus Thailand will have to promote its manufactured exports in a world market that will be less open than previously due to rising trade barriers in importing countries, and more intense competition from other developing economies that are also eager to expand their sales of such goods.

Prospects for Further Export Growth

Despite its problems, Thailand has quite promising medium-term prospects for expansion of its manufactured exports. Major manufactured export items such as textiles and garments may experience slower growth than in the past, due to increasing constraints on textile products in the world market as well as heightened competition from other developing economies. But further expansion of items such as gems and jewelry, leather products, ceramic products, plastic wares and toys, and artificial flowers will still be possible for a few years to come. Thailand could also maintain its comparative advantage in various processed food items. But as time passes, Thailand will have to gradually move up the comparative advantage ladder toward more skill-intensive products; the prospects for integrated circuits are particularly good. It will have to diversify both export markets and products, given the protectionistic trend among major importing countries and the limited growth potential of such items as rice, tin, tapioca products, and textiles.

The overall growth of Thailand's exports could decelerate in the near future because the bulk of its products will encounter more restraints abroad, although sales of some minor items will continue to increase rapidly. Nevertheless, manufactured exports will likely continue to grow faster than exports of primary commodities.

Several factors affect the competitiveness of manufactured exports from Thailand. The following positive influences will enable Thailand to remain competitive in the near future:

- A large pool of unskilled labor is still available in the rural sector. The agricultural labor force is still quite large, and underemployment is widespread. In the past the development of the manufacturing sector has been unable to absorb much labor from the agricultural sector. Thus further development of labor-intensive industries will not exert much pressure on its wage level, and Thailand will be able to enjoy a comparative advantage in such manufactures in the foreseeable future.

- Compared with most other developing economies in Asia, Thailand is relatively rich in natural resources. The country is expected to enjoy a continued competitive advantage in resource-based products, particularly food items.

- International exchange rate movements of recent years have been favorable to the expansion of manufactured exports from Thailand. The more flexible management of the external value of the baht will help to promote manufactured exports.

- Thailand will most likely maintain its policy of export promotion. The country's policy makers are well aware of the need to promote manufactured exports. Various mechanisms to achieve this have already been set out and will be improved gradually.

- The recent surge in foreign direct investment in Thailand's export-oriented industries will be helpful to its export expansion in the years to come.

At the same time, a number of negative factors will hinder the pace of manufactured export expansion. In addition to external threats of protectionism and increasing competition from low-wage economies, there are also internal obstacles to export expansion. These include:

- Thailand's tariff and tax regimes, which still favor industries producing for the domestic market and therefore discriminate against those producing for export .

- The country's lack of adequate supporting services and infrastructure facilities. Electricity and telephone services are inadequate, and port facilities in particular require improvement. The major port in Bangkok has become congested, while other smaller ports have not been utilized efficiently. The government recognizes the problem of inadequate infrastructure and remedies have been designed, but solution of these problems will take time.

- Lack of a qualified work force in various fields. The rapid inflow of foreign investment and increased domestic investment in recent years have increased the demand for well-trained workers in various industrial branches. It is now a common complaint among manufacturers that qualified engineers and technicians are in short supply. Again, the government has recognized the seriousness of this problem. But it will take time to increase the supply of qualified workers to match the increased demand. Lack of qualified personnel will also constrain Thailand's ability to move up the comparative-advantage ladder toward more sophisticated products as the country confronts competition from labor-intensive products exported by other low-wage economies.

References

Aknasanee, Narongchai, and Tambunlertchai, Somsak. 1990. "Transition from Import Substitution to Export Expansion: The Thai Experience." In *Economic Development in East and Southeast Asia: Essays in Honor of Professor Shinichi Nakamura,* eds., Seiji Naya and Akira Takayama. Honolulu: East-West Center, and Singapore: Institute of Southeast Asian Studies pp.104–20.

Bank of Thailand, *Monthly Bulletin*, various issues. (Bangkok).

———. 1993. *Economic Performance in 1992 and Outlook for 1993*. (Bangkok).

The Economist Intelligent Unit. "Country Report, Thailand," *The Economist,* (London) 1990–92 issues.

Ingram, James C. 1971. *Economic Change in Thailand: 1850–1970*. Stanford: Stanford University Press.

International Monetary Fund. 1993. *International Financial Statistics* pp. 516–520 (Washington, D.C.).

National Economic and Social Development Board (NESDB). National Income Statistics of Thailand, new series, various issues. (Bangkok).

Tambunlertchai, Somsak. 1989. "Economic Prospects and External Economic Relations of Thailand," *Asian Development Review*, Manila: Asian Development Bank, vol. 7, No.2.

———. 1992. "Manufacturing" in Peter G. Warr (ed.), *The Thai Economy in Transition*, (Cambridge) Cambridge University Press, Chapter 3.

World Bank, 1992. *Trends in Developing Economics*, pp. 513–14. (Washington, D.C.).

———. 1993. *World Development Report* (Washington, D.C.)

207.15

CHAPTER 10

Industrialization and Manufactured Export Strategy of Malaysia

PAUL CHAN AND SHU-CHIN YANG

Malaysia
019
L 60
014
F13
F14

Introduction

Malaysia is now confronted with uncertainties that arise from the changing global trade strategies of the industrial economies, intensifying competition from LDCs and other NIEs, and technological innovations.

The design of economic policies and choice of strategic options are now more globally-driven than in the early 1970s, when the total policy framework was dominated by national issues of the political economy. Thus, the management of the Malaysian economy requires a different strategic approach. In this regard, previous Malaysian government policy response to the challenges of the global environment has had somewhat mixed success.

This chapter will highlight the status of manufactured exports and major government policy strategies to promote industrial growth and manufactured export that have evolved since the country gained independence in 1957.

Industrial Policy Strategies for Manufactured Exports

Three stages of industrial development of the Malaysian economy are discernible since the independence in 1957:

(1) From 1958, when the Pioneer Industries Ordinance was introduced, to 1968, the focus was on import substitution.

(2) From 1968, when the Investment Incentives Act was introduced, to 1980, industrial export promotion was emphasized.

(3) From 1980 to date, coinciding with the Fourth and Fifth Malaysian Plans, the thrust has been toward heavy industries and the second round of import substitution. The Industrial Master Plan for 1986 to 1995 provided the strategic direction for industrialization and export manufacturing.

An important dimension of the import-substitution policy was the emphasis on the private sector, which was offered generous investment incentives and protection. The second round of import substitution focused on resource-based industries. In the structure of the fiscal incentives there was a bias in favor of capital-intensive industries. Direct foreign investment benefited significantly from this, as the government was keen to attract the foreign multinational corporations (MNCs) that provided capital, technology, and foreign market access. Thus, the initiative for export-oriented industrial expansion during this period came principally from foreign MNCs that relocated in low-cost centers like Malaysia. Recently, the change in cost structures due to currency appreciation, higher wage pressures, restrictive pollution regulations, and loss of GSP status in the region's other NIEs have caused medium-sized companies to relocate to Malaysia from other Asian NIEs.

The strategy in the second round of import substitution was accompanied by a second round of export expansion that emphasized capital- and technology-intensive products and other resource-based manufactures in which Malaysia has a comparative advantage. The public sector set the initiatives for the former.

The Industrial Master Plan (IMP) was formulated to provide a coherent industrial program. The IMP philosophy was based on a target-oriented strategy within the framework of a private enterprise economy. Various long-term objectives and development strategies were formulated for thirteen sectors. Quite apart from its socioeconomic objectives, the main strategic rationale of the IMP was to accelerate the growth and diversification of Malaysia's industrial export base.

An important macroeconomic assumption of the IMP during its target period is a GDP growth rate of 6.4 percent per year, with total investment paced to increase at 5.7 percent per annum. By 1995, the manufacturing share of GDP is projected at 24 percent.

The present manufacturing sector has three structural components. The first component comprises the Free Trade Zones (EPZs), where predominantly multinational subsidiaries assemble electronic products and electrical machinery. All these producers are export-oriented and are subsidized by various tax benefits, besides benefiting from GSP. Among East Asian developing countries, Malaysia has the largest number of EPZs that have contributed to expansion of its manufactured exports. In fact, because of its EPZs, Malaysia is now a top exporter of several manufactured items such as air conditioners, integrated circuits, and other precision instruments.

The second component is the domestic private sector, which has a significant amount of foreign investment. Here the focus is on light industrial product manufacturing with a high import content, particularly in intermediate and capital goods.

The third block of the structure comprises the heavy industry sector, which was launched by the public sector during the 1980s. This is the capital- and technology-intensive sector, whose development has been influenced by the South Korean model.

In short, the growth of the manufacturing sector in Malaysia has been encouraged by the use of fiscal and financial incentives, infrastructural and institutional development, and the active participation of both the public and private sectors.

Since the 1970s, industrial development has accelerated in order to achieve both a high economic growth rate and ethnic-distributional objectives of the National Economic Policy formulated more than two decades ago. Under the government's Outline Perspective Plan, the manufacturing sector was geared to grow at an average rate of 12 percent per year from 1970 to 1990. The manufacturing share of GDP was targeted to increase from 13 percent in 1970 to 26 percent by 1990. Manufactured exports were to increase their share of total export earnings from 32 percent in 1985 to 41 percent by 1990. As can be seen from tables 10.1 and 10.2, all these targets have been surpassed.

With momentum of the rapid development of the manufacturing industry and exports in place, the government began to modify its incentives offered. In the 1992 national budget, several investment and export incentives which had been liberally given to the manufacturing sector previously have been reduced and refocused. Meanwhile, some new incentives have been introduced to encourage the development of high technology industries, venture capital companies, and research and development. They are as follows (EIU 1991 No. 4: 12–14, 25):

• Newly granted pioneer status companies will no longer be exempted from the prevailing 30 percent corporate tax. In addition, there will be no further extension of the status period. The government is, however, prepared to consider 100 percent exemption on projects such as heavy industries and high technology industries which can have a significant impact on the economy.

• The maximum tax allowance on investment was reduced to 60 percent (from 100 percent). The amount is not to exceed 70 percent of the company's statutory income. Any unutilized allowance can be carried forward to subsequent years.

• Export allowances will now be accessible only to manufacturing and trading companies which are 70 percent owned by Malaysians. Only trading companies which export manufactured goods and agricultural produce are eligible.

• The development tax rate for individuals and companies was reduced from 3 percent to 2 percent in 1992 (abolished in 1993).

• Venture capital companies are allowed to deduct from income losses incurred on the disposal of shares in a venture company in line with government strategy to promote investments in high technology industries. To entice companies to set up their operational headquarters in Malaysia, the distributed income to shareholders of these companies will be treated as tax exempt dividends.

• Incentives for research and development will be increased for companies and institutions established specifically to carry out industrial research and for new technology based firms. The new incentives will take the form of tax exemption over five years. Already such firms are offered deductible expenses, building allowances, and capital allowances on plant and machinery. The move is part of the government's strategy to increase R&D expenditure from 0.8 percent of GDP to 2 percent by the year 2000.

The government has also made efforts in reducing tariff protection. Malaysia has offered to reduce and bind tariff levels for 1,387 import items, on a quid pro quo basis, that is, in return for similar concessions on a bilateral basis, in a move to help break the deadlock at the Uruguay Round of the GATT talks on freer trade. The proposed cuts cover mainly manufactures, and chemical and mineral items and would affect about one third of the country's imports. With the reductions, the country's average tariff rate would be 10.3 percent, which would be substantially lower than that of many countries in the region. In late 1991, import duties on textile, garment, food, chemical, and printing goods have been reduced. In late 1992, import duties on 600 items have been reduced by between 10 percent and 30 percent. Among the items affected are foodstuffs, household goods, clothing, electrical and electronic goods, and components parts for electrical goods (EIU No. 4 1991: 13, 31 and No. 4. 1992: 17). This would help to reduce the import-substitution bias which still exists in some areas in the incentive system.

Manufactured Export Performance

Malaysia has been endowed with rich natural resources. Before independence, its economy was a kind of colonial economy, exporting agricultural and mineral raw materials mainly rubber, timber, palm oil, and tin to the industrial countries in exchange for manufactured goods. As part of the British Commonwealth, trade was free within the Commonwealth and therefore there was no chance to develop manufacturing industry. Upon independence in 1957, Malaysia began to develop some processing and textile industries under protection. But even by 1965, the value-added of the manufacturing sector accounted for only 9 percent of GDP. Since 1968, the government began to promote more actively the development of the manufacturing industry. The manufactured sector had grown faster than the GDP, and its share in the GDP increased to almost 14 percent in 1970 (see Table 10.1). However, because of sharp increases in export value of petroleum and palm oil, the share of manufactured goods in total export value fell to almost 12 percent in 1971 from 13.7 percent in 1967 (see Table 10.2).

Incentives for manufacturing investment and export gradually worked out their effects and the growth of both manufacturing production and exports accelerated since the early 1970s. The share of manufacturing in GDP rose to 19.6 percent in 1980, 26.7 percent in 1990 and almost 30 percent in 1992. Correspondingly, the combined share of the primary producing sectors (agriculture, forest, fishery, mining and quarrying) fell continuously from 44.5 percent in 1970 to 24.7 percent in 1992, and was for the second year smaller than the manufacturing sector (see Table 10.1).

Manufactured exports showed even more drastic increases. In the 1970s, their share in the total export value almost doubled and in the 1980s almost tripled. Their share of total export value in 1991 was 65 percent, compared with 23

Table 10.1

Malaysia: Gross Domestic Product by Sector Origin, 1965–92 (at constant 1978 market prices) (in percent)

	1965[a]	1970	1980	1990	1992
Agriculture, forest and fishing	27.9	30.6	22.9	18.6	16.0
Mining and quarrying	11.1	13.9	10.1	9.7	8.7
Manufacturing	9.1	13.9	19.6	26.7	29.9
Other industry	0.5	0.5	0.6	3.5	5.9
Services	46.8	36.3	41.3	42.6	41.5
Adjustment items	4.6	4.8	5.5	1.1	−2.0
GNP	100.0	100.0	100.0	100.0	100.0
GNP value (M$billion)	15.6[a]	20.9	44.5	79.6	94.0
GNP growth rate per annum (%)	6.0	7.8	6.0	8.7	
	(1965–70)	(1970–80)	(1980–90)	(1990–92)	

Source: Bank Negara Malaysia, *Annual Report*, various issues (Kuala Lumpur).
[a]Based on value at 1965 prices.

percent in 1981; more than reversing the position with primary exports. Even the recent currency appreciation and recessions in the West did not slow down Malaysia's manufactured exports.

The structure of manufacturing exports also changed phenomenally. In the late 1960s and early 1970s, the resource-based processed exports, such as petroleum products, food products, wood and wood products, mineral and metal products, as well as the labor-intensive manufactured exports, such as textiles, clothing, footwear, and simple electrical machinery, appliances, and parts registered more rapid growth than other manufactured exports. This reflects the first stage of industrialization and industrial export promotion. Later, following the strategy of developing machinery, chemical, and other heavy industries, the investment of MNCs in such industries in the EPZs, and the initiation of such industries by the state, capital, and technology-intensive manufactured exports increased by leaps and bounds. Exports of electrical machinery, appliances and parts, and transport machinery was the largest category (12.2 percent) of total export value in 1981, and they increased sharply in the 1980s, accounted for 58 percent of the total export value in 1991. Exports of textiles, clothing, and footwear (the second largest category) accounted for only 7.7 percent of total export, followed by mineral and metal products (4.4 percent) (see Table 8.2). All this reflects that industrialization in Malaysia has been further upgraded.

During about twenty-five years of most export-led industrialization with intermittent import-substitution, the economy grew fairly rapidly, particularly during the export promotion period of 1970–80 with GDP growing at 7.8 percent per annum. In 1965–70 and 1980–90 GDP grew at 6.0 percent per annum. In 1991–1992, GDP grew by 8.7 percent per annum. The Malaysian economy, highly

Table 10.2

Malaysia: Gross Exports[a] by Major Products, 1967–91 (in percent)

	1967	1971	1981	1991
Agricultural products, including forestry and fisheries	57.3	59.5	42.8	19.2
Rubber	34.2	29.1	14.4	2.8
Saw logs	12.8	12.5	9.2	4.3
Sawn timber	2.9	3.9	4.4	3.2
Palm kernel and oil	3.4	7.7	12.2	5.8
Others	4.3	6.3	2.6	3.1
Minerals	27.7	26.9	36.2	15.5
Tin	20.3	18.1	8.3	0.7
Petroleum[b]	3.3	7.8	26.8	10.8
Others	4.1	1.0	1.9	4.0
Manufactures	13.7	11.9	23.2	64.9
Electrical machinery, appliances, and parts	1.5	1.7	11.1	58.0
(Electronic components)				21.2
(Electrical appliances)				5.9
(Other electrical machinery)				30.9
Transport equipment			1.1	5.4
Food products, beverages, and tobacco	3.1	2.1	2.2	3.7
Textiles, clothing, and footwear	0.8	10.1	2.9	7.7
Wood and wood products	0.8	2.4	1.7	2.8
Rubber products	0.3	0.4	0.3	2.8
Petroleum products	4.6	2.2		1.9
Chemical and chemical products	0.9	0.8	1.5	2.9
Mineral and metal products	0.7	0.7	0.8	4.4
Other manufactures	1.1	0.7	1.5	10.4
Miscellaneous[c]	1.3	1.7	1.4	0.5
TOTAL	100.0	100.0	100.0	100.0
Total value (in M$billion)	3.72	5.01	27.11	94.67

Total exports growth rate per annum (%)	7.7	18.4	13.3
	(1967–71)	(1971–81)	(1981–91)

Source: Bank Negara Malaysia, *Annual Report*, 1971, 1981, 1990, 1991. (Kuala Lumpur). Tables 42 and 43 (1971, Tables 9.1 and 9.3, 1981, 1990, and 1991).

[a]Gross exports include re-exports but exclude intra-regional exports among West Malaysia, Sabah and Sarawak.

[b]Mainly re-exports of crude petroleum imported from Brunei and partly refined petroleum produced in Sarawak and West Malaysia.

[c] Mainly special transactions and postal packages.

dependent on foreign trade, is vulnerable to changes of the world economic situation. The external sector of the Malaysian economy was critically threatened during the early–1980s recession. Aggregate exports stagnated during the 1981–82 period. In 1986 there was a commodity slump as prices of primary products collapsed simultaneously. However, prices recovered since 1987 and with a currency devaluation, Malaysia has been able to maintain its international competitiveness in its manufactured exports. Moreover, because of greater export diversification, wide fluctuations of prices of its major primary exports such as rubber, tin, and palm oil have less effect on export stability than before the onset of industrialization.

The composition of manufactured exports, however, is still structurally weak, because it is based on a narrow range of industrial goods. Electrical and electronic products, chemicals and textiles, and clothing and footwear are the dominant industrial exports. They constitute almost 70 percent of total manufactured exports. In view of this, it is the explicit policy strategy of the Industrial Master Plan to diversify the export structure to encourage other types of manufactured exports such as basic metals, metal products, and nonmetallic products.

Although Malaysia has attempted to diversify its export market, the country still depends on a few industrial economies as major buyers. Aside from Singapore (23 percent of total Malaysian exports) which is Malaysia's main destination for reexports, the United States (17 percent), Japan (16 percent), and the EC (15 percent) are the three largest markets for Malaysia's exports. They are the markets for primary commodities, manufactures, and resource-based industrial goods, as well as the suppliers of intermediate and capital goods. Regarding Malaysia's manufactured exports, besides Singapore (27.7 percent), the United States is the largest buyer (23.5 percent), followed by the EC (17.5 percent) and far behind by Japan, 9.2 percent in 1991 (Bank Negara Malaysia 1991: 251).

Electronic components, telecommunication equipment, textiles, and apparel account for 60 percent of the manufactured exports to the United States. A significant part of the United States–Malaysian trade is within the General System for Preference (GSP) framework. Malaysia ranks eighth among the beneficiaries of the United States' GSP. The declassification of other NIEs as of the United States' GSP, has boosted Malaysia's manufactured exports and industrialization. In 1981 the country's GSP exports to the United States totaled US$62 million. In 1988, the total was almost US$2 billion.

Malaysia's EC trade has not improved markedly since 1975. Manufactured exports constitute 22 percent of total trade with the EC. In light of this, Malaysia is apprehensive about the consequences of post–1992 EC integration, although it has been delayed.

As Asian NIEs, particularly South Korea and Taiwan, change their trade structure, Malaysia plans to increase its exports to such countries. For instance, South Korea is presently Malaysia's fourth largest export market. New trade links with Asian NIEs are being forged via their investment in Malaysian industry. Such investments are predominantly export-oriented, directed to the investors markets and to the industrial economies.

Challenge

Like other developing economies, Malaysia faces global challenges. Its choice of strategic options is influenced by trade and fiscal imbalances in the major industrial countries, trade conflicts, and increasing competition from LDC's as well as other NIEs.

In the coming years, Malaysia must overcome the following challenges if its manufacturing export program is to be successful:

• In the short term, Malaysia would be unable to penetrate the nontraditional export markets because of growing protectionism and intensified competition from other producers of manufactured goods.

• The IMP suffers from an overemphasis on resource-based industries. Its production strategy is not development- and market-oriented; it needs to create a new approach to comparative advantage dynamics. In general, as indicated by the export-output ratios of the various manufacturing subsectors, the resource-based industries have been poor exporters.

• The competitive edge of Malaysian manufactured exports is not clearly focused. Malaysia has always sold primary commodities; it is not a marketer of branded manufactured exports. The two types of exports require distinctly different strategic positions.

• R&D support for industrialization and manufactured export promotion is weak, the government has only recently tried to step it up. Malaysia's internal technological capacity is below that of other NIEs.

• The industrial work force quality required for export manufacturing is lacking. In particular, the entrepreneurial and managerial personnel for export promotion is unavailable. The infrastructure for training technical and marketing workers is inadequate.

• There is no institutional infrastructural support, including marketing organizations and quality control facilities, for a strong marketing drive.

• Malaysia has only a weak ancillary industrial sector to support its manufactured export sector. Most of the small- and medium-sized industries are backward and inefficient. There is no integrated subcontracting system.

• The investment and export incentive system does not provide an integrated support system for promoting export manufacturing because of the ad hoc nature of most of the government policy measures.

• The country's narrow manufactured export base is vulnerable to both foreign competition and protectionism.

• In its overall policy formation style, the government has been distracted by requirements of the New Economic Policy which overstresses the ethnic-distributional aspect of economies to the detriment of growth dynamics.

• Related to the above item is the overly interventionist role of the government. For some time it has crowded out the initiatives of the private sector.

Conclusion

Overall, the Malaysian government has been quite flexible in adjusting to the demands of the changed world economy. During the 1980s, it introduced numerous policy changes to encourage a greater role for the private sector, both local and foreign. A program of liberalization and deregulation is being implemented, particularly to attract direct foreign investment from the Asian NIEs. At the same time, production costs have been restrained by regulating labor's wages and increasing producer subsidies.

But Malaysia's policy does not embody a coherent set of strategies. Efforts to promote export trade, particularly manufactured exports, are governed by ad hoc measures rather than anticipatory planning. Countertrade, bilateral trade agreements, and trade missions are used to increase manufactured exports and diversifying markets.

At the regional ASEAN level, the basic institutional infrastructure is set up, but there has been no dramatic increase in the volume and value of regional manufactured export trade. The ASEAN Industrial Projects, the ASEAN Industrial Complementation Scheme, and the ASEAN Industrial Joint Ventures have been beset with implementation problems. They have not helped to increase complementary manufactured exports in ASEAN intra-trade. However, Malaysia has had more success in bilateral trade with other ASEAN members, particularly Singapore, which has created new economic complementarities.

Malaysia's success in its manufactured export drive will depend principally on the strategic positioning of its various policies and implementation capability to create a market segment for its manufactured products. It will not be an easy task, as the government's attention and energy is constantly diverted to other goals by the priority of the politics of ethnic economies. The urgent need for more manufactured exports is recognized, but the government still has to formulate a firm, integrated, and sustained policy to solve the problem.

References

Bank Negara Malaysia, *Annual Report*, various issues. (Kuala Lumpur).
Economists Intelligence Unit, 1991, 1992. *Malaysia, Brunei Country Report*, No. 4 1991, Nos. 3 and 4, 1992. *Economist* (London).
World Bank, 1992. *Trends in Developing Economies*, Chapter on Malaysia, pp. 327–33 (Washington, D.C.).

CHAPTER 11

Indonesia: From Dutch Disease
to Manufactured Exports

MARI PANGESTU

Manufactured exports have become important for Indonesia only in recent years. Before that, the growth of its non-oil exports, including manufactured goods, had been erratic. During the oil boom years, due to the so-called Dutch Disease effect as well as an unfavorable policy environment, non-oil exports and manufactured exports in particular even declined in 1975 and 1981–82. During those boom years, the Indonesian government had always recognized the need to diversify into non-oil exports, but in an economy buoyed by windfall oil revenues such action did not seem urgent. Since the rapid decline in oil prices beginning in 1986, a strong export-oriented drive has been evident, and the country has achieved spectacular growth in non-oil exports (see Table 11.1).

This chapter provides an overview of Indonesia's experience with manufactured exports. The first section gives a brief background regarding the factors that contributed to the stagnation of manufactured exports. The second section analyzes the period since 1987, in which manufactured exports have increased substantially.

Past Experience: Stagnating Manufactured Exports before 1986

Policy Environment

In an oil-exporting country like Indonesia, changes in the Indonesian economy and its industrialization, as well as growth of manufactured exports, have been closely linked to oil prices.

The appendix to this chapter summarizes changes in Indonesian policy direction and conditions, as well as economic reforms undertaken by the so-called new-order government (headed by General Sukarto as the President) since 1967. After a period of high growth during the rehabilitation and stabilization period came moderate growth of 7 percent to 8 percent. The new-order government undertook substantial liberalization measures, including trade and industrial reforms.

The oil boom years, which began with the quadrupling of oil prices in 1973 and continued with high prices until 1982, weakened much of the government's resolve to institute reforms that would provide a greater role for the private sector and non-oil exports. The oil boom and concomitant windfall oil revenues were accompanied by substantial adjustment problems related to absorption of that income by the domestic economy. Increased domestic spending led to excess demand for domestic or nontraded goods and put upward pressure on the price of nontraded goods relative to non-oil traded goods. Since exchange rates were fixed, the price adjustment had to occur through a rise in the prices of nontraded goods. There is some evidence that the relative price change caused resources to move from the non-oil traded goods sector to the nontraded goods sector. The deterioration of this sector is what is referred to as the Dutch Disease effect in the literature. (The term "Dutch Disease" derives from the difficulties experienced by the Dutch manufacturing sector as a result of the natural gas discoveries of the 1960s. The natural gas export boom caused a real currency appreciation, thereby reducing the international competitiveness of Dutch industry.)

Trade and industrial policies during this period sought to influence the pattern of industrialization by protecting domestic industries. Like other developing countries, Indonesia adopted an import substitution strategy, beginning with finished consumer goods and then moving upstream to intermediate and capital goods. The protectionist regime that developed was characterized by escalating protection through tariff and nontariff barriers; high and variable effective rates of protection that were biased against production of exports; and proliferation of administrative procedures and excessive government intervention. Bias toward non-oil exports, particularly manufactured goods, was evident in the protection system. Measures of effective rates of protection showed negative protection (or penalty) for manufactured exports.

Macroeconomic Policy

Macroeconomic policy was fairly sound during the new-order period. It was characterized by relatively prudent fiscal policy; there was an implicit rule of thumb that the external debt service ratio (DSR) should not exceed 22 percent of export earnings. The 50 percent devaluation of the currency in 1978, justified as a response to the Dutch Disease effect, showed the government's willingness to react quickly to changing conditions with appropriate exchange rate management. However, the government was less successful in controlling inflation during this period, since the substantial increase in the money supply resulting from higher oil prices could not be sterilized with the available monetary instruments. It is estimated that inflation eroded the effect of the devaluation within two years. Aside from this development, the devaluation did not provide a permanent stimulus to non-oil exports because it was not accompanied by deregulation measures. The existing protection system was still biased against manufactured exports.

Two important policies increased manufactured exports. First was the introduction of the export certificate scheme in 1978, which was supposed to be essentially a duty-rebate program. A substantial increase in shipments by textile exporters, the chief users of this scheme, can be attributed to the certificates. However, the huge increase of Indonesian export sales in American and European markets led to the imposition of quotas on the country's textiles and garments. There was also a threat of countervailing duties because the United States could show that the certificate scheme provided Indonesian manufacturers with a payment exceeding the duties they paid, so it was in effect an export subsidy. Furthermore, implementation of the scheme was subject to much abuse: for example, textile exporters sent empty containers and still obtained the rebate. Since the scheme was evaluated as an export subsidy, it had to be changed upon Indonesia's accession to the GATT Code on Subsidies and Countervailing Duties.

The second policy that boosted manufactured exports "artificially" was the phasing-out of log exports beginning in 1980 and their replacement by plywood exports. Due to a lag in plant and equipment investment, plywood exports did not begin until 1983, but they are now one of Indonesia's major manufactured exports.

No other government policy could be said to have promoted exports during the oil boom years. No export processing zones were developed. There was a trade promotion center at the Ministry of Trade, and trade attachés as well as investment promotion boards were located overseas, but they have not been effective.

Industrial Sector and Manufactured Export Performance

The manufacturing sector's share of total GDP increased from 8.3 percent in 1969 to 15.3 percent in 1980, and further to almost 20 percent in 1991. The manufacturing share decreased during the first half of the 1980s due to exhaustion of import-substitution potential, as well as the decline of economic activity as oil prices fell (see Table 11.3).

Tables 11.1 and 11.2 show the stagnation of non-oil exports and manufactured exports in particular during the oil boom period, as well as a substantial increase since the fall in oil prices, notably since 1986, when its share in total export rose from 11 percent in 1985 to 31 percent in 1988, when the oil price stabilized. Table 11.1 shows how the value of oil exports jumped with the first oil price shock in 1973–74 and the second shock in 1979. The decrease in the value of oil exports since 1982 is evident, particularly in 1986, when oil prices declined dramatically. As can be expected, price fluctuations are also reflected in the changing proportion of oil exports to total exports. Table 11.2 shows that oil exports were dominant for most of the oil boom years, accounting for more than 70 percent of all exports and reaching a high of 85 percent in 1982. Their share has declined rapidly since then, particularly since 1986. It was 40 percent in 1991 (same source as Table 11.2).

Table 11.1

Indonesia: Value of Exports, 1969–91 (U.S. $ billions)

Year	Value		
	Non-oil	Oil & Gas	Total
1969	.37	.37	.74
1970	.69	.45	1.14
1971	.70	.55	1.25
1972	.82	.72	1.53
1973	1.60	1.61	3.21
1974	2.21	5.21	7.43
1975	1.79	5.31	7.10
1976	2.54	6.00	8.55
1977	3.47	7.38	10.85
1978	3.66	7.98	11.64
1979	5.43	10.16	15.59
1980	6.17	17.78	23.95
1981	4.50	20.66	25.16
1982	3.93	18.40	22.33
1983	5.00	16.14	21.15
1984	5.87	16.02	21.89
1985	5.87	12.72	18.59
1986	6.53	8.28	14.80
1987	8.58	8.56	17.14
1988	11.54	7.68	19.22
1989	13.48	8.68	22.16
1990	14.60	11.07	25.68
1991	18.25	10.90	29.14

Compound Growth Rates (percent per annum)

Year	Non-oil	Oil & Gas	Total
1969–72	30.5	25.9	19.9
1972–81	21.5	45.0	36.2
1981–86	7.7	−20.1	−11.2
1986–91	22.9	5.6	14.5

Sources: Biro Pusat Statistik (BPS), *Monthly Statistical Bulletin,* January 1993 and earlier issues (Jakarta).

Growth in the value of non-oil exports has also fluctuated during the past two decades, due to changes in commodity prices. Until recent years, non-oil exports still comprised mainly primary products, and their high growth in the early 1970s reflects commodity prices.

Agricultural commodities constituted more than half of Indonesia's exports before the oil boom, and their share of total exports has declined since then. But until 1980, agricultural products still accounted for about 90 percent of the country's non-oil exports. Their share has declined as exports of manufactured products have increased.

Table 11.2

Indonesia: Composition of Exports, 1970–88 (percent)

Year	Agriculture	Oil & Gas & Minerals	Manufacturing
1970	55	44	1
1971	54	45	1
1972	42	57	1
1973	44	55	1
1974	25	75	1
1975	20	78	1
1976	25	74	1
1977	27	71	2
1978	26	72	2
1979	28	69	3
1980	22	76	2
1981	13	83	3
1982	11	85	4
1983	13	81	7
1984	14	77	8
1985	16	73	11
1986	21	61	18
1987	22	55	23
1988	24	45	31

Source: Biro Pusat, *Exports,* various issues (Jakarta).
Notes:
Agriculture: SITC 0, 1, 2 (except 27 & 28) and 4.
Oil & Gas & Minerals: SITC 27, 28, 3, 68.
Manufacturing: SITC 5, 6 (except 68), 7, 8, and 9.

The spectacular growth—more than 30 percent—per year of non-oil exports in 1987–88 and 23 percent per year in 1986–91 was due mostly to increased manufactured exports, although improvement of commodity prices has also had a favorable effect. Manufactured exports increased at a rate of about 40 percent to 50 percent, with a resulting increase in their share of non-oil exports. Manufactured exports represented a mere 2 percent of non-oil exports in 1980 but rose to 31 percent by 1988 (see Table 11.2).

Several points about this growth are noteworthy. First, rapid growth can be expected when one starts from a low base. Second, the product composition of manufactured exports is still confined to several commodities. Textiles, garments, and plywood are the major manufactured exports (see Tables 11.4 and 11.5). Furthermore, more than half of the manufactured exports are resource-based (mainly plywood). However, there has been a steady increase in labor-intensive manufactured exports (see Tables 11.4 and 11.5). Third, due to weak domestic economic conditions related to the oil price decline that began in 1986, there was excess production capacity. Thus manufactured export output could be

Table 11.3

Indonesia: Sectoral Share in GDP, 1976–91 (at 1983 market prices)

	1976	1980	1985	1990	1991
Agriculture, forestry and fishery	36.1	30.7	24.0	19.4	18.4
Mining and quarrying	11.7	9.3	17.5	15.2	15.6
Manufacturing	11.4	15.3	13.3	19.3	19.9
Public Utilities and Construction	5.3	6.4	6.3	6.4	6.7
Commerce	16.6	16.6	15.5	16.1	16.0
Transport and communication, and other financial services	9.1	10.1	12.6	13.4	13.5
Public administration and defense	7.3	8.7	8.1	7.6	7.4
Ownership of dwelling	2.5	3.0	2.7	2.6	2.5
GDP	100.0	100.0	100.0	100.0	100.0

Source: Bank of Indonesia, *Report of the Financial Year,* various issues (Jakarta).

increased in response to a more favorable policy environment without increasing investment.

Manufactured Export Expansion and Policy Changes

Indonesia does not have a sharply defined export promotion package along the lines of those formulated by the NIEs, although recent reforms have built in a favorable bias toward exports. Several of the recent significant reforms had more overriding objectives than export promotion. However, in most cases they have had a favorable effect on non-oil exports.

Falling oil prices had important implications for Indonesia. Since oil exports accounted for almost 70 percent of total exports at the time, foreign exchange earnings available to finance imports and debt service decreased. The terms of trade worsened, and appreciation of the yen, particularly after 1985, exacerbated the balance of payments situation because more than one-third of Indonesia's foreign debt was denominated in yen. External debt increased substantially, and the DSR rose sharply to more than 30 percent. Furthermore, about 60 percent of government revenue came from taxes on oil-producing corporations, so that public funds available for development expenditures decreased substantially.

Ambivalent Reform 1982–85

In the initial stage of oil price decline, the government response was ambivalent. The authorities recognized the problems of mobilizing increased domestic funds and raising foreign exchange reserves by promoting non-oil exports, but it took some time before political will became strong enough to push through the policy

Table 11.4

Indonesia: Major Manufactured Exports, 1980–88 (in U.S. $ millions)

	1980	1985	1986	1987	Jan.–July 1988	Average Annual Growth 1980–87 (percent) Nominal Value	Volume
Resource-Intensive							
Total	119	992	1,209	2,036	1,404	50.0	N/A
(% of all manufactures)	(24)	(49)	(46)	(52)	(48)		
Major items:							
plywood	68	941	1,127	1,901	1,291	60.9	35.9
cement	26	22	41	57	42	11.9	24.4
leather	6	8	15	45	41	33.4	40.7
Labor Intensive							
Total	287	785	1,054	1,303	1,024	24.1	N/A
(% of all manufactures)	(57)	(38)	(40)	(33)	(35)		
Major items:							
clothing	98	339	522	596	418	29.4	28.9
woven fabrics	43	227	287	385	304	36.8	42.3
yarn	3	13	20	84	64	61.0	59.9
oils & perfumes	21	23	27	34	20	7.1	1.0
glass & glassware	3	8	13	31	46	39.6	41.9
electronics	94	77	29	15	17	−23.1	32.5
musical instruments	n	39	43	28	19	n	n
furniture	3	7	9	27	33	36.9	50.1
footwear	1	8	8	22	36	n	n
Capital Intensive							
Total	97	266	377	556	467	28.3	N/A
(% of all manufactures)	(19)	(13)	(14)	(14)	(16)		
Major items:							
fertilizer	35	80	127	86	67	13.7	94.6
paper products	5	21	33	96	73	52.5	61.4
steel products	8	28	58	136	89	49.9	55.8
inorganic chemicals	n	35	27	25	12	n	48.5
rubber types	n	7	11	23	24	n	n
Total, all manufactures	501	2,044	2,639	3,895	2,895	34.1	N/A
Three largest as % of total	(52)	(74)	(73)	(74)	(70)		

Sources: Biro Pusat Statistik (BPS), *Ekspor (Exports)*, (Jakarta, various issues); Hall Hill 1989): Table 4.

Notes:

(1) The following definitions are used:

Resource-intensive—SITC items 61, 63, 66 (excluding 664–666), 671.

Table 11.4 *(continued)*

Labor-intensive—SITC items 54, 55, 65, 664–666, 695–697, 749, 776, 778, 793, 81–85, 89 (excluding 896–897).

Capital-intensive—SITC items 5 (excluding 54 and 55), 62, 64, 67 (excluding 671), 69 (excluding 695–697), 7 (excluding 749, 776, 778, 793), 86–88, 896–897.
(2) The following trade classification codes are used for the major exports (corresponding SITC codes are given in parentheses): plywood 634 (33113); cement 661 (3631); leather 611 (323); clothing 84 (322); woven fabrics 652–9 (32112); yarn 651 (32111); oils and perfumes 551 (35233); glass and glassware 664–5 (362); electronics 749, 776, 778 (3833); musical instruments 898 (3902); furniture 821 (332); footwear 851 (324); fertilizer 562 (3512); paper products 641 (341); steel products 672–3 (371); inorganic chemicals 522 (3511); rubber tires 625 (3551).
(3) "n" indicates less than $1 million, and growth rates rendered irrelevant by very small initial base.

Table 11.5

Indonesia: Exports of Industrial Products,[a] 1981, 1991 (in U.S. $ million)

	1981	1991
Processed wood	397	3,560
Articles of basic metal	604	594
Garments	95	2,290
Other textiles	31	1,785
Preparation rubber	812	960
Cattle fodder	88	167
Essential oils	16	153
Palm oil	107	335
Fatty acids	11	94
Electrical apparatus	81	669
Processed food	64	391
Cement	30	147
Painted articles	6	56
Chemicals	19	43
Fertilizer	4	298
Leather and leather goods	29	53
Paper and paper goods	1	268
Rattan	69	—
Others	177	3,104
Total	2,667	15,068
Share in total exports	10.6	51.7

Source: Same as Table 11.1.
[a]The coverage of exports of industrial products is broader than that of manufactured exports in Table 11.4.

reforms required to achieve these objectives. Not until oil prices fell to $10 a barrel in 1986 did it become politically feasible to implement several of the policy reforms that had been proposed for some time in political economy debates.

Unlike financial measures, trade and industrial policies were not liberalized but became more protectionist. Quantitative restrictions on imports were increased under the approved importers system (*Tata Niaga Impor*) that was introduced in 1982, under which goods specified in nine categories could be imported only by approved importers. The nine categories were electrical and electronic goods; chemical products; metal industries; machinery and spare parts; heavy equipment and spare parts; motor vehicle components; textiles; agricultural products; and food, beverages, and fresh fruits.

During the 1982–86 period many such import licenses were issued. In addition to direct balance of payments pressures, there was renewed support for import-substitution industrialization aimed at intermediate and upstream products such as iron, steel, synthetic fibers, cement, chemicals, fertilizers, and motor vehicle engines. The underlying argument was that such an industrialization strategy would relieve the balance of payments problems. Although tariff levels were already high, they did not provide the required protection. But instead of increasing tariffs, the nontariff barriers were raised because they were less visible.

In 1986, it was estimated that the approved importers system restricted 28 percent of the total number of items imported, 26 percent of the total import value, and 31 percent of the value added.

Despite the increased protectionist trend during the mid-1980s, two important and substantive reforms were undertaken with respect to tariffs and customs procedures toward the end of the first stage of declining oil prices. This marked the beginning of the deregulation drive that aimed to increase non-oil exports, improve efficiency of the economy, and expand participation by the private sector.

It is important to note that long before the actual reforms were undertaken the government recognized the problem of the popularly termed "high-cost economy": high costs due to protection; inefficiencies in the processing of government-related regulations; and the inevitable abuses inherent in a highly regulated system.

In 1985, the tariff system was rationalized considerably by across-the-board reduction in the range and level of nominal tariffs. The range of tariffs was reduced from zero to 225 percent to zero to 60 percent, and most tariff rates ranged 5 to 35 percent. The number of tariff levels was also reduced from twenty-five to eleven. Despite the imposition of higher nontariff barriers during this period, the rationalization of tariffs must be viewed as a positive development.

In March 1983, the rupiah was devalued by 50 percent in rupiah terms. The devaluation was undertaken after much speculation concerning the possibility of such a step in light of the oil price decline; and the speculation led to a significant anticipatory capital outflow. Devaluation was undertaken for budgetary reasons, so that the nominal value of government revenues in rupiah terms would increase despite the reduction in the price of oil. It also aimed to increase non-oil exports but failed to do so because devaluation was accompanied by more protectionist policies instead of the much needed deregulation in the real sector. This lack of direction by government policies underscores again the ambivalence toward implementation of reform measures during the initial stage of the oil price decline.

In April 1985, the whole customs department operation related to the import and export of goods was disbanded in one bold sweep. This reform was undertaken to reduce processing time and discretionary actions by customs officials, long recognized as a major problem and often cited as an important component of Indonesia's high-cost economy. The customs officials who had cleared goods for import were replaced by a private Swiss surveying company, SGS, at the point of importation. Evaluation of the duty rate and value of imports are now done at the point of origin of the goods, and the importer pays the duty directly to his bank. This permits a reduction in the number of customs officials required and limits their discretionary actions at the point of entry.

Active Promotion and Deregulation since 1986

The sharp decline in oil prices that began in 1986 marked the turning point in Indonesia's present deregulation phase. Ironically, declining oil revenues and the deteriorating balance of payments provided the political will for substantive deregulation to take place. At this stage, deregulation usually aims to remove the bias against exports that is caused by the prevailing system of protection; it does not yet aim to remove the source of distortion.

The first step toward reducing the exporters' high costs was the customs cleanup in 1985. Subsequent deregulation had a similar objective: to offset exporters' costs by simplifying procedures; allowing them special facilities; and slowly dismantling the system of protection by changing from nontariff barriers to tariffs, which are believed to cause less distortion.

In the 1986–87 period, the resolve to deregulate was very strong. In May 1986 a package of policy measures for removing export bias and encouraging foreign investment (PAKEM) was introduced. It provided a new and improved duty-rebate system in response to objections to the previous export certificate scheme. Under the new scheme exporters can obtain a refund of the duty paid on imports that are used to produce exports, and they are allowed to bypass the import monopolies as long as the item is used in export production.

Exporters were defined as producers who exported 85 percent or more of their total production. The unique feature of the new system was that the applicants for duty rebate were not allowed to meet face to face with the officials who processed their applications. Applications had to be sent by mail or courier, and all inquiries had to be made by telephone. This computerized and arm's-length application procedure was designed to reduce the abuses that existed under the old system.

Other important features of PAKEM were that Indonesian exporting firms with foreign investors could be up to 95 percent foreign-owned; foreign firms operating in the country could utilize low-interest export credits; and joint ventures with 75 percent or more Indonesian equity could undertake domestic distribution.

However, the most important reason for the rapid increase of manufactured exports since 1986 was the 1986 devaluation of the rupiah in response to plummeting oil prices. Unlike the depreciations of 1978 and 1983, this one succeeded in increasing non-oil exports because deregulation measures were undertaken, and inflation rates were low: 9 percent during 1987 and 8 percent during 1988. In 1988, a tight monetary policy was adopted, and the rupiah was depreciated with the objective of maintaining competitive real effective exchange rates. Deregulation also began to alleviate the problems associated with the high-cost economy and the general direction of export promotion (see appendix).

On the trade side, many nontariff barriers were removed and replaced by tariffs in October 1986 and January 1987. The approved-importers system was rationalized at the same time. In line with efforts to improve the investment climate, the investment and capacity licensing requirements for domestic firms were substantially deregulated. Before this, renewal of licenses (for terms varying between two and five years) and any capacity expansion exceeding 30 percent required approval. Furthermore, the categories of licenses were broadened considerably to encourage diversification of the same type of product; manufacturers no longer had to apply for a new license to modify a product. The "closed" (or restricted) sector under the DSP list could also be opened to investors who exported 85 percent or more of their production.

Textiles and garments constitute a major component of Indonesia's non-oil exports. In July 1987 the system of textile quota allocation to Indonesian exporters was rationalized, after much press coverage of quota-allocation system abuses and dissatisfaction with the existing Textile Producers Association. The main changes aimed to reduce the discretionary powers of officials and eliminate unnecessary administrative procedures and costs. While the initial allocation was still based on past performance, allocations by company and size were henceforth published in the media. The questionable fee to the Textile Association that had been linked to allocation of quotas was removed. Unused quotas could now be exchanged at an auction, but quotas would be reduced in the next year's allocation.

The remaining major deregulations were in the financial and capital market sectors. In November 1988, another significant nontariff barrier, the monopoly on plastics and steel, was removed. Deregulation of interisland shipping was announced at the same time. The most important recent deregulation has been the elimination of the highly complex priority investment list and its replacement by a simplified negative (restriction) list.

Table 11.6

Indonesia: Approved Export-Oriented Investments, 1986–88

	1986	1987	1988	Cumulative 1986–88
Domestic Investments				
Total new projects:				
number	316	565	765	1,646
Value (Rp. billions)	4,417	10,265	13,200	27,882
Export-oriented projects	169	375	578	1,122
(% of total)	(53.5)	(65.1)	(75.6)	(68.2)
Planned exports per year (US$ millions)	1,778	3,943	6,116	11,838
Foreign Investments				
Total new projects:				
number	50	70	133	253
Value (US$ millions)	826	1,457	4,166	6,449
Export-oriented projects	19	43	96	158
(% of total)	(38.0)	(61.4)	(72.1)	(62.5)
Planned exports per year (US$ millions)	243	507	1,556	2,307

Source: Board of Investment (Jakarta).
Note: Figures refer to "approved" investments, excluding the financial and oil sectors.

Prospects

The recent expansion of manufactured exports shortly after 1986 has been largely based on existing excess capacity. Future growth of manufactured exports will require new investment. There are encouraging signs of interest in export-oriented activities among domestic as well as foreign investors, who have planned large increases in approved investments for the export market (see Table 11.6). Some of the investments have already taken place. The major sectors receiving export-oriented foreign investment are food, textile and leather, wood and wood products, chemical and rubber products, and metal products.

Data on approved export-oriented foreign investment by country of origin indicate a strong interest from Japan and the NIEs that are undergoing structural changes. (see Table 11.7 for a country and product breakdown of investments.) Preliminary evidence suggests that most of the exports from Japanese firms in Indonesia are destined for the Japanese market. In addition, smaller and medium-sized Japanese companies are relocating their manufacturing to Indonesia, among other Asian NIEs. Most of the exports from NIEs' investments are destined for third markets, notably the United States.

Table 11.7

Indonesia: Major Source Countries Investing in Export-Oriented Projects, 1986–87 (number of projects)

	1986	1987	Major Sectors
Japan	7	25	Machinery, electrical machinery and appliances, wood manufactures, rubber manufactures, equipment
South Korea	1	7	Wood manufactures, footwear, garments, food processing, chemicals, forestry
Hong Kong	1	11	Textiles, wood manufactures
Taiwan	1	5	Paper and paper products, textiles, rubber manufactures, wood manufactures
Singapore	5	1	Wood manufactures, rubber manufactures, electrical machinery
Subtotal of countries above	15	49	
Total (for all countries)	50	70	

Source: Board of Investment (Jakarta).

Future growth of manufactured exports will depend on increased investment along with continued consistent implementation of trade and industry as well as financial reforms (as a source of finance). Thus far, the real effective exchange rates have been kept competitive.

References

Hill, Hal. 1989. "Indonesia: Export Promotion in the Post-OPEC Era." Working Papers in trade and development (Australia) No. 89/8:1–42, August; Australian National University, Department of Economics and National Center for Development Studies (Canbera).

Pangestu, Mari, and Boediono. 1986. "The Structure and Causes of Manufacturing Sector Protection in Indonesia." In *The Political Economy of Manufacturing Protection: Experience of ASEAN and Australia*, eds. Christopher Findlay and Ross Garnaut. Allen and Unwin, Sydney.

Pangestu, Mari, and Habir, Achmad. 1989. "Trends and Prospects in Privatization and Deregulation in Indonesia." *Asean Economic Bulletin* (March).

Wardhana, Ali. 1989. "Structural Adjustment in Indonesia: Export and the 'High Cost' Economy." Keynote address at the Twenty-Fourth Conference of Southeast Asian Central Bank Governors, Bangkok, January 25.

Appendix

Indonesia: Changes in Policy Direction and Economic Conditions

Policy Areas		1967–72; Rehabilitation & Stabilization	1973–81; Oil Boom	1982–85; Initial Oil Price Decline	1986–1988; Rapid Oil Price Decline
Direction		Liberal	Increasing Intervention	Some Reforms but Still Ambivalent	Serious Reforms, Some Mixed Signals
Economic setting	GDP	High growth, 10%	Moderate high growth, 7–8% p.a.	Slow growth, 3–5% p.a.	Slow growth, 3–5% p.a.
	DSR (% exports)	14–20%	14–20%	20–25%	30–38%
	Inflation	1–10% p.a. (av. 6%)	10–47% p.a. (av. 20%)	4–12% p.a. (av. 8%)	5–9% p.a. (av. 7%)
	Oil Exports	60%	60–80%	60–70%	50%
	Manuf./exports	1%	1–3%	4–11%	18–25%
	Oil/govt. revenues	50%	60–70%	50–60%	40–50%
Macro	Fiscal		Large revenue, govt. spending, Pertamina debt.	Tax reform (84)	Continued tax reform
	Monetary	Tight	Steriliz. oil money; credit ceilings; unsuccessful	Tight, introducing new monetary instruments	Tight; improvement of monetary instruments
	Exchange Rate	Unify multiple exchange rates and devaluation 1971 Open capital account	Devaluation, 1978–Dutch disease Begin 78–managed		Devaluation, 1986 1988–depreciation Effective exchange rate management
Industrial policy		Initial phase Import substitution (IS) (final consumer goods)	Continued import substitution (intermediate and capital goods)	Continued IS—industrial deepening; localization; Beginning export oriented	Export oriented Strong non-oil exports
Trade Policy		Beginning protection	Increased protection, mainly tariffs (some decline 1980) High and variable "effective rate of protection" Duty drawback (78)	Increased use NTBs Tariff reforms (85) Export credit (82) Shipping deregulation (85)	Decline in protection from NTBs to tariffs Improved duty drawback (86) Improved textiles quota allocation (87)
Investment		Open-door policy, liberal; except domestic distribution	Increasingly restrictive in ownership, priority list, capital limits, licensing; but administrative reform, BOI–one step	Still restrictive	Open, increased foreign ownership to 95% and access to export credit and domestic distribution for export oriented industries Deregulation of investments, licensing and renewal
Financial		Open entry	Closed; banks channel oil money	Deregulation of interest rates (83), removal of credit ceilings	Open for new entry Deregulation of insurance and capital markets

CHAPTER 12

The Development of Philippine Manufactured Exports

FLORIAN A. ALBURO

There were striking changes in the composition of Philippine exports since 1960, and changes in the product composition of nontraditional manufactures since 1970 have also been great. The share of nontraditional manufactured exports increased dramatically from 1.2 percent of all exports in 1960 to 36.4 percent by 1980 and 73.2 percent in 1990 (see Table 12.1). The trend in nontraditional manufactured exports followed the pattern of other developing countries and, more recently, the newly industrializing economies (see Table 12.2), reflecting the abundance of labor resources for producing such exports as electrical components, garments, food products, furniture, and footwear.

As Table 12.2 shows, electrical components and garments constitute a significant proportion, more than 50 percent, of nontraditional manufactured exports. In fact, this share rose from 40 percent in 1975 to over 60 percent since 1985. On the other hand, the more indigenous Philippine products have experienced either a lower rate of increase or an outright decline in exports. (see Tables 12.1 and 12.2).

There is no doubt, however, that the increasing proportion of manufactured goods among the country's exports is now a permanent structural characteristic. The Philippines has also seen an increase in the magnitude of its exports of nontraditional nonmanufactured items, which include such products as bananas, iron ores, fresh or simply preserved fish, and textile fibers.

Given this changing export performance and pattern, the basic question is whether the development of Philippine manufactured exports has led to broader changes in the economy in general and industry in particular that are consistent with this trend. More pointedly, does this augur well for a sustainable structural change in the economy toward a trade structure that reflects the country's comparative advantage and resource endowments?

We have argued elsewhere (Alburo 1987) that these trends have developed on top of the country's existing protectionist regime, rather than by simultaneously reducing the protection. We think a complete departure from the country's past

Table 12.1

Philippine Exports, 1960–90

Sector	1960	1970	1980	1990
Traditional primary	49.3	40.0	7.8	}17.6
Traditional manufactured	48.4	49.8	47.2	
Non-traditional primary		1.1	8.0	7.8
Non-traditional manufactured	1.2	8.3	36.4	73.2
Re-exports and special transactions	1.1	0.8	0.6	1.4
Total	100.0	100.0	100.0	100.0

Source: National Census and Statistics Office, *Foreign Trade Statistics*, various years (Manila).

import-substitution era is needed. Certain aspects of the development of manufactured exports put a drag on the country's ability to transform its structure.

First of all, the spurt of manufactured export growth in the 1970s did not really set in motion a snowball effect on overall export growth, which was the case in the NIEs. In fact, it was only in the early and mid-1970s that both total and manufactured exports registered respectable growth. In the 1980s growth rates for manufactured exports decreased. This decline was further aggravated by the 1983 crisis, which set back any gains achieved earlier.

Second, the development of manufactured exports has been overly concentrated in a few products, mainly electrical components (semiconductors and microcomponents) and garments or handicrafts. Manufacturing processes for the first two product groups are characterized by packaging and assembly. These weaknesses (overconcentration and packaging) were also found in the import-substitution regime of the three preceding decades, which did not build a strong industrial base.

Third, the real foreign exchange contribution of these manufactured exports is less than indicated, in the sense that many are import-intensive. Where we net out the value of import inputs for manufacture of electronics exports, we find they have a lower contribution to foreign exchange earnings. In contrast, exports of handicrafts, footwear, furniture, and food products, which have more domestic contents earned more foreign exchange per peso of exports.

Fourth, it is questionable whether this development of manufactured exports has resulted in broader-based growth. Although this question extends beyond trade and into the realm of macroeconomic and equity policies, it is relevant. For one thing, this has not stimulated a greater export orientation by Philippine manufacturing. For example, between 1960 and 1980 the proportion of manufactures to total exports grew faster than the proportion of manufacturing output that was exported. This suggests a slow change in the structure of the manufacturing sector. For another, while the factor content of manufactured exports has de-

Table 12.2

Philippine Exports of Nontraditional Manufactures, 1970–90
(in U.S. $ millions)

	1970	1975	1980	1985	1987	1990
Electrical & electronic equip.						
& components	—	47.3	671	993	1,100	1,964
Garments	36.2	107.0	500	622	1,096	1,776
Chemicals	5.4	22.1	95	152	246	268
Processed food & beverages	8.2	14.7	170	157	153	207
Furniture & parts	1.1	5.2	77	84	130	189
Footwear	1.1	3.0	67	39	31	78
Machinery & trans.						
equipment	1.1	9.5	46	37	86	150
Textile yarn, fabrics &						
related products	2.8	8.7	49	25	56	93
Wood manufactures	4.0	16.9	24	26	43	117
Nonmetallic mineral manu-						
factures, particularly						
cement	3.0	32.2	59	23	19	57
Other	32.8	115.9	348	408	643	726
Total exports of						
nontraditional						
manufactures	6.7	382.5	2,107	2,564	3,604	5,994
Total exports	1,142	2,294	5,788	4,629	5,720	8,186

Sources: National Economic and Development Authority, *Philippines Statistical Yearbook,* 1988, and *Philippine Development Report,* 1990 (Manila).

clined among capital-using products, the content of the largest share of the country's exports remains in the low-capital, low-skill category with only marginal increases in the low-capital, high-skill category (see Table 12.3). To the extent that public policy inhibits backward linkages or fails to promote broader rural development, the impact of the development of manufactured exports is more limited.

Finally, a significant portion of Philippine exports are classified under SITC 931 as "special transactions not classified according to kind." These transactions are defined as exports of products that are manufactured from imported materials on a consignment basis. In the Philippines, these products are mostly electronic equipment and garments.

The country's share of exports by all developing countries has expanded rapidly (see Table 12.4). But it is not clear whether this has changed Philippine trade structurally in the sense of adequately testing the country's marketing capacities through exposure of production decisions to more external or global factors.

Overall, recent data suggest that the development of Philippine manufactured exports has achieved the scale of trade experienced by the NIEs. However, it is

Table 12.3

Philippines: Value and Distribution of Nontraditional Manufactured Exports
(in 1972 U.S. $ millions; percentages in parentheses)

Factor Content	1971	1975	1980	1982
Low capital-low skill	56.8 (67.4)	117.6 (74.3)	361.8 (80.6)	455.4 (78.1)
Low capital-high skill	2.0 (2.4)	4.9 (3.1)	18.9 (3.7)	25.0 (4.3)
High capital-low skill	18.9 (22.4)	24.3 (15.3)	93.2 (18.2)	54.9 (9.4)
High capital-high skill	6.6 (7.8)	11.5 (7.3)	38.6 (7.5)	47.9 (8.2)

Source: F.A. Alburo, 1987.
Note: Figures do not include nontraditional manufactured exports classified under "Other" in previous tables.

doubtful that such development translates into a sustainable structural change that is consistent with a country's participation in a world trading system. Without concomitant policy reforms to harness this development, the Philippines is unlikely to experience the transformation characteristic of countries that have expanded their manufactured exports.

The following actions are needed now:

• Depart completely from the import-substitution and protectionist regime of the past. To embark on programs or policies to promote manufactured exports in the existing environment would be distortionary and would simply inhibit widespread structural change.

• Rationalize the protective structure of the economy along with trade liberalization that eliminates import restrictions.

• Implement an active exchange rate policy that seeks to maintain the competitiveness of Philippine tradable goods. (The nominal exchange rate stayed at a level of peso 20.4–21.7 to US$1 during 1986–89 was depreciated to P24.3 in 1990 and P27.5 in 1991. It was however, appreciated in 1992 to P25.5 and the real effective exchange rate was consequently slightly appreciated as compared with 1986. [IMF 1993])

• Pursue complementary policies that foster greater equity and broader distribution of growth, which, in turn, provide the necessary domestic support for manufactured export development.

• Safeguard the positive aspects of manufactured export development from other policies that may negate it. Continuous efforts must be made to facilitate

Table 12.4

Share of the Philippines in Leading Commodity Exports of Developing Countries (percent)

SITC	1970	1975	1980	1988–89
Organic chemicals	n	n	3.90	n
Veneers, plywood	15.81	6.29	8.93	2.48
Textiles	n	n	0.57	1.44
Floor Covering	n	1.05[a]	—	—
Iron and steel plates	n	n	3.01	—
Machinery, nonelectrical	0.02	0.69	—	—
Electrical machinery	n	n	1.10	1.25
Motor vehicles	n	n	1.05	—
Travel goods	n	n	0.67	0.98
Clothing	0.04	0.75	2.02	12.41
Footwear	n	n	2.08	0.63
Watches and clocks	n	n	1.02	1.66
Plastic	n	n	0.87	0.62
Toys	0.07	0.77	1.05	0.62
Other manufactures	0.94	11.18	6.72	6.76

Source: UNCTAD, *Handbook of International Trade and Development Statistics* (New York: United Nations, various issues).

Notes: SITC 0–4 not included. "n" indicates a value less than 0.05%.

[a]1978.

employment-promoting policies, because they, in turn, improve the prospects for manufactured exports. Broader macroeconomic policies must continue to focus on rural development that is complementary to the long-run transition from export production that uses low-skill labor to capital-intensive output that uses high skills.

Since 1986, the Philippine government has formulated and implemented a range of structural reforms and policies that seem to address many of these weaknesses in the development of manufactured exports. Trade liberalization has resumed, although there are signs of increased protection through either higher tariffs on outputs or lower rates on inputs. There are no exchange restrictions, although exchange rate policy seems passive. Macroeconomic policy appears to respond to the need for expansion.

Perhaps the crucial issue is not the details of policy making but the acceptance of a vision for the country that must recognize its need for openness, its need for finding its comparative advantage and thereby creating an efficient trade sector. In the initial and subsequent stages of development it will be necessary to undertake painful reforms. And that takes a strong political will. The restoration of the country's democracy will test the dynamics of its political economy in policy formulation and collective decision making.

References

Alburo, Florian A. 1987. "Manufactured Exports and Industrialization: Trade Patterns and Trends of the Philippines." In *Trade and Structural Change in Pacific Asia*, eds. C.I. Bradford, Jr., and W.H. Branson. Chicago: University of Chicago, National Bureau of Economic Research.

Central Bank of the Philippines. 1990. *Forty-Second Annual Report* (Manila).

International Monetary Fund (IMF). 1993. *International Financial Statistics*, May. p.430.

National Economic and Development Authority (NEDA). 1990. *Philippine Development Report* (Manila).

CHAPTER 13

Prospects of Trade and Regional Cooperation of the Industrializing Economies of East Asia

BELA BALASSA AND MARCUS NOLAND*

Introduction

The industrializing economies of East Asia are increasingly important participants in the global trading system.[1] Between 1963 and 1988 they doubled their share of world production and more than tripled their share of world trade. Historically, there has been little economic interaction among the developing countries of the Pacific Basin. The share of intraregional trade actually fell from 18.8 percent in 1963 to 18.4 percent in 1988. But the emergence of sizable trade surpluses in Taiwan and South Korea, combined with exchange rate realignment and relaxation of capital controls, has led to an explosion of intraregional investment. Investment from the four NIEs (Hong Kong, Singapore, Taiwan, and South Korea) to the ASEAN–4 (Malaysia, Thailand, the Philippines, and Indonesia) quadrupled from $126 million in 1985 to $554 million in 1987, or more than 20 percent of the total inward foreign direct investment (FDI) into these countries in 1987. Investment figures for 1988 are even higher. These capital flows are encouraging the kinds of intercorporate penetration and technology transfer that may spur the emergence of a far more genuinely integrated regional economy.

We examine here the future trade outlook for the East Asian industrializing economies. Using an econometric model, we project the trade patterns of these economies for the year 2000. We then analyze how trade policies pursued in both the East Asian industrializing economies and the rest of the world may affect these prospects.

---

* We would like to thank participants at the seminar for helpful comments on the preliminary version of this paper. The second part of this chapter on "prospects" (particularly in China) was updated and slightly expanded by Dr. Shu-Chin Yang.

Trade Projections

We have used a multicountry econometric model of international trade to generate forecasts for the year 2000. (The technical appendix on the equations of the model and sources of data is not included here; interested readers may contact Professor Noland. See Appendix for his address.) In this model, trade flows are a function of factor endowments (labor, capital, human capital, arable land, pasture land, forest land, oil reserves, coal reserves, and mineral reserves) and transport costs. The model was estimated for forty-six industries that encompass the universe of traded goods. In general, the results were quite good. To generate trade forecasts we used the estimated regression coefficients and forecasts of the factor endowments for the year 2000.[2] We obtained the factor endowment forecasts by estimating autoregressive integrated moving average (ARIMA) time series models for each series and using the time series models to forecast.

For this presentation, the forecasts for each of the forty-six industries have been aggregated into twelve trade categories. The results for Hong Kong, in percentage terms, appear in Table 13.1. Interpretation of these figures is somewhat problematic, since the export figures exclude re-exports, which are included in imports. The model forecasts indicate a considerable decline in the share of textile, apparel, and leather exports. In 2000, engineering products replace them as the largest export sector. The largest export share increase is in the capital-intensive chemicals sector, where the share rises from 5.6 percent to 16.7 percent. This is due mainly to a large projected increase in plastics exports.

Results for Singapore appear in Table 13.2. Significant export share increases are predicted in the capital-intensive sectors of chemicals and iron and steel. Within the chemicals sector, the export share of basic chemicals is forecast to increase from 2.3 percent to 5 percent. One sector, wood products, a net export sector in 1988, is projected to become a net import sector in 2000. Conversely, five sectors go from net import to net export status: paper, chemicals, iron and steel, engineering products, and miscellaneous manufactures.

Trade forecasts for Taiwan appear in Table 13.3. According to these projections, there would be a decrease of 10 percentage points in the textiles, apparel, and leather export share (from 24.4 percent to 14.4 percent) and a rise of 10 percentage points in the chemicals share (from 9.6 percent to 19.6 percent). Within the chemicals sector, the plastics share is projected to increase from 5.1 percent to 11.5 percent, and the share of basic chemicals is forecast to grow from 1 percent to 4.9 percent. Two capital-intensive sectors, paper and chemicals, are projected to go from net imports to net exports in 2000.

Trade forecasts for South Korea appear in Table 13.4. According to the model, there is a significant decrease in the textiles, apparel, and footwear export share, and an important increase in the iron and steel and chemicals shares. The basic chemical share is projected to rise from 1.2 percent to 8 percent, and the

Table 13.1

Trade Composition of Hong Kong (percentage share)

Industry	Exports		Imports	
	1988	2000	1988	2000
Fuels	0.5	0.5	3.7	8.2
Nonfuel primary	3.4	3.2	14.2	20.0
Food & live animals	0.8	0.5	6.7	6.6
Beverages & tobacco	1.1	1.0	1.9	1.2
Industrial materials	1.6	1.7	5.6	12.2
Manufacturing	96.0	96.3	82.1	71.8
Textiles, apparel & leather	41.2	13.0	26.3	18.3
Wood products & furniture	0.4	1.0	1.1	2.6
Paper & paper products	2.3	2.6	1.9	1.8
Chemicals	5.6	16.7	10.2	9.5
Nonmetallic mineral products	0.6	0.7	1.2	1.1
Iron & steel	0.1	0.7	2.3	3.0
Engineering products	38.6	47.5	33.5	29.1
Other industries	7.3	14.1	5.6	6.5

Table 13.2

Trade Composition of Singapore (percentage share)

Industry	Exports		Imports	
	1988	2000	1988	2000
Fuels	24.5	23.8	27.0	30.3
Nonfuel primary	14.5	10.4	13.6	13.0
Food & live animals	4.4	3.1	5.4	4.7
Beverages & tobacco	0.9	0.7	1.0	0.9
Industrial materials	9.2	6.6	7.3	7.4
Manufacturing	61.0	65.8	59.4	56.7
Textiles, apparel & leather	5.2	2.4	5.6	3.8
Wood products & furniture	1.8	0.9	0.9	1.7
Paper & paper products	1.1	1.1	1.3	1.2
Chemicals	6.5	9.7	6.9	5.4
Nonmetallic mineral products	0.3	0.3	1.0	1.1
Iron & steel	0.8	7.3	2.6	1.2
Engineering products	44.3	42.5	40.0	41.2
Other industries	1.1	1.6	1.1	1.0

plastics share increases from 2.2 percent to 5.7 percent. Paper and chemicals go from net imports in 1987 to net exports in 2000.

The results for Malaysia are shown in Table 13.5. The share of fuel exports is predicted to fall significantly, while the share of agricultural products is pro-

Table 13.3

Trade Composition of Taiwan (percentage share)

Industry	Exports		Imports	
	1988	2000	1988	2000
Fuels	1.3	0.9	16.5	24.4
Nonfuel primary	7.9	6.3	20.7	23.8
Food & live animals	5.1	3.8	5.0	4.6
Beverages & tobacco	0.1	0.2	0.7	0.6
Industrial materials	2.7	2.3	15.1	18.7
Manufacturing	90.8	92.8	62.8	51.8
Textiles, apparel & leather	24.4	14.4	3.6	3.0
Wood products & furniture	3.7	6.2	1.4	3.8
Paper & paper products	1.0	2.7	1.8	1.6
Chemicals	9.6	19.6	13.9	11.9
Nonmetallic mineral products	2.0	1.5	0.8	0.7
Iron & steel	1.5	3.2	5.6	5.7
Engineering products	41.5	37.4	34.9	24.5
Other industries	7.2	7.8	0.7	0.6

Table 13.4

Trade Composition of South Korea (percentage share)

Industry	Exports		Imports	
	1987	2000	1987	2000
Fuels	2.5	1.8	20.9	31.0
Nonfuel primary	6.8	5.2	22.9	28.6
Food & live animals	4.5	1.6	6.0	5.9
Beverages & tobacco	0.2	0.7	0.1	0.5
Industrial materials	2.1	2.8	16.8	22.2
Manufacturing	90.7	93.1	56.2	40.4
Textiles, apparel & leather	34.1	15.8	6.1	5.1
Wood products & furniture	0.7	1.3	0.4	1.0
Paper & paper products	1.1	4.7	1.7	1.5
Chemicals	6.7	16.6	11.7	8.6
Nonmetallic mineral products	1.2	1.1	0.8	0.8
Iron & steel	5.0	15.9	4.1	3.3
Engineering products	38.3	34.8	30.9	19.8
Other industries	3.6	3.0	0.5	0.4

jected to rise. The largest increase in manufactured exports is projected in engineering products, where the export share will rise from 19.4 percent to 24.3 percent. The nonmetallic mineral products sector, a net importer in 1987, is projected to exhibit net exports in 2000.

Table 13.5

Trade Composition of Malaysia (percentage share)

Industry	Exports		Imports	
	1987	2000	1987	2000
Fuels	26.0	14.5	11.6	11.3
Nonfuel primary	41.6	44.4	19.2	27.9
Food & live animals	5.4	10.6	8.6	7.5
Beverages & tobacco	0.2	0.4	0.8	0.7
Industrial materials	36.1	33.3	9.9	19.7
Manufacturing	32.4	41.1	69.2	60.7
Textiles, apparel & leather	4.4	3.9	5.4	2.5
Wood products & furniture	4.9	6.7	0.2	0.3
Paper & paper products	0.2	1.5	2.7	2.1
Chemicals	1.7	2.9	10.7	8.5
Nonmetallic mineral products	0.3	0.7	0.7	0.6
Iron & steel	0.7	0.2	4.1	14.3
Engineering products	19.4	24.3	44.3	31.5
Other industries	0.7	1.0	1.1	0.9

Table 13.6

Trade Composition of Thailand (percentage share)

Industry	Exports		Imports	
	1987	2000	1987	2000
Fuels	1.1	0.8	21.2	20.8
Nonfuel primary	51.4	50.1	16.5	32.0
Food & live animals	34.2	33.2	4.2	6.6
Beverages & tobacco	0.5	1.0	0.6	0.7
Industrial materials	16.7	15.9	11.7	24.8
Manufacturing	47.6	49.1	62.3	47.2
Textiles, apparel & leather	21.1	11.2	4.3	2.0
Wood products & furniture	2.1	2.6	0.8	1.7
Paper & paper products	0.6	1.2	2.0	2.1
Chemicals	3.1	7.6	14.6	11.0
Nonmetallic mineral products	0.7	0.7	0.7	0.5
Iron & steel	0.7	0.9	7.0	6.6
Engineering products	11.6	11.0	30.9	20.4
Other industries	7.7	13.9	2.1	2.9

Results for Thailand are reported in Table 13.6. The country is projected to change from a net importer to a net exporter of manufactures. The greatest export increases are projected in the miscellaneous manufactures. The nonmetallic mineral products sector is projected to shift from net imports in 1987 to net exports in 2000.

Trade projections for the Philippines are reported in Table 13.7. Manufactured exports are projected to account for more than half of the Philippines exports in 2000. The largest export share increase will occur in chemicals; nonmetallic mineral products are projected to change from net import to net export status.

Finally, the results for Indonesia are shown in Table 13.8. According to the projections, the share of fuels in exports will decline and the share of manufactures will rise over the forecast period. The export share of engineering products is projected to rise from 0.4 percent to 13.3 percent. The largest increase will occur in shipbuilding and repairing, where the export share is projected to rise from 0.0 percent to 5.4 percent. Paper, nonmetallic minerals products, and iron and steel are all projected to switch from net import sectors in 1987 to net export sectors in 2000.

All these trade projections are conditional on the factor endowment forecasts.[3] It may be desirable to perform sensitivity tests in particular cases. For example, in the case of Hong Kong, it might be useful to model possible future emigration as reductions in the rates of labor force growth and human capital accumulation. Similarly, recent high rates of inward foreign direct investment in Thailand could be modeled as an acceleration in the rate of physical capital accumulation. It is not difficult to think of many other possibilities.

Last, there is the issue of trade policy. The trade policies pursued worldwide during the sample period are embedded in the estimated coefficients of the regression model. The trade forecasts, then, are conditional on the continuance of the same international trade regime through the forecast period. A significant change in the world trade regime would obviously change trade patterns in ways not captured by this model.

Prospects of Trade Policy Changes and Regional Cooperation

Obviously, the trade policies undertaken in each of the East Asian industrializing economies will have the most significant impact on their respective trade patterns. However, the future of these economies depends not only on actions at home but on the external economic environment as well. In particular, the prospects for the East Asian industrializing economies may be greatly influenced by the policies of their major trading partners, their policies toward each other, and their collective policy stance toward the world as a whole. Accordingly, we examine the prospect for future economic cooperation among the Pacific Basin economies and then broaden the discussion to consider the interests of these countries in global economic cooperation. We then analyze the potential impact of actions by other regional economic powers on the Pacific Rim economies.

Potential for Regional Cooperation

The only notable international organization in East Asia is the Association of Southeast Asian Nations (ASEAN).[4] Its founding members in 1967 were Indone-

Table 13.7

Trade Composition of Philippines (percentage share)

Industry	Exports 1988	Exports 2000	Imports 1988	Imports 2000
Fuels	5.8	3.9	30.4	35.0
Nonfuel primary	48.3	43.0	19.8	27.7
Food & live animals	19.3	17.4	7.8	10.0
Beverages & tobacco	0.7	1.3	1.4	1.7
Industrial materials	28.4	24.4	10.6	16.0
Manufacturing	45.8	53.1	49.8	37.2
Textiles, apparel & leather	10.6	8.0	5.6	3.7
Wood products & furniture	10.4	12.7	0.1	0.2
Paper & paper products	0.4	1.0	2.1	2.1
Chemicals	4.4	9.1	13.7	10.6
Nonmetallic mineral products	0.5	1.5	0.8	0.5
Iron & steel	1.3	1.1	6.1	8.8
Engineering products	13.5	13.7	20.7	10.8
Other industries	4.7	5.9	0.6	0.6

Table 13.8

Trade Composition of Indonesia (percentage share)

Industry	Exports 1987	Exports 2000	Imports 1987	Imports 2000
Fuels	57.2	36.4	14.1	23.4
Nonfuel primary	24.0	22.7	18.2	34.3
Food & live animals	7.5	4.4	4.0	8.2
Beverages & tobacco	0.3	1.4	0.3	1.6
Industrial materials	16.2	16.9	14.0	24.5
Manufacturing	18.8	40.9	67.7	42.2
Textiles, apparel & leather	5.5	5.2	2.3	1.3
Wood products & furniture	10.3	11.2	0.1	0.1
Paper & paper products	0.4	2.0	2.6	2.7
Chemicals	0.9	3.9	19.7	13.2
Nonmetallic mineral products	0.4	1.4	1.1	1.1
Iron & steel	0.8	3.8	5.3	4.7
Engineering products	0.4	13.3	36.3	18.8
Other industries	0.1	0.2	0.4	0.3

sia, Malaysia, the Philippines, Singapore, and Thailand. Brunei joined the group subsequently. The charter stated that ASEAN's goal would be "to accelerate economic growth, social progress and cultural development in the region through joint endeavor in the spirit of equality and partnership in order to strengthen the foundation for a prosperous and peaceful community of Southeast Asian Nations" (quoted in Krause 1982: 6).

In the economic sphere, the founding document called for cooperation on basic commodities, particularly food and energy; industrial cooperation; cooperation in trade; and a joint approach to international commodity problems and other world economic problems. The program of action further included political, social, cultural, and security issues.

Cooperation in trade was to be served by the establishment of preferential trading arrangements. These arrangements took the form of product-by-product negotiations for tariff reductions on intra-area trade and across-the-board tariff reductions on small items. Tariff reductions have been small though, and there have been numerous exceptions, so that only about 5 percent of intra-ASEAN trade is covered by preferential tariff arrangements. Trade creation has been negligible (Ariff 1989). Intraregional trade was US$30 billion or about 20 percent of member states' trade in 1991.

According to the Bangkok Declaration of 1977, industrial cooperation was to be promoted by the establishment of large-scale ASEAN industrial plants, particularly to meet regional requirements of essential commodities. Initially, five projects were identified: urea plants in Indonesia and Malaysia, a superphosphates plant in the Philippines, a diesel engine plant in Singapore, and a soda ash plant in Thailand. The urea fertilizer plants were eventually constructed. In the Philippines, the superphosphate project was replaced by a pulp and paper project, which itself was replaced by a copper fabrication plant, which has yet to be built. Thailand decided to liquidate the soda ash plant. In Singapore, the diesel engine project had to be scrapped because Indonesia wished to undertake a similar project. In the end, Singapore chose a small hepatitis B vaccine project and reduced its equity participation in the other projects from 10 to 1 percent (Krause 1982).

The Bali summit of 1976 called for complementarity agreements involving joint ventures among private firms in a regional context. Eventually seven such projects were approved, and a few were implemented. However, new rules adopted at the Manila summit of 1987 made these private cooperative ventures more feasible (Ariff 1989).

The Bali summit also called for the creation of an ASEAN Finance Corporation. This corporation was set up by 140 commercial banks and individual shareholders to promote economic cooperation among ASEAN member countries. It did not prove to be particularly successful in this regard, and, following its 1987–88 restructuring, the corporation is now acting as a merchant bank, with limited lending to bankable projects.

Although ASEAN has made little progress in the trade and industrial fields, it has established modest cooperative ventures in areas covered by eleven permanent committees. They include food and agriculture; shipping; civil air transportation; communication; air traffic services; meteorology; finance; commerce and industry; transportation and telecommunications; tourism; science and technology; sociocultural activities; and mass media.

Perhaps ASEAN's greatest achievement in the economic field has been its role as a pressure group in trade negotiations with industrial countries and in the GATT. ASEAN has succeeded in inducing the EC to modify its trade preference system and in inducing Japan to forego increasing the production of synthetic rubber.

ASEAN has also acted as a political force. In particular, its opposition to Vietnam's occupation of Kampuchea has contributed to the negotiations undertaken by the warring parties and to Vietnam's eventual withdrawal.

In January 1992, ASEAN took further cooperative steps, aiming at creating a regional free-trade zone by year 2008 and forging closer ties with the other southeast Asian countries, that is, Vietnam, Cambodia (formerly Kampuchea), Laos, and Myanmar (formerly Burma). Three accords were signed in Singapore. The Framework Agreement and a common Effective Preferential Tariff Scheme are aimed at gradually implementing an ASEAN free-trade area, starting in January 1993. The agreements commit ASEAN member countries to open its market sector by sector by reducing tariffs over the next fifteen years. The tariff reductions apply to fifteen types of manufactured goods, ranging from cement to jewelry (*The Washington Post*, January 29, 1992). The ASEAN members believe that the ASEAN Free-trade Area (AFTA) will be useful not only to promote intra-regional trade but also to make investments in the area equally attractive as in Mexico under NAFTA. While AFTA may succeed in due course, the long time period, the narrow coverage of preferential tariffs, as well as the right accorded to members to take the option of excluding certain products and categories unilaterally may reduce substantially its effectiveness.

The future of ASEAN is likely to lie in increasing the bargaining power of its member countries through joint action. It is unlikely that member countries will grant significant preferences to each other involving purchases at higher than world market prices. Similarly industrial projects are likely to be oriented toward world rather than regional markets. Nonetheless, ASEAN may play a positive role in such areas as harmonization of rules for investment and taxation.

There is even less intra-area trade among the East Asian NIEs than among the ASEAN countries. The share of this trade was 8.7 percent in 1973, 10 percent in 1981, and 10.5 percent in 1988. At the same time, a substantial part of intra-area trade involves trade with China. Nor is it likely that the East Asian NIEs would enter into preferential trade arrangements among themselves, if for no other reason than that Hong Kong and Singapore are practically free traders and consequently there is little scope for trade preferences.

It has been suggested, however, that the East Asian NIEs would gain from adopting a common basket currency peg. This would avoid the dilemma of each country being reluctant to revalue its currency for fear of losing markets to the others. At the same time, revaluation would permit correction of imbalances in trade and the current account.

The four East Asian NIEs would have to correct their existing current account imbalances before the adoption of a common basket peg. Yet this could be envisaged for some future period, since rapid productivity growth will engender the need for future appreciation of the currencies of the four countries. At the same time, similarities in their geographical trade patterns support the establishment of a common basket peg.

Finally, the East Asian NIEs may contemplate joining the OECD and participating in the establishment of a similar organization on the Pacific level. Singapore and Hong Kong have surpassed per capita incomes of Italy and Spain; Taiwan and South Korea will reach similar income levels at the end of the century. Thus, their claims on membership will be similar to those Japan had when it joined the OECD.

OECD membership by South Korea and Singapore should not encounter major obstacles. But membership by Hong Kong and Taiwan could be politically problematic; some sort of observer status might be possible, however.

There has been growing interest in an OECD-type organization in the Pacific area to serve as a forum for consultation on issues of regional interest, and act as a pressure group to promote greater international openness. Attention has coalesced around the proposal of Australian Prime Minister Hawke for an Asia-Pacific dialogue involving the United States, Canada, Australia, New Zealand, and Japan, in addition to the East Asian industrializing economies.[5] Eventually, the organization called Asia Pacific Economic Cooperation, with fifteen countries/ areas, including China, Taiwan, and Hong Kong participating, established a small secretariat in Singapore in 1991, and ten working groups were formed to deal with investment and technology policy, trade data, tourism, transportation, fisheries, etc. Its aim is to become an Asia Pacific kind of OECD (*The Washington Times*, March 25, 1993). A similar proposal by Japan's Ministry of International Trade and Industry (MITI) has been incorporated into the Hawke initiative (Schott 1989).

Given the widely differing levels of economic development, trade regimes, and political structures of the potential member countries, it is doubtful that such an organization could promote the development of a meaningful preferential trading area on the model of the European Community. Rather, it is more likely that the organization could more successfully develop into a consultative forum, perhaps focusing initially on trade policy issues and later extending to encompass broader economic issues, cultural exchange, and environmental concerns (Baker 1989). In this way it could serve as a useful complement to existing organizations, especially the GATT.

Potential for Global Economic Cooperation

The last point leads to the question of global economic cooperation for the East Asian industrializing economies. These countries are highly dependent on international trade and thus have a great interest in the maintenance of an open trade regime. This means that they have a major interest in a well-functioning GATT.

The interests of the East Asian industrializing economies range over the whole set of issues currently under discussion in the Uruguay Round of multilateral trade negotiations. They have an especial interest in maintaining the openness of trade in manufactured goods, in particular strengthening the Safeguard Code to ensure that import controls are temporary and degressive, outlawing protectionist measures outside the GATT such as "voluntary" export restraints (VERs), and banning discrimination in the application of trade restraints. The East Asian industrializing economies (particularly South Korea and Taiwan) have been increasingly pressured into VERs and other forms of discriminatory trade restrictions.

The single most important source of trade restrictions in manufacturing goods has been the Multifiber Arrangement (MFA), which consists of a set of bilateral quotas covering trade in textiles and apparel. MFA quota allocations tend to reflect past history, not current production costs, and thus discriminate against recent and low-cost producers to the benefit of long-standing and high-cost producers. Also, the MFA provides rents to the quota recipients, and the inefficiencies generated internationally are reproduced at the firm level in the exporting countries through the domestic allocation of quotas.

At the same time, the rents derived from the quota system are dwarfed by the limitations imposed on the exporting countries under the MFA. Thus, the East Asian industrializing economies would gain substantively from the liberalization of trade in textiles and clothing. One recent study concluded that all of the Pacific Basin countries would gain from a global liberalization of textile and apparel trade. Elimination of tariffs and quotas under the MFA would result in export volume increases ranging from a low of 45 percent in the case of Hong Kong to 407 percent in the case of Indonesia. Even if only the bilateral quotas were eliminated, export volumes would increase anywhere from Hong Kong's 24 percent to Indonesia's 275 percent (Trela and Whalley 1988).

East Asian industrializing economies and, in particular, the East Asian NIEs encountered problems in developed country markets related to the application of countervailing and antidumping duties as well as safeguard measures. The issues here are complex and center on reconciling the desires to protect importers from unfair trade practices with the need to prevent the application of trade laws from becoming a convenient way for import-competing industries to harass efficient exporters.

The potential negative impact of these measures on the East Asian industrializing economies is substantial. In this respect, the 1988 U.S. trade act, which expanded the scope of unfair trade practices, relaxed the criteria for affirmative findings, and increased the automaticity of retaliation, provides an example of the drift toward unilateralism in trade policy that the East Asian industrializing economies seek to prevent. Thus, these countries have a major interest in strengthening disciplines on countervailing and antidumping action.

In the area of agriculture, the interests of the individual East Asian industrializing economies vary widely, as some countries are principally importers of agricultural commodities, while others are exporters of such commodities.[6] For exporters, agricultural protection has a substantial impact. A recent study (Anderson and Tyers 1987) concluded that agricultural protection in the European Common Market and Japan cost nearly $1 billion a year in net foreign exchange earnings to Thailand, for example. Subsidization by developed country producers has also depressed world market prices, reducing the agricultural export receipts of several East Asian industrializing economies.

In the area of services, too, the interests of the East Asian industrializing economies differ. South Korea has a comparative advantage in some labor-intensive construction and engineering services and would benefit from liberalization in this area. Singapore and Hong Kong have a comparative advantage in financial services and may benefit from liberalization. However, in the less developed countries of the area, financial services are weak and their domestic development is a first priority. Thus, while the East Asian industrializing economies should support the development of a liberal international trading regime for financial services, the ASEAN–4 will need special and differential treatment for the time being.

Likewise, it is in the long-run self-interest of the East Asian industrializing economies to strengthen intellectual property rights. While in the short run this will involve costs, in the long run several East Asian industrializing economies, in particular South Korea and Taiwan, will become producers of intellectual property, including computer software. And, in the meantime, the strengthening of intellectual property rights will facilitate the smooth transfer of technology.

Yet it must be recognized that the enforcement of intellectual property rights may impose substantial budgetary costs on the recipient countries. A variety of solutions combining stricter intellectual property rights standards with a mechanism to share enforcement and adjudication costs internationally may be envisaged. Possibilities include the reform of national codes to increase allowable damage awards in civil suits and the establishment of a common fund to subsidize enforcement costs. Thus, the East Asian industrializing economies would agree to stricter standards, thereby reducing the costs of the transfer of technology to the proprietary firm, while enforcement costs would be spread internationally.

With regard to trade-related investment measures (TRIMS), East Asian industrializing economies have pursued a variety of policies. Export performance requirements are trade distorting and may well deter investment projects that are economically desirable. Domestic content legislation is essentially a form of protection for domestic parts manufactures; it is difficult to quantify the economic effects, and it distorts investment decisions. Such legislation should be avoided in favor of explicit tariff protection when protection is considered desirable.

There is also the issue of incentives to foreign direct investment. In some cases, competition among potential recipients has led to foreign firms receiving preferential treatment over domestic firms, particularly through tax benefits. This should be avoided.

One solution to investment bidding wars would be to harmonize investment codes regionally and ensure equal treatment to domestic as well as foreign investors.

Another global trade issue the East Asian industrializing economies face is the future of the Generalized System of Preferences (GSP). Under GSP, certain developing country exports enter developed country markets duty free. While trade under GSP is substantial, the impact of the program is less certain. First, the effect of GSP should be measured in terms of the additional trade it creates, which may not be large. Furthermore, developed countries have imposed both product and source ceilings, many of which are binding. And several product categories of interest to the East Asian industrializing economies, such as textiles, apparel, and footwear, are excluded from GSP.

Finally, there is the issue of graduation. In principle, graduation is to ensure that the less developed countries, those with greatest need of preferential access, are the main beneficiaries of the program. Thus, as countries develop, preferential access is withdrawn, thereby limiting trade preferences to less developed countries. In January 1989, the United States withdrew GSP privileges from Hong Kong, South Korea, Singapore, and Taiwan, affecting $10 billion of its imports from these countries. While it is clear that the four East Asian NIEs developed into highly successful exporters of manufactured goods, the removal of their GSP privileges may have had more to do with U.S. trade deficits than with the principle of graduation. In a separate action, the United States has also partially suspended GSP privileges to Thailand in a dispute over intellectual property rights.

GSP privileges in the European Common Market have also been withdrawn from South Korea, although this was done because of a trade dispute, not as a result of graduation. In fact, the uncertainty surrounding GSP due to the arbitrary determination of product exclusion, ceilings, and graduation by developed countries, may have reduced the program's beneficial impact by discouraging investment in the affected countries and industries.

Thus, it would be in the interest of the East Asian industrializing economies to secure greater adherence to internationally recognized principles and rules in the conduct of trade policy. But the same lack of commitment to internationally recognized standards emerges on the other side of the ledger in relation to the "special and differential" provisions for the benefits of the developing countries. As Bergsten (1988: 141) noted, these "have enabled LDCs to apply far-reaching restrictions of their own, and have frustrated all GATT efforts to achieve meaningful liberalization of LDC trade barriers."

These provisions also provide an excuse for developed countries to apply discriminatory measures against developing country exports. As long as developing countries insist on special and differential treatment, it may be difficult to negotiate greater discipline in developed country trade practices under a strengthened safeguards code. Thus, it may well be in the interest of the East Asian industrializing economies to give up special and differential treatment in merchandise trade on the grounds that such a move would secure a commitment to greater discipline and liberalization from the developed countries in the context of the Uruguay Round of negotiations.

There is further need to increase reliance on multilateral forums in trade disputes. A case in point is the U.S.–South Korean negotiations on intellectual property rights. The United States secured retroactive protection that in some cases exceeded the protection afforded South Korean firms. While the United States achieved its narrow negotiating goals, the agreements are widely regarded in South Korea as unfair and may actually impede the liberalization of intellectual property rights. It may be added that when the South Korean government rejected the European Common Market's demand for equal treatment, the Common Market suspended South Korea's GSP privileges.

In retrospect, it may have been in the interest of all the parties to conduct negotiations multilaterally. These cases, then, strengthen the argument for the multilateral adjudication of trade disputes.

Influence of Other Regional Powers

Beyond policies pursued domestically and participation in international organizations, the economic fortunes of the East Asian industrializing economies will also be affected by economic developments in other countries of the region. Among these countries, Russian Federation and the newly independent eastern states of the former Soviet Union, Vietnam, and North Korea have not had major economic ties to the East Asian industrializing economies.

In the case of Russia, the area east of the Urals is rich in natural resources and is potentially an important source of supply for the manufacturing economies of East Asia. In turn, the Soviet Union may become a market for these countries if it makes progress in its economic reforms.

Vietnam is one of the world's poorest countries, but it could be an exporter of some agricultural goods and labor-intensive manufactures in exchange for machinery and equipment if it makes progress in economic reforms. The country has improved its macroeconomic performance, reformed its agricultural policies, and emerged as a major exporter of rice. It is already the recipient of limited amounts of foreign direct investment, mostly from Japan and the East Asian industrializing economies. But the U.S. trade and investment embargo remains a significant handicap. Neighboring Laos has also initiated economic reforms and begun to receive aid from the United States and Japan (among others) as well as private investment, mostly from Thailand.

The economic fortunes of North Korea may be closely tied to its progress in normalizing relations with the South. Such normalization could also have an appreciable impact on South Korea by providing a new outlet for trade and investment and permitting a reduction in military expenditures.

In all three communist countries, greater participation in trade with the East Asian industrializing economies is highly contingent on the successful implementation of fundamental economic reforms, and it is by no means clear that such reforms will be implemented. In any case, these countries are unlikely to become major factors in the trade of the East Asian industrializing economies before the end of the century.

Complementarity in economic structure and geographic proximity make Australia and New Zealand natural trading partners for the East Asian industrializing economies. Indeed, the greatest contribution Australia and New Zealand could make to the economic fortunes of the East Asian industrializing economies would be to lower and bind their high tariff rates on a variety of manufactured goods. However, trade with these two countries would remain a relatively small percentage of the overall trade of the East Asian industrializing economies.

Policies in China

China differs from the other communist countries in the region in that its size, extent of economic reforms, and assumption of sovereignty over Hong Kong in 1997 ensure that it will have an important impact on the East Asian industrializing economies over the next decade. China looms large in the trade of these countries. Official figures understate its importance because of the substantial unreported trade between China and South Korea and Taiwan. (In 1992, China's trade with Taiwan via Hong Kong has reached US$8 billion.) Following the establishment of the communist government in 1949, China adopted a centrally planned economic system similar to those in the Soviet Union and Eastern Europe. It encompassed central determination of the firms' output targets, material allocation, employment, investment, and foreign trade. Targets were set in physical volume terms, with prices serving only an accounting function. Over the next three decades living standards stagnated, as agricultural, industrial, and service output barely kept pace with population growth.

Economic reforms were begun in the late 1970s. In agriculture, they included establishment of the family responsibility system, reduction of procurement targets, and freeing of some agricultural prices. The result was a dramatic rise in production and real income in the agricultural sector.

Since 1984, however, agricultural growth has slowed down as maintenance of low prices on major crops and reduction of funds available for investment have discouraged the expansion of production. The slowdown of agricultural growth, together with rising population and urban incomes, has required increased agricultural imports. China has become the world's third largest agricultural importer, behind Japan and Russia. Some projections foresee its rise to the rank of leading food importer over the next decade. While favorably affecting the food-exporting East Asian industrializing economies, this will put pressure on China to generate foreign exchange through the exports of manufactured goods, thereby creating increased competition with the East Asian industrializing economies.

Industrial sector reforms have included changes in the allocation and incentives system, the establishment of special export-oriented zones, and the encouragement of foreign direct investment. Foreign investment has been encouraged through the establishment of fourteen "open cities" and five "special economic zones" on China's coast. By the end of 1992, China had 84,371 foreign investment investment enterprises, of which 70 percent were joint ventures (New China News agency news, February 2, 1993). A substantial number of these enterprises involved Hong Kong–based firms, and, more recently, there have been increasing investments by Taiwanese and South Korean firms. (China and South Korea established their diplomatic relations in 1992.) In 1992, Taiwan companies invested about US$2.5 billion in the mainland, up from about US$1.9 billion in 1991 (*The Washington Post*, December 1, 1992).

The East Asian NIEs are interested in investing in China to offset their rising labor costs. From the Chinese point of view, such ventures have the advantage that they involve the transfer of simpler, and more appropriate, technology than do investments by the developed countries. At the same time, the Chinese can obtain the benefits of the worldwide marketing and distribution expertise in labor-intensive manufactures that firms of the East Asian NIEs possess. But investment is not a one-way street: funds are moving in and out of China. Guangdong province, adjacent to Hong Kong, absorbs one-half of foreign investment and reportedly controls 3,000 firms in Hong Kong (*Economist*, December 10, 1988).

The piecemeal and incomplete reforms in China's industrial sector have been less successful than its early reforms in agriculture. While under the family responsibility system there is a close correspondence between performance and reward, this link is less direct in industry. Firm managers attempt to increase profits by negotiating higher prices, lower planning targets, higher material allocation, and increases in subsidies or reductions in taxes, rather than by cutting costs.

Industrial efficiency has been hampered further by the lack of competition and the prevalence of sellers' markets in the Chinese industrial sector. These incentive problems have been compounded by a fragmented and irrational pricing system in which dual (one official, one market) prices may coexist for the same good, none reflecting true scarcity value.

This incomplete liberalization has encouraged the generation of excess demand by creating super-normal profit opportunities on one hand without curtailing loss-making activities on the other. The main channel has been an unplanned investment boom, undertaken by regional and local authorities and financed by local bank lending. The credit expansion resulted in a sharp increase in the money supply, which was rising at an annual rate of 40 percent by August 1988. The rate of inflation reached 30 percent in 1989.

These developments prompted the Chinese authorities to initiate austerity measures to reduce aggregate demand and roll back some of the reforms. The tightening up of bank credit and the cut in public investment succeeded at reducing aggregate demand and slowing inflation, but at a considerable cost in output, employment, and the reapplication of some administrative regulations. According to China's State Statistical Bureau, GNP growth slowed to 4.6 percent in 1989 and 5.6 percent in 1990, down from 11.2 percent in 1988.

The economic difficulties were compounded by additional shocks following the political unrest in June 1989. First, the immediate fall in tourism revenues and foreign direct investment worsened the external deficit problem, sparking internal debate about the need for further devaluation. Second, in response to the June events, the multilateral development banks and bilateral development agencies suspended or delayed loans. Private lenders canceled loans in response to slowing demand and the perception of increased political risk. Meanwhile, foreign debt reached US$40 billion with a peak repayment period to begin in 1992. All this exacerbated China's external financing problems. The June events also slowed China's progress toward accession to the GATT, which would presumably enhance its long-run access to foreign markets. China's subsequent political retrenchment and movement away from economic liberalization have further clouded its prospects.

Nevertheless, while the austerity program resulted in slow growth and higher unemployment, it also checked inflation. The relative price stability (official retail price index increased only 2.1 percent in 1990 and 2.9 percent in 1991) provided a favorable environment for further price reform which China was unable to do during 1988–89. Thus, the Chinese government has taken advantage of the sluggish market to adjust administrative prices, to eliminate or reduce the gaps of dual prices, and to decontrol prices of a number of commodities and services. Most notable were the increases of over 60 percent in urban grain prices, of over 150 percent in edible oil prices, of over 20 percent for crude oil and coal, over 25 percent for rail and water freight and passenger fares, and 15 percent for steel, etc. The number of commodities under price control imposed in 1989 was reduced from 50 to 6 by mid-1991. This has helped to expand the market economy at the expense of planning. Also important were the continuous reforms in the fields of foreign trade and investment. To encourage exports as well as foreign investment, the currency was devalued twice (first by 21 percent in December 1989 and then by 10 percent in 1990) from RMB3.72 = US$1 to RMB5.3 = US$1. This, together with the rather flexible exchange rate at the foreign exchange centers, helped greatly the competitiveness of Chinese exports. Beginning in 1992 the government stopped export subsidies.

Meanwhile, being concerned about the unemployment, the sluggish sales and high indebtedness of the state enterprises, the Chinese authorities gradually relaxed bank credit and revived government investment in 1991. This has brought about economic recovery with GNP increased by 7 percent in 1991. However, the paramount leader, Deng Xiao-ping was not satisfied with the rather "slow" growth and with the ambivalence of the new administration toward reform. Thus, in early 1992, he pronounced that China should and could grow faster by practically expending the market economy system to substitute planning and by opening the door more widely to the outside world, without the burden of ideology. This was followed by substantial increases in government investment expenditures and bank credit expansion. A large number of coastal cities as well as those further inland have been opened to foreign trade and investment and numerous development zones have been established with favorable taxes and incentives granted to foreign investors. Thus, GNP grew in 1992 by over 12 percent. Exports, aided by currency devaluations, increased from US$43 billion in 1989 to US$59 billion in 1991, and an estimated US$75 billion in 1992. Direct foreign investment revived to about US$11 billion, for the first time it exceeded foreign loans, which amounted to US$7.3 billion in 1992.

The main objective of the economic reform now clearly defined as to achieve a "socialist market economy system," has been included in the country's revised constitution by the People's Congress in March 1993. While the long-term development path is now clarified, the road is by no means straight and smooth. New trends of inflation have already emerged. The cost-of-living index of thirty-five cities rose by almost 11 percent in 1992 and there are no signs of slowing down. Prices of building materials, such as cement and lumber are rising sharply, some more than doubled. One cannot rule out that sooner or later a brake on the economy may have to be applied. More fundamentally, reforms in many important fields, such as tax system, banking system, and state enterprises, still have a long way to go.

Future Chinese political and economic policies will have ramifications beyond their immediate impact on China itself. China is scheduled to assume sovereignty over Hong Kong in 1997. The draft of the Basic Law, which is supposed to set out the rules governing Hong Kong's affairs for at least fifty years after 1997, appears to give sweeping powers to the central government in Beijing. This conflicts with growing demands for greater self-government within Hong Kong.

The resulting uneasiness has led to substantial increases in emigration from Hong Kong, which is running around 55,000 a year, five times the number in 1985. A survey found that 46 percent of professional households polled had plans to move to a country with a clearer political future (*South China Morning Post*, February 1, 1988). The June 1989 events in China gave further impetus to emigration. Businesses are also leaving the colony. Of the 296 companies listed on the Hong Kong stock exchange, 70 are now based in Bermuda and more are expected to follow. Major firms have been purchasing large stakes in companies based in the United States and Europe.

Any diminution of Hong Kong's economic vitality would be against China's interest. China receives a large share of its foreign exchange earnings through trade with Hong Kong. Furthermore, the existence of a modern, sophisticated market economy in Hong Kong is important for the Chinese reforms.

In the case of Taiwan, China maintains a claim to govern the island as a province. The Chinese government announced a policy of the reunification of China by the year 2000. With sovereignty over Hong Kong reverting to China in 1997 and the small Portuguese colony of Macao returning to Chinese rule in 1999, Taiwan will remain the only outstanding claim. It is unlikely, however, that the Chinese government would attempt to seize Taiwan by force. Taiwan maintains a considerable defense capability and given the growing economic ties between the two countries, any diminution of Taiwan's economic vitality would ultimately work against China's self-interest. In fact, in late April 1993, a conference was held in Singapore between two semi-official delegations, one from Beijing and one from Taipei to discuss civil problems concerning both sides. Several agreements were reached, among which two were economic affairs, one about Taipei's investment in mainland and economic relations between Taiwan and the mainland and the other on cooperation in emerging development. (*People's Daily,* overseas edition, April 30, 1993).

Prospective developments in China can have a substantial impact on the East Asian industrializing economies. Successful reform of the Chinese economy would create further opportunities for trade and investment for the East Asian NIEs. At the same time, it would represent a boon for agricultural exporters in the region, as rising incomes in China would generate greater demand for agricultural imports. However, successful reforms of the Chinese economy would also lead to increases in the exports of labor-intensive manufactures, putting other exporters in the East Asian industrializing economies under pressure.

Policies in Japan

Japan will be increasingly important for the economies of the East Asian industrializing economies. Japanese direct investment in these countries nearly quadrupled between fiscal years 1985 and 1988, reaching $4.7 billion. Investment in this area has traditionally gone into trade-related operations, including natural-resource–extracting industries and manufacturing.

Investment in extractive industries has generally been undertaken with a view to supplying the Japanese market, frequently with government support. In manufacturing, investment followed Japan's declining comparative advantage, initially in unskilled-labor–intensive sectors, more recently in more capital-intensive sectors such as metals, machinery, and automobiles. Once established, Japanese firms have tended to export a greater share of output back to their home market than have non-Japanese firms. While manufacturing firms in the East Asian industrializing economies have encountered considerable difficulty in penetrating the

Japanese market, Japanese firms have used their knowledge of domestic conditions and access to distribution channels to export successfully to the home market.

The flow of private money to the East Asian industrializing economies has been accompanied by increasing flows of official funds to the less developed of these countries. Japan's foreign aid budget has grown considerably in recent years, and the country is by far the largest bilateral contributor to aid in the region.

The Japanese aid programs consist mainly of yen-denominated loans. The appreciation of the yen against the U.S. dollar has caused repayment difficulties for Pacific area aid recipients because their exports are denominated mostly in U.S. dollars. Japan has also been criticized by the Development Assistance Committee of the OECD for tying loans either directly or indirectly to exports by concentrating development assistance in capital-intensive projects. Nearly 35 percent of Japanese aid is earmarked for public utilities and another 10 percent for mining and manufacturing projects. Implementation of these projects often involves purchases of sophisticated equipment from the donor country, particularly for power generation, transportation, and telecommunications.

There have been efforts to increase Japanese aid to Africa and Latin America, but rising domestic concern about possible fragmentation of world trade into regional blocs has reinforced the historical tendency to target Japanese aid to Southeast Asia, reinforcing private investment there. The desire to enhance regional influence has contributed to the establishment of a $2 billion aid package to ASEAN, announced in December 1987, and to Japan's determination to increase influence over the Asian Development Bank. Ideas for Japanese-led regional economic schemes, such as a preferential trade area or an Asian currency system modeled after the European Monetary System, have also been floated.

Although such ideas have gained popularity in Japan, political sensitivities make it difficult to sell them in the East Asian industrializing economies—and in the United States. Any attempt to create a regional preferential trade area that diverts trade from the United States would be viewed unfavorably by Washington, which could probably block any such initiative with a credible retaliatory threat.

Setting aside regional schemes, Japan's role in trade and investment in the East Asian industrializing economies is bound to grow. Rising labor costs in Japan drive manufacturing firms offshore, while growing demand pulls in imports, thereby increasing opportunities for East Asian exporters. Whether firms based in those countries will achieve greater success in penetrating the Japanese market or this trade will be dominated by Japanese firms exporting back to Japan remains an open question. Either way, Japan's importance as a market will increase.

United States

Economic relations between the United States and the East Asian industrializing economies have been and will be dominated by the United States' efforts to reduce its global current account deficit, which, although it has continuously declined since 1987, was still US$90.5 billion in 1990 and US$62.5 billion in 1992. The merchandise trade deficit was US$109 billion in 1990 and US$96 billion in 1992 (the merchandise trade deficit was $109 billion in 1990 and $96 billion in 1992). Some sources, such as the Joint Economic Committee of the U.S. Congress, have urged that the United States seek to restore the current account to its traditional surplus position. Others have argued for the more modest goal of stabilizing the net foreign debt export ratio, which would be consistent with a current account deficit on the order of $50–75 billion.[7] An intermediate target of achieving current account balance over the medium run would require deficit reductions of $30–35 billion annually for several years.

Moreover, due to mounting interest payments on the accumulated foreign debt, the improvement in the merchandise trade balance (as distinct from the current account balance) would have to be even greater, on the order of $100 billion to $175 billion to achieve the current account targets outlined above. Real volume change would have to be even greater, depending on the extent of the dollar depreciation associated with this external adjustment: possibly in the range of $125 billion to $250 billion, or 4 to 6 percent of real GNP at its current level (Bergsten 1988: 81–84).

In this situation, a nonrecessionary adjustment path requires a dramatic increase in export growth combined with a significant and sustained slowdown in the growth rate of imports. Moreover, reductions in the U.S. trade deficits must be matched, by definition, by reduced surpluses (or increased deficits) abroad.

For the East Asian industrializing economies, this means that diversification away from the U.S. market will be required if rapid export growth rates are to be maintained. Furthermore, trading partners with large surpluses (notably Taiwan and South Korea) will come under increasing political pressure to reduce these surpluses as part of the global macroeconomic adjustment.

The United States can be expected to pursue an activist trade strategy to support its macroeconomic adjustment efforts. This will combine the threat of reducing access to the U.S. market with an aggressive emphasis on opening export markets abroad. Increasingly, such target markets will involve the politically sensitive areas of agriculture and services, raising the specter of continuing and publicly acrimonious bilateral disputes between the United States and its trading partners.

This is not in the interest of the East Asian industrializing economies. First, bilateral disputes between major trading countries are often resolved at the expense of third parties. A recent case in point was the preferential treatment accorded by Japan to U.S. plywood, discriminating against substitute products from other Pacific Basin countries (Ariff 1988). Second, as the East Asian industrializing economies become more important markets in their own right, they will increasingly be the target of U.S. bilateral pressure, as is already occurring.

All this underlies the imperative interest that the East Asian industrializing economies have in promoting effectively functioning multilateral forums for the resolution of international economic disputes. The East Asian industrializing economies have a vital interest in an international trade regime that would be characterized by adherence to predictable and internationally recognized rules, not bilateral negotiating strength. Moreover, they have an interest in being at the negotiating table when those rules are formulated.

Conclusion

This chapter has examined the trade prospects of the industrializing economies of East Asia. We used an econometric model to generate forecasts of the East Asian countries trade patterns in 2000. The forecasts indicated that these industrializing economies would increase their specialization in manufactured exports. Two countries, Thailand and Malaysia, would go from net importers to net exporters of manufactured goods during the forecast period.

The trade outlook for the East Asian industrializing economies will also depend on both the trade policies they apply domestically and those pursued by their trading partners abroad. In this context, the industrializing economies of East Asia have a large stake in the maintenance of an open, rules-oriented international trade regime and the further development of multilateral forums for trade negotiations.

At present, the only notable intergovernmental organization in the region is ASEAN. While ASEAN has made little progress in promoting intraregional trade and industrial development, it may continue to play an important role as a pressure group in trade negotiations with the industrialized countries and the GATT.

Likewise, the development of preferential trade arrangements among the NIEs is neither likely nor advisable. They might, however, benefit from adoption of a common basket peg once current imbalances in their balance of payments positions are corrected. In addition, their participation in the OECD as full members or observers may be envisaged.

It may also be desirable to establish an OECD-type organization in the Pacific area. In addition to the industrializing countries of East Asia, such an organization could include Australia, New Zealand, Japan, Canada, and the United States. To a large extent, the organization would be oriented toward trade issues, with the goal of ensuring the openness of the international economic system.

The East Asian industrializing economies have a great stake in the future openness of the international trade system. They have a particular interest in strengthening the Safeguard Code to ensure that import controls are temporary and digressive, outlawing protectionist measures outside of the GATT, and banning discrimination in the application of trade restraints. With these goals in mind, it may be desirable for the industrializing economies of East Asia to consider giving up special and differential treatment in merchandise trade in order to secure a commitment to greater discipline from the industrialized countries in the Uruguay Round.

Last, the trade prospects of the East Asian industrializing economies will be affected by the policies of major regional powers. Successful economic reforms in China would provide new opportunities for some economies in the region but could pose a threat to others. These could take the form of increased trade and investment opportunities for the NIEs and agricultural exporters on one hand and increased competition for labor-intensive manufactures exporters on the other. Rising levels of trade and investment are expected between the East Asian industrializing economies and Japan. This is important, as balance of payments adjustment in the United States will exert pressure on the East Asian industrializing economies to diversify their exports from the United States to other markets.

Notes

1. The East Asian industrializing economies are the People's Republic of China, Taiwan, Hong Kong, Indonesia, the Republic of Korea (South Korea), Malaysia, the Philippines, Singapore, and Thailand.
2. The exception is the textiles and apparel sector, where the Multifiber Agreement has seriously distorted the pattern of trade. For textiles and apparel the forecasts were generated by using the Trela and Whalley (1988) model under the assumption that the bilateral quotas were removed but existing tariff protection was retained.
3. The results are also conditional on the relative prices prevailing in 1980. Changes in relative prices (particularly those of certain commodities such as oil) could have a considerable impact on the projected results.
4. At times there have been proposals for a Pacific Free Trade Area (PAFTA) and an OECD-type organization, the Organization for Pacific Trade and Development (OPTAD), but neither progressed beyond the proposal stage. There are also various informal organizations, such as the Pacific Cooperation Council (PECC), Pacific Basin Economic Council (PBEC), and the Pacific Area Trade and Development Conference (PATADC), but they lack official government representation.
5. The original Hawke proposal did not include the United States or Canada and consequently did not generate much enthusiasm in the smaller states that feared Japanese domination of such an organization.
6. Indonesia, Malaysia, the Philippines, and Thailand are participants in the Cairns group of agricultural exporters in the GATT.
7. See Bergsten 1988: 79–80 for references.

References

Anderson, Kym, and Tyers, Rod. 1987. "Japan's Agricultural Policy in International Perspective." *Journal of Japanese and International Economies* 1 (June):131–46.
Ariff, Mohamed. 1988. "Multilateral Trade Negotiations: ASEAN Perspectives." In Mohamed Ariff and Tan Loong-Hoe (eds). *The Uruguay Round ASEAN Trade Policy Options*. Singapore: Institute for Southeast Asian Studies.
————.1989. "The Changing Role of ASEAN in the Coming Decades: Post Manila Summit Perspectives." In *Global Adjustment and the Future of Asian-Pacific Economy*, Miyohei Shinohara and Fu-chen Lo (eds.). Kuala Lumpur: Asian and Pacific Development Center.
Baker, James A. III. 1989. "A New Pacific Partnership: Framework for the Future." Address to the Asia Society, New York, June 26.

Belsley, David A.; Kuh, Edwin; and Welsch, Roy E. 1980. *Regression Diagnostics*. New York: Wiley.

Bergsten, C. Fred. 1988. *America in the World Economy*. Washington, D.C.: Institute for International Economics.

Bowen, Harry P. 1983. "Changes in the International Distribution of Resources and Their Impact on U.S. Comparative Advantage." *Review of Economics and Statistics* 65: 404–14.

Breusch, T. S., and Pagan, A. R. 1979. "A Simple Test for Heteroskedasticity and Random Coefficient Variation." *Econometrica* 47: 1287–94.

Cline, William R. 1987. *The Future of World Trade in Textiles and Apparel*. Washington, D.C.: Institute for International Economics.

Hausman, J. A. 1978. "Specification Tests in Econometrics," *Econometrica* 46: 1251–72.

Hill, Hal, and Johns, Brian. 1985. "The Role of Direct Foreign Investment in Developing East Asian Countries." ASEAN-Australian Working Papers 18.

Krause, Lawrence B. 1982. *U.S. Economic Policy Toward the Association of Southeast Asian Nations Meeting the Japanese Challenge*. Washington, D.C.: Brookings Institution.

International Monetary Fund. 1993. *International Financial Statistics*. August. Washington, D.C.: International Monetary Fund.

Leamer, Edward E. 1974. "The Commodity Composition of International Trade in Manufactures: An Empirical Analysis." *Oxford Economic Papers* 26: 350–74.

———.1984. *Sources of International Comparative Advantage*. Cambridge, Mass.: MIT Press.

Leamer, Edward E., and Bowen, Harry P. 1981. "Cross-Section Tests of the Heckscher-Ohlin Theorem: Comment." *American Economic Review*. 71:1040–43.

Saxonhouse, Gary R. 1983. "The Micro- and Macro-Economics of Foreign Sales to Japan." In *Trade Policies in the 1980's*, ed. William R. Cline, 259–304. Washington, D.C.: Institute for International Economics.

———.1985. "What's Wrong with Japanese Trade Structure." Seminar Discussion Paper No. 166, Research Seminar in International Economics, University of Michigan, Ann Arbor.

Schott, Jeffrey J. 1989. "Is the World Developing into Regional Trading Blocs?" Washington, D.C.: Institute for International Economics. Mimeo.

Trela, Irene, and Whalley, John. 1988. "Do Developing Countries Lose from the MFA?" NBER Working Paper No. 2618. Cambridge, Mass.: National Bureau of Economic Research.

World Bank. 1985. *China: Long-Term Development Issues and Options*. Baltimore, Johns Hopkins University Press.

———. 1992, 1993. *World Development Report*, 1992, 1993. Washington, D.C.: World Bank.

CONTRIBUTORS

ALBURO, Florian A.
Deputy Director General of National Economic and Development Authority and Professor of Economics at the School of Economics, University of the Philippines. He is a member of the Advisory Committee of the ASEAN Economic Research Unit, Institute of Southeast Asian Studies in Singapore. He obtained his M.A. degree from the University of Philippines and received his Ph.D. from the University of Colorado. He has written more than 40 papers in Economics (especially rural development and agriculture, trade, and trade issues) and has been published in several journals in the Philippines and abroad.

BALASSA, Bela (deceased)
Former Professor of Political Economy, Johns Hopkins University and long-term consultant to the World Bank. He was also adviser to several other international organizations and to a number of governments and industries. He received his Ph.D. degrees from the University of Budapest in 1951 and Yale University in 1959. He was conferred honorary doctorate by the University of Paris in 1988. His research and teaching concentrated in the fields of international trade, trade policies, and development strategies. He had published extensively in these fields, most notably *The Theory of Economic Integration* (1961), "The Purchasing Power Parity Doctrine: A Reappraisal" (1964), "Tariff Protection in Industrial Countries" (1965), and *The Structure of Protection in Developing Countries* (1971). His latest books include *Development Strategies in Semi-Industrial Economies* (1982) and *Change and Challenge in the World Economy* (1985).

CHAN, Paul
Chairman, Asia Pacific Capital Corporation, Malaysia.

CHEN, K.Y. Edward
Professor and Director of the Center of Asian Studies, University of Hong Kong. He graduated from the University of Hong Kong and obtained his Ph.D. in

Economics from Oxford University. He specializes in Asian economic development, the economics of transnational corporation, and technical change. He has been Visiting Professor at the University of California, and Consultant to various United Nations Agencies. His publications include *Hyper-Growth in Asian Economies* (1979), *Multinational Corporations, Technology and Employment* (1983), and *Small Industry in Asia's Export-Oriented Growth* (1986).

CHEN, Pochih

Professor and Chairman of the Department of Economics, National Taiwan University. He received his Ph.D. in Economics from National Taiwan University. He specializes in international trade and finance, macroeconomics, and labor economics. He has been Visiting Associate Professor at Brown University. He has published several articles and papers including "Price Contracts to Reduce Cash-in-Advance Constraint," *Economic Essays* (1986) and "Output and Price Effect of Exchange Rate Adjustment under Flexible Wages," *Economic Essays* (1980). He is also a member of the Committee on Price Statistics, DGBAS and Research Consultant of the Taiwan Institute of Economic Research.

LI, Kui-wai

Senior Lecturer of the Department of Economics and Finance, City Polytechnic of Hong Kong. He received his M.Sc. in Economics from the University of London and his M.A. in Development Studies from the Institute of Social Studies, and his Ph.D. from City University, London. He has contributed articles on Asian economy to a number of scholarly conferences and has published many articles and books including *Advanced Microeconomics*.

LIN, Yuhua

Deputy Director and Senior Economist of International Trade Research Institute, Ministry of Foreign Economic Relations and Trade (MOFERT), China. He graduated from School of Cadres of Ministry of Trade. He was formerly Commercial Secretary and Counselor of the Chinese embassy in Morocco, Ethiopia and Liberia; and Deputy Special Commissioner of MOFERT in Tianjin.

NG, F.A. Victor

Managing Director of Chong Brothers Jewelry Pte Ltd. and CBJ Manufacturing Sdn Bhd, Malaysia. He received a B.Sc. and M.Sc. degree in Economics from the University of London. He has had a varied career as a journalist, civil servant, corporate entrepreneur, and as a partner in an international management consultancy firm. He has written several articles including "Econometrics Model: Demand for Money Function in Singapore" and "Prospects and Growth, Intra-ASEAN Trade."

NOLAND, Marcus

Research Associate of Institute for International Economics, Washington, D.C., and Visiting Professor of Graduate School of Policy Science, Saitama University. He received his Ph.D. from Johns Hopkins University. He has published many articles and co-authored books including *Japan in the World Economy* and *Pacific Area Trade: Threat or Opportunity?*

PANGESTU, Mari

Lecturer of University of Indonesia. She graduated from Australian National University and received her Ph.D. from the University of California, Davis. She specializes in international trade and finance. Her papers, "Prospects of Privatization and Deregulation in Indonesia" (1989) and "The Pattern of Direct Foreign Investment in ASEAN: U.S. vs. Japan" (1987), were published in *ASEAN Economic Bulletin*. She is also a Research Fellow of the Centre for Strategic and International Studies.

PEARSON, Charles S.

Professor and Director of International Economics at SAIS, Johns Hopkins University in Washington, D.C. He received a Master's degree in International Relations from Johns Hopkins, SAIS, and Master's and Ph.D. degrees in Economics from Cornell University. His teaching and professional research are in the areas of international economics and international environmental issues; and he consults extensively for international organizations, the U.S. government, and private industry. His publications include *Free Trade, Fair Trade: The Reagan Record* and *Import Surges: The Roles of Japan and the Developing Countries.*

RHEE, Yung Whee

Principal Economist of the Industry and Energy Department, The World Bank. He graduated from Seoul University and received his Ph.D. in Economics from Johns Hopkins University. He specializes in industrial and trade policies for developing countries. His publications include *Korea's Competitive Edge* (1984).

TAMBUNLERTCHAI, Somsak

Associate Professor of the Faculty of Economics, Thammsat University. He received his B.A. from Thammasat University and his Ph.D. degree from Duke University, specializing in international and industrial economics. He was Economic Adviser to the Minister of Science, Technology, and Energy (1984–85) and a Member of the Industrial Policy Committee of the Thai government (1985–87). He has published several papers related to manufactured exports.

WANG, Rui

Associate Research Fellow and Deputy Chief of Asian and African Studies for the International Trade Research Institute, Ministry of International Economic Relations and Trade, China. He graduated from Beijing Foreign Economic Relations and

Trade University in 1960. He has been Deputy Manager of Market Research Department of China Resources (Holding) Co. Ltd. and Director and Deputy-General Manager of China Resources Trade Consultancy Co. Ltd. He has published articles in *International Trade Tribune and Reunificated Tribune.*

WU, XIAOTIAN
He obtained his Ph.D. from the Institute of International Economics, Nankai University, Tianjin, China.

XIONG, Xingmei
Deputy Director of the Institute of International Economics, Nankai University, China. He received his B.A. from Huachong University, 1950 and his M.A. from Nankai University, 1952. He has published several books including *An Introduction to Business Cycles* (1974), *Contemporary Monopolistic Capitalism* (1982), and *A Guide to Develop Outward Economy* (1988). He has undertaken several study and lecture tours in the United States.

YANG, Shu-Chin
Professor and Director of the Institute of International Economics, Nankai University, China. He received his M.A. from Nankai University and his Ph.D. from the University of Wisconsin-Madison. He was economist and branch chief of the United Nations Economic Commission for Asia and the Far East in economic survey and development planning, 1950–1963; Senior Economist, Asia Department, Department of Policy and Review, and Economic Development Institute of the World Bank, 1963–1982; and Program Coordinator of the training program in economic management and project planning in China for the World Bank's Economic Development Institute and the United Nations Development Program, 1983–1986. He led several World Bank economic missions to developing countries. He has been consultant to the World Bank and UNDP. His publications include numerous professional articles and *A Multiple Exchange Rate System: An Appraisal of Thailand's Experience, South Korea's Trade Policy and Industrialization, Economic Development Theory and Strategies,* and *International Trading Systems and Developing Countries* (jointly with William J. Davey and Richard H. Snape).

YOO, Jung-ho
Senior Fellow of Korea Development Institute. He graduated from Seoul National University and received his Ph.D. in Economics from the University of Wisconsin. He has held the position of Guest Scholar at the Brookings Institution and Assistant Professor of Economics at Wheaton College, Massachusetts. He has published several articles and papers including "The Government in Korean Economic Growth," *KDI Working Paper* (1989).

ZHU, Tong

Associate Professor, the Institute of International Economics, Nankai University. He received his Master's degree from Nankai University and studied at Swarthmore College, specializing in international economics. His major publications include articles on China's balance of payments, economic special zones, and U.S. multinational corporations.

INDEX